With lo

To Pepi on your 50th
Much love Hilary, Martin
Holly Amber & Cressie xxx

The Sunshine Land

Ghana Fifty: Memories of Independence, 1957

David Wedd

Bloomington, IN  Milton Keynes, UK

authorHOUSE®

AuthorHouse™
1663 Liberty Drive, Suite 200
Bloomington, IN 47403
www.authorhouse.com
Phone: 1-800-839-8640

AuthorHouse™ UK Ltd.
500 Avebury Boulevard
Central Milton Keynes, MK9 2BE
www.authorhouse.co.uk
Phone: 08001974150

First published by AuthorHouse 2/9/2007

ISBN: 978-1-4259-8030-6 (sc)

Printed in the United States of America
Bloomington, Indiana

This book is printed on acid-free paper.

For my daughter, Ruth

Contents

Preface   ix

PART ONE: THE GOLD COAST   **1**

1. The Way There   3
2. Accra   13
3. Learning   26
4. Power Too Plenty   34
5. The Waste Ground   41
6. Chopmaster   49
7. Politics   58
8. Intelligence Palaver   66
9. Corps of Drums   73
10. Independence Snapshots   88
– Countdown   88
– *Saturday, 2nd March 1957*: WELCOME QUEEN   92
– *Tuesday, 5th March*: INDEPENDENCE EVE   95
– OSAGYEFO   96
– *Wednesday 6th March*: INDEPENDENCE MORNING   99
– *Thursday, 7th March*: FLAGSTEAL   100
– *Friday, 8th March*: THE NEW LAND   101

PART TWO: THE GHANA REGIMENT   **105**

1. In the Mid-day Sun   107
2. Senchi   120
3. Dreamtime   130
4. The Coming of the Rains   137
5. The Prime Minister   147

6. Adenkrebi   156

7. Look People   168

8. Voyage to Timbuktu   173

9. Farewell   240

PART THREE: A LONG POSTSCRIPT   **245**

1. Rumours   247

2. Accra Again, August 1968   252

3. The Last Time   274

PREFACE

On 6th March 1957 the Gold Coast gained its Independence from British rule and became Ghana, the first of a string of black African colonies to achieve this status. It was a time of pageantry, excitement and optimism, and I was privileged to be there, as a young army officer in the Gold Coast Regiment.

I had the time of my life. At a period of massive changes, I found myself holding several posts in an African army that were ridiculously senior for a 19-year-old, so had to grow up fast. From the start of my service, however, I was made welcome in my Battalion: the enthusiasm of the soldiers impressed me and their generosity and loyalty eased my way, so that I made friendships that have lasted for fifty years.

Recently some associates who knew how much I had enjoyed my time in West Africa suggested that I should write an article about those early days of Independence, half a century ago. The idea appealed, and I promptly searched out diaries and notebooks I had kept at the time. Once I had started, I found that the article quickly became an extended memoir, then grew and carried on growing. This book is the result.

It does not pretend to be a historical assessment, but is an account of the last days of the old Gold Coast colony and the beginning of the new state of Ghana, as seen by one enthusiastic but impressionable British officer. If my opinions appear to change from chapter to chapter, that is indeed how it happened, and I have tried to present events as they seemed to me then. I hope I have caught the spirit of that time.

Ghana has altered greatly since the heady days of Independence. There have been physical changes, in particular the damming of the River Volta at Akosombo, which has created one of the world's largest artificial lakes, some 250 miles long and still growing, and the disappearance of much of the rain-forest, which so delighted me in the 1950s. New towns have developed, including what is now the main port, Tema, and a network of modern roads connects them, where in many cases there used to be only dusty tracks. Place-names have changed, especially in and around Accra, Ghana's capital, where countless roads and buildings have since been re-titled at least once. There has been much rebuilding of old districts and creating of new ones, to cope with the city's population, which has grown from 200,000 at Independence to more than two million today... I have kept the place-names that were in use in 1957-8, although where it is helpful I have also given the 'modern' versions.

Names outside Ghana have changed, too. The country north of the border, formerly Haute Volta ('Upper Volta'), has become Burkina Faso, and beyond it, what used to be the Soudan Francais is now Mali. Both lands have since gained their own independence, and are no longer French colonies. Travelling within these regions has become easier – the journey from Accra to Timbuktu that in 1958 proved so challenging for James Ankumah and me became, for my parents fifteen years later, a simple flight from the coast to the new Timbuktu airport, something about which I confess I had mixed feelings! And when, recently, I examined several guide-books, including the *Lonely Planet* series, and the brilliant *Bradt Travel Guides*, to check the route James and I had taken, I was astonished to find that not only were the maps and descriptions of the places we visited much changed from what I recalled – but the accounts also differed from each other... On the internet, however, I was reassured by photos in several American websites, which depicted the Niger towns much as I remembered them, so much so that I found myself wishing we had had the benefit of digital cameras in the 1950s!

This is a true story, but I have had to take liberties in depicting the young British officers who were my colleagues. This is because, at fifty years' recall, I cannot always remember precisely which individual did what, and since I lost touch with most of them after I (and they) left West Africa, I decided to 'compress' the characters, change some names, and reduce their number. All the events portrayed took place, however, and I am confident that should any of my then colleagues read these pages, they will recognise their own portraits and their contributions to events that occurred, even if they sometimes find these given to the wrong person! I hope they will not be disappointed or offended.

Except in a few minor instances, where I have been unable to check the correct versions, I have had no such problems with the Ghanaians, who are given their own names. I met many of them again in the 1960s and 1970s when I revisited the country, and while researching this account I have been pleased to renew contact with several people I feared I had lost touch with for ever, although I have been saddened to learn how many old friends have died.

During my time in the Ghana Army I was grateful to many, many people in my Battalion for their friendliness and support, but to nine, in particular, this gratitude went deeper. Firstly, Major Douglas Ives, who features many times in this story, initially terrified me, for he was a much-travelled colonial officer who expected high standards from his subordinates, both African and British, and did not consider inexperience an excuse for inefficiency. I soon came to value his help and support, however, and it has been a source of real pleasure to have kept in touch with him and his wife Shirley for fifty years. Now in his late eighties, Doug's astonishing recall of events and people has been of great help in checking the accuracy of what I have written.

Emmanuel Kotoka and Albert Ocran were Ghanaian officers of flair and integrity who taught me how to earn respect as a white European in an African army. They were valued companions, whose advice I often sought, and it was no surprise to me when both became important figures in the subsequent history of their new country.

Six Ghanaians of my own age became particular friends. Joseph Halm and Joseph Mensah ('the Two Josephs') were intellectuals, well-read and multilingual, keen to discuss and argue about everything; Peter Kamerling and William Stevens were extraverts, always laughing and exuberant, with whom one could never feel depressed for long; and Boadu Bekoe ('BB') and James Ankumah ('JB') were confident, sociable characters who introduced me to people and places I would otherwise never have known. Through this group of clever, witty inseparables and their families I came to understand and love the culture of their country, and after I left Africa, for many years their letters and cards kept me in touch with the nation's roller-coaster progress.

Six of the nine are still alive, and I hope that for them this book will bring back some happy memories, and that they will pardon its inaccuracies.

It was Joseph Halm who first spoke to me of his country as *The Sunshine Land,* and that is how I have thought of Ghana ever since. It seems wholly apt, for not only does the sun shine almost every day, but no people I have met with, before or since, have smiled more, been more straightforward, or offered me more genuine trust. Ghana is often called 'the friendliest country in West Africa'. Of course it is impossible to prove this, but the frequency with which one hears and reads these words suggests that there may be more than a hint of truth in them. The former colony has suffered plenty of setbacks in the fifty years since Independence came in with such joy and promise, but now the country seems to be stable again, and sure of itself, and it has been pleasing recently to follow the success of Ghanaians as diversely distinguished as the Secretary-General of the United Nations and the 'Black Star' footballers! A few months ago, on a rare visit to London, there was a breakdown on the underground, and I was ferried across the city by a delightfully garrulous taxi-driver. I thought I recognised the accent and asked him where he came from.

"Accra," he said. "We Ghanaians get everywhere, and we always talk plenty!"

Which is perhaps the key to the celebrated 'friendliness', for even in the worst of times, the people of the Sunshine Land have refused to stay downcast and, whatever their circumstances, have laughed freely, made music, and danced. And talked and talked and talked! I was intrigued to discover that there are more internet cafés in Accra alone, than in the whole of London...

An endearing trait of Ghanaians is that they always think of each other as brothers and sisters, even when totally unrelated and far from home. I hope that in March 2007 they will celebrate fifty years of Freedom with a non-stop pageant of colour, music, fun – and brotherhood – and that the world will look on and marvel!

David Wedd,
Alderney, Channel Islands, 2006

PART ONE
THE GOLD COAST

Chapter One

THE WAY THERE

I arrived in West Africa by a round-about route. The story began in Lancashire, in the spring of 1956, when I joined the British Army for my National Service. My home was in Devon, and I had been educated in Essex, but my family regiment (for many generations) had been the Lancashire Fusiliers, and I had been brought up on the legend of 20 VCs, including 'six before breakfast' at Gallipoli. My charismatic Uncle Kenneth was not only a Colonel in the Regiment (later Brigadier), with service all over the world, but had led a Company of the West African Frontier Force with dash and distinction on the Burma Campaign.

In fact I was not at first called to serve with the Fusiliers, but with the South Lancashire Regiment, at its Warrington depot. When I enquired later I was told there had been a 'slip of the pen', which was apparently not unusual! After initial disappointment, however, I realised I had struck lucky, and found my time at Warrington both entertaining and worthwhile. Many of my friends who were also called up for their National Service at this period told me later that they had either disliked their two years in the forces, or had been thoroughly bored. I could not have disagreed more.

Admittedly, it began with terror. I found myself in a large barracks with factory workers from Lancashire towns, who spoke in a dialect foreign to me and seemed confident and streetwise, until I realised that this was almost wholly bravado. They were as scared as I was, and in many cases had never been away from home before. We were worked so hard, however, and the days went by so quickly, that there was little time for worry, and soon we were genuinely enjoying the hectic routine. To get everything done, we found we were rising not at the reveille bugle-call but at 4 a.m., to polish our boots and brasses and make our bed-packs spotless, and this communal work-rate made for a communal spirit. Some of the formalities were so ludicrous that we actually took pleasure in completing them. We put blacking on the big stove that heated our billet, and shone it to mirror-like perfection, then ruined our efforts with coal-dust and had to black it again. It had been rumoured that we would cut the grass outside our billet with scissors, and sure enough, we did. We painted the edging stones white – after which we were informed that the nearby pile of coal, for the stove, looked incongruous, so we painted that white, too, piece by piece. Far from mutinying against these absurdities, my new friends found them hilarious, and carried out their tasks with gusto, chatting and even singing as they worked. Mike, a big, freckled lad who had toiled in a factory, sorting ball-bearings into correct sizes for hour after hour, remarked that he'd sooner paint coal for a living any day.

My admiration for my fellow recruits soared when we had our first instructions on how to use a bren gun. After four years' cadet-force service at school I thought I would have a big advantage, yet I found that after just one lesson the factory-hands, with their training in repetitive skills, could strip and re-assemble a machine-gun far faster than I could. Sports time also was illuminating. We played rugby league, at which I held my own, even though it was a sport new to me, since I was a reasonable rugby union player and few of my fellows had even seen a rugby game. Soccer was a different matter, however, for in our unit there were at least a dozen players of real ability, several of whom later made careers in league football. When I took part with them, I was treated as a threat, instead of a harmless novice, and finished each session bruised all over. In the NAAFI afterwards I jokingly asked the massive Billy McLardy why he needed to batter me, when he could so easily have just waltzed past, and was told that if he 'went soft' other people would take advantage. Billy, who had already played for Manchester City, said I should wait and see what happened when they played together as a unit against other local army sides. 'Sugar' Anderton, a teenage professional with Shrewsbury Town, said jokingly that I should come on the team coach, and watch them play. 'Sugar' was a charming fellow off the pitch, although frightening on it, and I said I would be delighted. I went once, and they won absurdly easily. The score was, I believe, 22-1, and there was a furious argument on the way home, because they had conceded an unnecessary goal.

One day, for a change, we had swimming, at the Warrington baths. The sergeant who was in charge on this occasion thought we would be going there by bus, so ordered us to put on our swimming trunks and carry our towels, so that we would waste no time. He then learnt that there was no transport, so we marched through the town in our swimming gear, attracting strange looks from passing shoppers, and applause from some school children going home for lunch. We had a wonderful hour of swimming and then, feeling exhilarated, doubled smartly back to the barracks – to find the Commanding Officer and Adjutant waiting for us. The sergeant was threatened with demotion, for deliberately demeaning the unit, leaving him bewildered and us incensed. It was decided that we must see our platoon commander, and explain that it was not the sergeant's fault. It was further decided that, although everyone would be present, I, the 'educated booger', should be the spokesman. In fact, I never made my speech, and we never even had to have a meeting, for the platoon commander was completely sympathetic. He was not much older than we were, indeed this was his first posting, and as he also had a high regard for his sergeant, he took up the case as soon as the situation was mentioned to him by our deputation. The three stripes were returned, before they had even been removed. We had an impromptu celebration in the NAAFI that evening, at which the platoon commander put in an appearance, and to our surprise, the Adjutant also, who told us with what seemed like a grin that he had never known such bloody cheek in his life.

Strangely, the swimming fiasco led to a relaxing of the regime. We had evenings free, when we watched Warrington rugby league team, and even, once, went to see Manchester United at Old Trafford. We also had a 36-hour pass, during which in my first real break I put on civilian clothes, stayed in a bed-and-breakfast at Windermere and got up at 9 o'clock. Partly because I had so recently escaped from school, and even more because I found my platoon-mates such engaging characters, I really enjoyed my time in Warrington. I had expected to be shouted and sworn at ceaselessly, which had indeed happened at first on the parade-ground and in the billet, where the NCOs needed to assert their authority. They were working-class Lancastrians, however, and the flow of abuse was seldom cruel and often genuinely witty. They quickly realised that, with a unit like ours, praise worked far better than blame. My fellow soldiers were funny, extremely friendly and loyal, and I have had a real affection for Lancastrians ever since. I was genuinely sorry to leave them when I was posted to Harrington Barracks, at Formby, near Southport, to a potential-officers' platoon.

Whereas in Warrington I had been billeted in the centre of town, and for six weeks had hardly seen a tree, let alone countryside, I now found myself in the most beautiful coastal setting. The next few weeks consisted of more intense soldiering than I had previously experienced, however, so there was little time at first to explore the surroundings. I was in any case the only one from my Warrington intake to be sent to Formby, so had to start making friends anew, and this was harder in the cut-throat atmosphere of potential officers' training. The Formby sandhills were a wildlife paradise, and I found it frustrating to have to practise fieldcraft for hour after hour, when there were crossbills and red squirrels in the pine-woods all around us, and fantastic flowers and natterjack toads in the sand-dunes and meadows.

My wildlife enthusiasm was not wholly wasted, however. As part of the syllabus, each of us was required to deliver a five-minute talk to the other recruits, on whatever subject we liked. Most of these talks were competent but routine, on 'Welsh Rugby', 'Collecting Coins', and 'Our Holiday in France'. Not one was amusing, and I found myself wishing that some of my Warrington intake had been present, to make us laugh. I chose a serious subject, too, and decided to speak on 'The Dawn Chorus in Devon.'

One of my favourite radio broadcasters was Percy Edwards, who could imitate innumerable birds, but also animals, farm machinery – indeed almost every country sound. From an early age I had tried to do the same, and could manage several bird songs rather successfully. I had also learnt to follow the Edwards pattern of linking them into a story. This was the first time I had risked it in public, and common sense might have suggested that an audience of some thirty young soldiers with a leavening of officers and NCOs was hardly an ideal occasion to make my whistling debut. But it worked. Not only that, but I quickly realised firstly, that everyone was listening intently and secondly, that I was enjoying myself.

Twice in my time at Formby I had to do a night's guard-duty. This entailed a group of us manning the gates at the entrance to the barracks, and while one stood duty outside, the others waited in the guard-room until it was their turn. Our commanding officer told us that nobody must be permitted to enter without a pass. There had been a certain amount of IRA trouble at other barracks, and we were told to be fully prepared.

The first time I was on duty, the occasion passed uneventfully. It was a very cold evening, but no untoward events disturbed us. The second time was very different, because there was a dinner night at the officers' mess, and various red-braided VIPs came in their sleek black limousines. We all paraded smartly, and saluted efficiently when passes had been checked and the gates opened. Then came an even sleeker, starred vehicle with pennant flying, in which sat an elderly man in a dark suit, with grey hair and moustache.

He had no pass. He was sure that we would recognise him. We didn't. We said he could not enter without a pass.

It was terrifying. He shook his fist and shouted, threatening to have us sent back to our units. "You know who I am!" he kept braying. But we didn't, and still refused him entry. He may well have given us his name, but we didn't take it in. If he had simply asked to telephone the officers' mess from the guard-room, we would have been very relieved, but probably his pride would not let him. Eventually, he ordered his driver to turn round, and left Harrington Barracks in high dudgeon, uttering awful threats about how disastrous it would prove to young whippersnappers who thought they were potential officers. He did not return. We completed our guard-duty feeling subdued and apprehensive. Someone said they thought he must be an 'important bloke – a war hero or something.' We felt we were on a hiding to nothing: either we should have let him in without a pass, which we had been forbidden to do, or we had refused entry to someone of real stature, who would make life awkward for us.

Next day, we were all summoned to see the Adjutant, and made our way to his office wondering if we would be returned to our units. To our surprise, he told us that 'the Field Marshall' had telephoned the Mess to apologise for missing the dinner, explaining that he had forgotten his pass, and had been refused entry at the gate by some courageous young lads who had done their job very well and deserved congratulation. Much later I realised, from photos, that we had refused entry to Sir Oliver Leese, whom Montgomery had called 'the best soldier in the British Army'…

While we were at Formby there were numerous training exercises. For one of these we went by truck to Cark in Cartmel, a beautiful stretch of moorland near the coast where, for the first time, we were issued with live ammunition for our rifles, with which we were required to fire at selected targets in the landscape 'to get the feel of it'. The climax came when our sergeant ordered us to take aim at a white rock, perhaps seventy yards away, under a lone pine tree. When he shouted an apoplectic "FIRE!" we loosed off a round each and the rock leapt into the air bleating loudly and dropped back, twitching. Not in the least nonplussed, the sergeant himself fired a single shot and the twitching stopped. The sheep was put into the back of a truck and returned with us to Harrington Barracks. There was 'lamb stew' for lunch a couple of days later, although we never discovered whether it was our target that we ate.

Another event, details of which I remember vividly, happened on a night exercise, when it was my turn to act as platoon commander. I was given a Very pistol and two live rounds, to signal 'if we got lost'. A Captain Lloyd-Jones was in charge of this exercise, and told all of us that he expected some real initiative. "Go on – surprise me!" he said.

I cannot remember exactly what the challenge was, although I know we had to discover some important 'secret' information and, I think, capture a building. In fact we achieved our objective quickly and decisively, because I crept up behind the Captain in the dark, threatened him with my Very pistol, and quietly demanded the details from him… He complied at once.

I was unsure whether this was acceptable behaviour, but Lloyd-

Jones was very fair. He congratulated me on my initiative, and did not even question the legitimacy of the tactics. Then he asked: "Was it loaded?"

"Yes, sir."

"And would you have used it?"

"I don't think so, sir. But I reckoned you wouldn't risk it."

The days at Formby raced by, and almost before I had realised it, I had moved on again, to Eaton Hall, the Officer Cadet Training School in its huge estate in Cheshire where, if possible, the time passed even more rapidly. Our training there lasted four months, but it seemed like half that. It was not enjoyable, as by now we were all set on becoming officers, so there could be no relaxation of effort, but equally there was never time to dwell on our woes.

We were living in a stately home, but under spartan conditions, and from the start, three men dominated our lives, whose personalities – and names – seemed born of music-hall. Our platoon commander, Captain Oddie, was a freckled-faced, broken-nosed, indestructible Para-trooper, who led by example and spoke as little as possible. Company Sergeant-major Blood was a diminutive Scots Guardsman, who actually enhanced his parade-ground authority by an alarming and unpredictable stammer. The third of the trio, Regimental Sergeant-major Lynch, was a giant Irish Guardsman, at least six-foot-five and heavily built, who seemed to scare even the officers. His opening speech to us, and apparently to every other intake, began: "Gentlemen, we have no time in this establishment for bullshit and red tape" and ended with a catalogue of misdemeanours for which we would wish for death rather than his punishment. RSM Lynch was a much-decorated soldier, and rumour had it that his Distinguished Conduct Medal would have been a Victoria Cross, had he been less abrasive with the senior officers who recommended him. At Eaton Hall, ornamental ponds full of goldfish and water-lilies fringed the big parade ground, where our turnout and rifles were inspected each morning, and after CSM Blood had b-b-barked and s-s-screamed at us, the final indignities were applied by RSM Lynch, who without compunction flung any rifle that was not immaculate and gleaming into the middle of the nearest pond. At the end of the parade, the shell-shocked cadet would have to wade in and

9

fetch it. The water was not deep, but the shame was massive.

After we had completed our first few weeks of non-stop pressure, our syllabus became more varied and, although the pace was just as hectic, the panic diminished, since we realised that our instructors actually wanted us to do well. Exchanges between non-commissioned officers and officer-cadets were often surreal, since however much they insulted us, the NCOs had to address us as "Sir!" We particularly enjoyed the abuse a short, red-faced corporal fired at a tall, gangling Etonian: "You 'orrible man! You habsolute hinsult to a giraffe - SIR!"

As always in the army, sport was taken very seriously. I played for the hockey team, against local clubs in Cheshire and Lancashire, and after a while found myself captain of the Eaton Hall side. We had a useful squad and did well, until one occasion when I was required to take the team to play against Widnes, across the Mersey. We set off in plenty of time, and as I had been told that our opponents' club-house was just the other side of the river, we negotiated the swing-bridge without much delay, and looked for the pitch – only to discover that it was in fact on the south side of the Mersey, back the way we had come. The return crossing took us a full hour, and by the time we reached the Widnes club there was no chance of completing the match. In the twenty minutes that were possible, we scored twice, before 'night stopped play'. Our opponents were very understanding, and gave us an excellent tea. We returned to Eaton Hall somewhat deflated, but the result was put down as a victory... Not long afterwards we beat Mons, our sister Officers' Training School, which warranted genuine celebrations.

The periodic written examinations presented few terrors to those of us who had been brought up on constant testing at school. I recall our feeling inordinately jealous, however, of the actor Jeremy Spenser, who was in our unit. He was a charming person, unspoilt by fame, and when he was given several weeks' leave, to film *The Prince and the Showgirl* with Marilyn Monroe and Laurence Olivier, we were delighted for him – although we thought his passing-out from Eaton Hall must surely be delayed. Not a bit of it. The day before our final Military Knowledge examination, Jeremy reappeared, bubbling with enthusiasm and full of wonderful stories of his co-stars. He stayed up until three a.m. learning his MK facts from the pamphlets we had collected for him, rose again at five-thirty – and sailed through the exam. with hardly an error! We were jealous not of his success, but of the photographic memory that had enabled him to achieve it.

Our course came to a head in October, when we took part in a big three day exercise at Trawsfynydd, in the Welsh mountains, which we were told was 'the real thing' and would influence whether we became officers or not. Like much that happened during those four months, the exercise as a whole is now a blur, leaving a few vivid memories. I recall two things in particular. The first indelible moment came when a group of us went into a small valley pub, where the locals were chatting in English as we entered, but on seeing who we were, they proved able to speak only Welsh. We were with our officers, so there was no sense of guilt, only humiliation.

The other vivid memory is of waking in my trench at 3 a.m., to find an officer addressing our sentry, who had apparently dozed off. The officer spoke very quietly, but with an icy edge to his words:

"If this was the Western Front," he hissed, "you would be put in front of a firing-squad and bloody *shot*!"

After successfully negotiating that exercise, we were confident of becoming officers, and spent many evenings discussing what we hoped to do if, and now almost certainly when, we were successful. Most people knew what units they hoped to join, and I was naturally keen to be commissioned into the Lancashire Fusiliers. I was desperate to be sent abroad, however, and above all, I wanted to go to Africa. I asked Captain Oddie if I could do both. "Of course," he said, "put down for LF and ask to be seconded to wherever you are keen to go."

My choice lay with either the King's African Rifles, in Kenya, or the West African Frontier Force. My uncle Kenneth had served with both regiments. I thought it was probably unethical to contact him, so I telephoned my father about my dilemma. He said: "You obviously don't want a cushy time, so what about trying for the Gold Coast? They'll be getting their Independence from us in about four months, so you could be making history. Of course, it's the White Man's Grave, but I don't expect that bothers you…!" As a result I put down my choice as the Lancashire Fusiliers, seconded to the Gold Coast Regiment of the West African Frontier Force.

❖   ❖   ❖

Passing-out parades at Eaton Hall were sometimes memorable. All the cadets at the Training School took part, although obviously those just about to be commissioned were the stars. On one occasion, when we were all standing smartly out on the huge field where the parade was to take place, our turnout immaculate and our lines ruler-straight, it started to rain. As the car carrying the inspecting officer, Field-Marshal Sir Gerald Templar, drove onto the field, the drizzle turned to heavy rain, then a torrential storm. We stood on the grass in our sodden uniforms, with white streams running down our trousers from the blancoed belts and gaiters. The tiny Field Marshal stepped out into the downpour, strode quickly along the lines of soaked cadets without inspecting anyone, then mounted his dais and, very distinctly above the drumming of the rain, congratulated everyone on a superb turnout and drill. After which he ordered the Adjutant to march us off. We were discussing this decisiveness that evening when, with his usual succinctness, Captain Oddie said: "That's why he's a Field Marshall."

Our own passing-out parade had better weather and was utterly unmemorable because it went without a hitch. I cannot even remember who took the parade, or any of the muted celebrations that followed, although doubtless there were some. I found myself, as I had hoped, commissioned into the Lancashire Fusiliers, seconded to the Gold Coast Regiment, in the West African Frontier Force.

Chapter Two

ACCRA

Shortly before Christmas 1956, nine of us met up at London Airport in grey drizzle, wearing army mackintoshes over our battledress, not because of the rain but to hide the newly-acquired pips on our shoulders. Despite our excitement, we were tired after the exertions of our training and the whirlwind visits home that had followed, so slept through much of the first part of the journey, waking to more rain at Rome, and to cicada-loud darkness when we stopped to refuel at Tripoli. Here we were able to stretch our legs on the airport for half an hour and for the first time the heat of Africa hit us. The next stop was again in darkness, at Kano in Northern Nigeria, after a smooth flight over the Sahara, and not long afterwards we arrived at Accra Airport in dazzling morning sunshine.

The long snake of passengers in light frocks and tropical suits wound its way slowly towards the customs shed, casting a single black shadow. On the tarmac big red-and-grey agama lizards lay stretched out, basking. As the shadow swayed near, they scampered aside on spindly legs, did a few press-ups, and stretched out again a few yards away.

We were almost the last to leave the Stratocruiser, and before we had moved twenty yards from the aircraft, we were sweating uncomfortably in our thick battledress. All the other passengers seemed to have friends or families to meet them. There was a huge crowd behind the barrier, a tapestry of bright clothes, waving arms and pennants, and faces black, brown and white. The passengers were signalling back frantically as they recognised people in the throng. Car horns hooted. There was even a small welcoming band for one family, with a wailing flute and gongongs clicking. The nine of us kept together and moved uncertainly towards the Customs, dragging our luggage with us. Alec's heavy raincoat slipped off his arm. He threw down his cases, swept off his cap and mopped his face.

"You'd have thought," he declared sarcastically, "they might have sent someone to meet us…"

"Allow me," a voice answered.

An African lieutenant in khaki-drill and wide slouch-hat sprouting green feathers had come out from among the crowd behind the barrier. He picked up Alec's baggage and we followed him to the Customs. He guided us through with the barest of formalities, so that we hardly had time to draw breath. No one was asked to open a single bag or case. The lieutenant barely spoke.

Two land rovers were waiting in the airport car-park, one small and worn, the other a new long-wheel-base model. We put our luggage into the small one.

"All right, Amadu. You may go," said the lieutenant to the African driver, who saluted smartly. Away went the land rover. No directions. No instructions as to what to do with our luggage. I suddenly felt exhausted and dazed. What were we doing here? Even who were we? Eight other faces reflected the same doubts.

"Don't worry," the lieutenant said. "Your luggage is going ahead of you. It will be there when we arrive. We will travel in the other land rover."

He took off his slouch-hat and made the suggestion of a bow.

"I must introduce myself," he said. "My name is Emmanuel Koto-ka. Welcome to the Gold Coast!"

We were whisked from the airport in a flurry of red dust, and hurried through a line of hooting taxis. We followed the main road for about a mile through green scrubland, from which rose huge, russet termite mounds; then our vehicle swung off into an avenue of flame-of-the-forest trees. Soon we had reached the gateway of an old fort.

"First stop," said Kotoka, "El Wak, our headquarters. You may be able to see the Adjutant right away."

As we clambered out of the land rover a tall, very thin African Regimental Sergeant Major appeared. He had obviously been awaiting us, and saluted fiercely so that his wispy moustache quivered. His shirtsleeves and shorts accentuated his leanness. Kotoka returned the salute.

"Sargy Major," he said, "these be the new officers for see Aggitant. I bring um from airport . We fit see Aggitant nownow?"

The RSM saluted again and disappeared through a doorway.

"This is where you get very tired very quickly," Kotoka said.

"Why?"

"Major Ives," he said enigmatically. "You'll see."

The RSM reappeared: "Sah, Aggitant he ready."

"Good luck!" said Kotoka. We went in.

The nine of us stood in a line in front of the Adjutant. Major Ives leant back in his chair, clasped his hands behind his head; peered at us with his head on one side. He was a big, florid man with slicked-back ginger hair. In spite of the electric fan whirling from the ceiling, sweat was dribbling down his forehead and there were large damp patches at the armpits of his bush-shirt. We felt hotter than ever. If only he would tell us to sit down... He said nothing at all. We stood awkwardly, fidgeting, nine schoolboys in a line.

Suddenly: "What do you know about this country?" he asked.

A pause.

"Not very much, sir."

A long pause. Major Ives tilted his chair further back, looked at the ceiling as if counting the revolutions of the fan; closed his eyes as if he had forgotten us altogether. Then he rocked forward suddenly, crashing his elbows onto the table, clenched his fists and knocked the knuckles together with a crunching sound.

Another long pause. Then the words gushed out in a distinctive kind of shorthand.

"Not to waste time," he said, "there are three Battalions, nine of you, all right? Two are wanted urgently I don't care which two for the Tamale Battalion, that's in the North, there'll be more needed later. Three at Takoradi. Here in Accra we need a dozen officers at least, we've

15

all bloody worn ourselves out lately trying to make ends meet but four will have to do, all right?"

There was no time to decipher this before he had started again.

"Tamale's got plenty of sun, good shooting if you like that, nothing to disturb you there not like this place, no red tape, very peaceful, OK? Takoradi's west along the coast, swimming, sailing, fishing, not too hot, not like Tamale anyway, quite a civilised place with some shops, Tak's all right. Then there's here. Accra's got a bit of most things, you know what's happening some of the time, even get news from England now and again. Sports, quite good nightlife. Surprisingly good nightlife. But no privacy at all and bloody hard work and with Independence coming it'll be harder still, OK? Now you know everything you need to know, so we'd better settle who's going where. You get a free choice."

It was like being buffeted by a very powerful wave. No one offered a word in reply.

"Well, come on," said Ives. "I've not got all day. Nor have you."

It took us about five minutes, with his help, to divide our numbers exactly as he wished. Those who were going to the First Battalion at Tamale and the Third at Takoradi went out immediately to learn further details of their move. They left looking dazed, still stunned by the wave. Mike, Jock, Alec and I stayed where we were.

For the first time, Ives half smiled.

"And then there were four," he said.

Kotoka was waiting outside in the land rover. Ives came across with us.

"*Gidas* first," he said. "They can change into mufti; they must be hot like that. Then QM stores and the tailors', then back here by noon to meet the Colonel. That gives you nearly two hours, OK?"

"So!" said Kotoka as we moved off. "Now you've met Major Ives, welcome to his Second Battalion…"

No one said anything. We too were still feeling the wave's impact.

Half a mile along the main road the land rover turned onto a bumpy red-clay path between tall, feathery cassava plants. The track opened into a wide space in which stood two long, low buildings painted green and cream, with a veranda running the length of each. We stopped in front of the first block, where two African servants were sitting, polishing boots. They stood up as Kotoka got out of the land rover.

"No be any officer here, Awuni?" he asked the taller servant, who was wearing khaki shorts and a vivid green shirt patterned with giraffes.

"No sah. Dey say dey come back 'leben o'clock for meet de new hofficers."

The other servant scratched his head with one hand, pointed at the land rover with the other and said shyly, "I tink, sah, dis-all be de new hofficers, no be so?"

Each bungalow-block contained six *gidas* of two rooms each. They were sparsely furnished. Mine had a desk, a table and a few chairs in one room, several cupboards and a bed with mosquito-net in the other. There were various basins and buckets. The bathroom hut was at the end of the block. A yell came from Mike next door. He had with difficulty opened one of his cupboards and a large cockroach had whirred out.

We changed into shirts and flannels, and wished we had added shorts to the few clothes we had brought from England. Nonetheless the change made us feel alive again, even remotely African. Jock glided along the veranda strumming an imaginary guitar.

"Slowly," he announced theatrically, "I am beginning to understand what's happening..."

Now another land rover appeared, bumping along the path, horn tooting loudly, and halted with a jerk alongside ours. Clouds of red dust billowed up. Out clambered four young second-lieutenants in khaki-drill, all wearing slouch-hats like Kotoka's, sprouting similar green and black plumes. All were Europeans, three dark, one very fair. They chimed in breathlessly, like a music-hall turn.

"I'm Simon," the tallest.

"And I'm Tom," craggy, with a North-Country accent.

"Jeremy." The fair one.

"I'm Geoff." Very dark and swarthy, with mobile eyebrows that functioned independently.

"Sorry we weren't here when you arrived –"

"We didn't think you'd be here so soon…"

"Hope you've found your way around –"

"—the rooms and everything?"

"We've been here two months," Simon said more calmly. "So we're expected to know everything."

Said Jeremy, "Well, welcome, anyway!"

Meanwhile four more Africans in vivid shirts had appeared quietly, as if from nowhere.

"These are your batmen," Simon said. "They'll look after you."

The four had obviously decided which rooms they were going to look after, regardless of occupants. It was probably the best way of deciding. So Abongo Frafra became my batman, and quickly took charge of every item of kit I had brought with me. Within minutes he had stowed away shirts, socks, underwear in the drawers, hung up my battledress and my only suit, arranged my few books on a shelf, wound up my small alarm clock…

He was a short and very muscular man, aged about thirty, with a broad flat face patterned with tribal scars like a spider's web. He heaved up all my heavy basins in one hand to pile them tidily in a corner, then set out the chairs and fluffed up the cushions.

"Ebryting be hall-light?" The spider's web wavered comically as he spoke.

"Fine pass all," I replied, risking my first pidgin-English. I sank back in an armchair.

The tailors measured us for our tropical kit: shirts, bush-jackets, shorts, long khaki-drill, white mess-jackets… the list seemed unending.

"We'll be able to parade in civilian clothes for weeks, which is something," Alec said. "They'll not have made this lot for ages."

"Sirt-an-sorts no be long time attall," the earnest tailor-corporal assured us. "I finish him today six o'clock."

The Quartermaster loaded each of us with a pile of kit: puttees, hose-tops, belts, slouch-hat, regimental buttons, badges... I gave everything to Abongo.

We went back to the Adjutant's office in some trepidation. Major Ives was not there. There was a row of comfortable chairs along one wall, but we did not dare to sit down. Instead, we examined the room gingerly. The Adjutant's own large table with three empty trays; a shelf of manuals and files; a large glass-fronted cupboard containing ten ceremonial swords.

"It'd need a giant to lift one of those," Alec said.

Two wall-safes. An open doorway leading to the Orderly Room, where several African clerks seemed to be attending very closely to their work. Perhaps Ives was in there. A closed door opposite, which said 'Commanding Officer'. Hell. Wish Ives would come and get it over.

Meet the Colonel. Commanding Officer, Colonel Quinn. Lieutenant-Colonel Neville Quinn, T.D., to be precise, according to the plaque. Behind the door, the ogre. 'Commanding Officer': All Hope Abandon. If the door opens, run. The door opened.

He came forward quietly, shook hands with each of us.

"Glad you've joined us. We need some new blood."

A thickset man with a kind, gentle face, he looked old and tired, with bags under his eyes. He seemed slightly apprehensive. A man nearing the end of his second West African tour, hoping to finish safely. A considerate man.

"Finding your feet all right?" he asked. "Met the Adjutant, have you? Ah, of course you have. There you are, Douglas, I didn't see you come in. Make sure they know the ropes."

"Yes, sir." Major Ives's voice had a softer, civil note.

"Met my Second-in-Command yet?"

Major Watkin-Williams appeared on his cue, a stocky man with sandy hair and a spry moustache, a mischievous face.

"Glad you've joined us. We need some new blood."

And a new line in patter, perhaps, or was he taking the mickey? But the Major was affable, understanding.

"Bit bewildering, wrrrwrrr? Rushing around, trying to learn everything at once. Bet the Adjutant's frightened you already, wrrrwrrr? He always does. But you'll soon learn the ropes."

"I'm sure you must all feel done in," said the Colonel.

"There's a lot they've still got to do –" Ives tried to interpose.

"Lunch first, Douglas."

Unbelievably, it was only one o'clock.

◆　◆　◆

By the end of our first day we were fully-fledged Battalion officers. Major Ives made the appointments and silenced every query. Mike found himself in charge of a platoon of 'A' Company, with instructions to teach his men Internal Security Drill thoroughly enough to put on a demonstration ("Say, within a week. All right?") Jock and Alec were platoon commanders in 'C' Company, which was to move out to the Shai Hills in a few days' time on a big training exercise. In addition, knowledge of Jock's background in vehicle maintenance had preceded him, so he was to start understudying the Motor Transport Officer, in order to take over as MTO himself next month, when the present incumbent returned to England ("And it's no good wondering when there's time to do it, young man. You *make* time here.") I was posted to Headquarter Company and given three days to learn the duties of Education Officer ("You're a budding University-wallah, aren't you?") so that I could take over from Jeremy. I was also to help Emmanuel Kotoka reorganise all the HQ Company documents ("They're a screaming shambles".)

By five o'clock the tailors had finished our khaki shirts and shorts.

At eight o'clock, after dinner at the Mess, the four of us were taken by Simon and Jeremy to the Ridgeway pub, where we were joined by Emmanuel and another African lieutenant, Sam Lartey. As we sat outside, drinking beer, while huge moths and praying mantises fluttered around the lights, I felt I was already beginning to enjoy Africa.

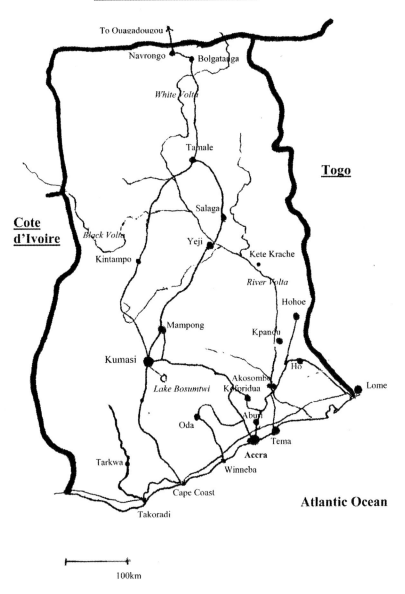

Haute Volta (Burkina Faso)

To Ouagadougou

Navrongo
Bolgatanga

White Volta

Tamale

Togo

Salaga

Cote d'Ivoire

Black Volta

Yeji

Kete Krache

Kintampo

River Volta

Hohoe

Mampong

Kpandu

Kumasi

Ho

Lake Bosumtwi

Akosombo
Koforidua

Lome

Aburi

Oda

Tema

Tarkwa

Accra

Winneba

Cape Coast

Atlantic Ocean

Takoradi

100km

The Gold Coast 1956-8

21

Our home, Junior Officers' Lines

The path through the cassava fields

At Giffard Camp

Training

Cannon outside the Mess

Mess Staff 'conga'

Welcome from the staff children

Baragu hanging out washing

Chapter Three

LEARNING

The Officers' Mess was raised six feet above the ground on squat stone pillars, to deceive the termites and prevent snakes and crawling vermin from entering. It was set in a picturesque garden of hibiscus and bougainvillea, with a lawn at the back which led straight onto the parade-ground. The whole area was surrounded by feathery neem trees, where by day fruit bats roosted in the highest branches, looking from the ground like clusters of brown rags.

From the comfort of the Mess, gazing out over the Battalion's neat, compact domain, it was easy to become for the moment Sanders of the River, lacking only his white pith-helmet, and in the evenings especially, while crickets and cicadas zithered in the garden, the romance was heightened.

Two heavy black cannons stood at the foot of the front steps. The enormous barrels were tilted at a menacing angle, as if about to fire, but they were corroded, useless, and beside each, fixed firm to a concrete block, was a single giant cannonball, far wider than the barrel. The guns were from antiquity, slave-trade relics, dead - or nearly. If you lighted a thunderflash or large firework and dropped it into one of the tilted barrels, then rolled an orange down after it and then stood clear, there would come a muffled sizzling followed by a devastating roar and away would fly the orange two hundred yards and more. Up it would soar, over the garden, the neem trees and the road, high over the old red fort of El Wak, to land with a squelch in the waste ground beyond, while

26

around the Mess the fruit bats flapped frantically on pterodactyl wings. M'shimba M'shamba had spoken.

In December 1956, when we arrived in Accra, the Mess was a convenient geographical centre of the Battalion. At the back, beyond the parade-ground, lay the Cantonments, part senior officers' houses, part soldiers' quarters, row upon row of mud-walled huts. The Battalion offices at El Wak were directly across the road. From the front veranda of the Mess you could just see, away to the left, our *gidas*, the junior officers' quarters, almost hidden by the trees and bushes of the waste ground. Every part of the Battalion was near, easily reached on foot.

In the New Year, however, the geographical balance swung, as the Battalion moved in entirety to Giffard Camp, a new site a mile and a half away, with only our quarters and the Mess remaining as they had been. For major administrative purposes this was admirable, since the Battalion offices were now situated alongside those of Brigade Headquarters. The soldiers were better off, too, for they now occupied the fine, modern Arakan Barracks, only a little way from the offices and training area. There was also a new, enormous parade-ground. But the officers now had to travel by car or land rover from the Mess to the Battalion area, instead of merely walking next door.

For the subalterns this arrangement was bliss, since a land rover was now provided to take us to and from work. Jeremy's small grey Volkswagen had previously been the only means of transport from our quarters, and a rather unreliable one at that. Now we had much more than a mere duty-service, for the land rover's work ticket was not restrictive, and if the vehicle happened to return from Giffard Camp to the Mess via the shopping centre in Accra, a detour of some six miles, no questions were asked. Even if we chose to detour further still, via Labadi Beach, we could argue – with some truth – that we had gone there to buy crayfish or fruit or coconuts for the Mess dinner-menu. Between swims, we often did bargain for food with the market-women on the beach.

In those early days our Battalion duties were not strenuous, and I think we did what was required of us conscientiously. The initial panic, when everything was strange and deadly, and a subaltern seemed less than nobody, did not last long. It was replaced by a new, assertive period, as soon as we realised that for all our inexperience we did have some authority, and that the soldiers serving under us were astonishingly loyal, and would obey our orders even if they thought them foolish.

The junior officers who were in infantry companies spent many hours supervising drill on the square or fieldcraft in the surrounding countryside. I sometimes watched the drill, which was impressive. The soldiers had a natural timing, and were hard as rock. They would stand uncomplaining in fierce sunlight, statues at attention, motionless as the termite-hillocks ringing the parade-ground. They marched firmly in line, with a confidence that would not have disappointed the Guards, and I found it easy to accept the dictum that they were the 'perfect soldiers in adversity' that I had heard about from my Uncle Ken, who had led a regiment of this very Frontier Force with much success on the Burma Campaign.

I watched Mike's platoon practising Internal Security Drill. His soldiers were wearing denims and tin hats, and carried rifles. Mike had a sten carbine. A three-ton truck stood nearby, with the back let down and the driver already in his seat.

"Get on board NOW!" Mike yelled, and checked his watch.

The soldiers rushed to the truck and clambered in two by two. Several of them carried large, furled banners; one had a roll of white tape. The last man flung up the back of the three-tonner, and was himself hauled inside. Five or six faces grinned out.

"We finish, sah! We ready!"

"Twenty seconds better," said Mike. "Not bad. Now drive off."

The truck was driven once round the clearing, and returned to exactly where it had been before. It was now in Accra town centre. The men were to dispel a rioting mob. They leapt out, still grinning hugely, and formed up. They unrolled the tape and tied the ends to two trees about thirty yards apart. The white tape billowed waist-high: this was the barrier beyond which the rioters must not come.

The flag-bearers unfurled their message. *'Disperse or we fire'*, one banner proclaimed, and the others apparently said the same in different local languages.

"Much better!" said Mike. "We'll do it once more, then tomorrow we'll have Two Platoon to act as rioters. Left small, we gettum Two Platoon for Enemy, you savvy?"

My own work at first was mainly that of a clerk. Emmanuel and I sat at desks in the sun outside Headquarters, cataloguing the Company records, disposing of irrelevant material so that we could find our way more easily through the maze of documents. Emmanuel was quite ruthless. Anything unimportant we threw into a large cartridge-box, and every ten minutes or so one of the junior clerks came for replenishment of 'Leften' Kotoka's bookfire' which was burning at the back of the office block. When we were re-filing the soldiers' conduct-sheets I was surprised at some of the names: Daniel Brown and William Stevens seemed hardly African; P White William seemed stranger still. Emmanuel told me that the anglicised names belonged to Southerners, who had had long contact with England ("going back to the slave trade...") but at this stage I found the names multiplying at such a rate that I was unable to follow up details of persons or tribes. Emmanuel himself was friendly, but quiet and detached. He told me that he too had been commissioned at Eaton Hall. He had just returned from another visit to England, to a mortar course at Nether Avon, and would soon be going once more. He needed 'as many qualifications as possible', with an eye to the reorganisation of the army after Independence. He said he liked English people, but qualified this with 'most of them', quietly but so emphatically that for the present I did not ask him to explain. It was clear, however, that he had a high regard for Major Ives. "I was frightened of him at first," Kotoka said, "but he was kind and helpful to me. He is a strong man, but fair – and he likes Africans..."

With Jeremy I spent some time each morning at the Education Centre. The sergeants worked out the timetable and did most of the instruction, but if they needed new equipment, maps or stationary, an officer had to sign for it. If an important examination was due, requiring a soldier to miss drill parade, for example, and arrive at the Centre armed with a pen, an officer had to authorise the change. Otherwise we watched the NCOs at their work, teaching their subjects slowly, painstakingly, very surely. Colour-Sergeant Moses, in particular, seemed a teacher of great talent. He was articulate, firm but kind, and we enjoyed seeing him at work. After a week or so, Jeremy handed over everything to me. I signed a form to prove that, nominally, I was in charge of each table, chair, book and blackboard – after which I went to the Centre every day by myself.

Soon after I took over, lessons were halted for a week while a number of soldiers sat their GCE examinations. They were taking many of the same subjects and papers as in England, and I was impressed by their knowledge and confidence – and their flowing copperplate handwriting. A few were studying tribal languages, and in at least one case the candidate had to set his own paper, as there was no Examining Board capable of doing it for him! Not only soldiers from the Battalion were involved, for a group from the Signals Brigade turned up, and another from the Battery Field Squadron, all smart and exuberant. There were a few others, apparently civilian entries. Sergeant Moses, who was one of the supervisors, was suddenly very alert as this group entered. He checked through the documentation they had brought with them.

"I do not believe these are *bona fide* candidates," he said. "They are too old. That one is supposed to be eighteen, and he has *grey hair*! I think we should get the Military Police to enquire about them."

Sergeant Moses was right. They proved to be teachers, who had been paid to sit the exam. for their pupils. The Colonel congratulated me on 'unmasking' them, and although I explained that the Sergeant deserved all the credit, I quite enjoyed the undeserved glory.

There was a four-day break in routine when the Headquarter Company soldiers fired their annual rifle course. To the infantry platoons, rifle-handling was second nature: something they did every day; but HQ Company contained among its huge numbers people who were normally employed in such non-athletic pursuits as cooking, tailoring or electrical work, who consequently seldom even saw a rifle during the greater part of the year. Their shooting was dreadful, but for most of them this annual visit to the range was a wonderful holiday, a red-letter day. It mattered little to them whether they were classified as 'Marksmen' or first, second or third-class shots, or failed to qualify at all. The day-out was what counted.

My own first day at Teshie Range was memorable, but for a different reason. A marksman myself, and keen to show how thorough my training had been, I was over-confident. I said I thought I was capable of organising everything: just give me the men, and the weapons and ammunition. So it was agreed that I should start the first few sections myself. This was not strictly legal, as there should be more than one officer present – but various majors and captains said they would be coming out later, and undoubtedly it would be a help if I could manage alone for the first hour or so.

"He'll have Owusu today," someone said, and someone else laughed, but the joke meant nothing to me. I was thoroughly happy. Anyway, I was to have a sergeant-major and two sergeants to help me.

Behind the butts at Teshie Range there was a protecting bank of shifting sand and, beyond that, the sea. On this sunny morning the view from the two-hundred-yard firing point was beautiful in its vivid, contrasting colours: the dusty range red-green, the yellow sandbank, the sea stretching blue and unbroken to meet the paler blue of the sky. A red flag waved from the higher ground to the East, as a warning to the townsfolk that the range was being used. Another flag, far away to the West, was supposed to tell fishermen that firing was in progress and that for a while no boats must be rowed or sailed past Teshie Range.

For some time everything went well. Sergeant-Major Binchity and his fellow NCOs were very efficient: they lined the men up in order, explained exactly what was required, and pushed them forward at the proper time. They made sure that the soldiers remembered their safety precautions.

Then a furtive, weak-lipped man arrived at the firing-point. The Sergeant-Major came up to me, worried.

"Dis be Owusu," he said. "He be fool man. Ebry time he de shoot, something go bush, *nyama-nyama*. I tink, sah, you look um proper."

I remembered the name, and the laughter in the Mess, but Owusu seemed very quiet, very insignificant. He lay down at the firing-point and positioned himself in a practice aim at his target. Four other soldiers did likewise.

"Dis man," Binchity whispered, "he no fit shoot attall. No be any time he de hit target. Ebry time he done do some bloo'fool ting. Be so I tell you." He shook his head sadly.

"He's all right now," I assured the Sergeant-Major. "Just let him do the same as the others."

Weeks later, I was told of some of Owusu's legendary range-exploits. I was assured that he had once contrived to bring down the target number-plate from the bank beyond, by putting two shots neatly through its slender supporting pole; and there was a story that he had once fired a shot directly into the protecting wall in front of the butts, thereby slaying a puff adder that had been basking unseen; and rumour of a rumour said that this was why some superstitious men credited Owusu even now with a snake juju and treated him with profound respect. Fact or fiction, the NCOs regarded the man as a liability.

But he seemed safe enough now.

"He'll be all right today," I again assured the Sergeant-Major.

Slowly Owusu pushed a round into the magazine, another into the breach. These were to be 'sighters', practise shots to get the feel of the rifle and, for the experts, to see whether they must aim higher or lower, or further left or right... Unhurriedly Owusu fired once, and soon afterwards the familiar red flag was waved vigorously across his target. A miss. He fired again, slowly, with no show of emotion... and the markers signalled that the shot had just clipped the top of the circle. This created a minor sensation. Owusu had hit the target...

"With five rounds – LOAD!"

Owusu loaded as he had been told, as did the other four soldiers, and waited until I told him to carry on firing, grouping, at the target before him; all formal, all correct.

His first shot ploughed into the bank in front of the butts, and there was an interval of respite while Owusu waited for a 'washout' signal that never came. Meanwhile, far beyond the targets, a small fishing-boat had appeared, silhouetted black against the sea. The others who were firing noticed it and put down their rifles, but Owusu had taken aim again and was concentrating, his face deadpan. He paid no attention to my frantic "STOP!" Perhaps he never heard me.

Slowly and deliberately he squeezed the trigger. A shot rang out. The watching soldiers were awed and silent… but the next moment there was a loud cheer, in which I found myself joining, as we saw the fishing-boat swing round sharply and hurry back the way it had come at remarkable speed.

Owusu fired one more shot that day. With it he shattered the range-telephone that had been unwisely left on a table at the hundred-yard firing-point. He ruined the table, too. After this, it seemed that he had done enough damage for one year and he was relieved of his rifle.

Chapter Four

POWER TOO PLENTY

The Second Battalion was understaffed, so the young British officers inevitably found themselves in positions of responsibility they could never have expected to hold. At the beginning of 1957 there were less than thirty commissioned Africans scattered throughout the entire Gold Coast Army, which then consisted of three full Battalions, a Training Depot at Kumasi, an Officers' Training School at Teshie, the Military Hospital and a number of individual Brigade units stationed at Giffard Camp.

In our Battalion there was a solid base of British regular officers seconded from home regiments but, before Independence, very few African officers to fill the main balance of positions. As a result, inexperienced National Servicemen found themselves credited with a multiplicity of posts, some of which were asking a great deal of second-lieutenants.

Several subalterns found themselves Acting Company Commanders at the age of nineteen or twenty, although fortunately never for long at a time, while Jock was responsible for the entire Battalion transport organisation before he had been in Accra for a month. He was slightly older than the rest of us, an acute-brained Scot, whose premature baldness gave him a venerable air and thus made him seem less like a boy taking over a man's job. He seemed to thrive on the responsibility.

Dai, who had already been on the Coast a year, held joint posts as Intelligence Officer and Ives's Assistant Adjutant. The partnership was not a success, for the two men were in total contrast. Major Ives was

34

a hectic, compulsive worker, never still, who believed in tackling every new problem as soon as it arose, while Dai was clever but rather lazy, with a neat line in excuses for why things had not been done when they should have been. In addition, his Welsh repartee was alien to Ives's sense of humour. We were envious of Dai's position as I.O., which gave him the excuse to travel far and wide in the country on 'reconnaissance', and were even more jealous of the girl friends he collected like stamps in all sizes, shapes and colours. But we reckoned that anyone who had to work under the Adjutant deserved some privileges.

Others of us held complex positions as subalterns, with a variety of minor posts which, added together, made us feel very important. My own initially included Education Officer, Company Records and Officers' Mess Catering, and this last job, which I enjoyed, led to yet another post, that of Battalion Rations Officer. The Quartermaster actually ordered the food, but each day I was driven to the Supply Depot in the Ration Truck to collect sacks of rice and groundnuts; oceans of red peppers, bananas and plantains; sides of beef – all that was required for the soldiers' meals. Corporal Marsel Dagarti, who drove the truck, knew exactly what had been ordered and from what part of the Depot it should be collected, and on the rare occasions when I had to sign for some more exotic supplies, he knew how the form should be filled in. He supplied the food: I merely took the credit for providing it.

We all had too much authority too soon. This was inevitable, with so few officers, and I suppose it was equally inevitable that the authority would go to our heads. A dose of Major Ives every few days would have sobered us, but our paths and his seldom crossed. As it was, most of us quickly decided that the Battalion could not survive without us.

I had two jolts to my over-confidence, early on, which should have made a lasting impression. The first arose out of my position as Rations Officer, and taught me very abruptly that in the Army you must never sign for anything, even on good authority, unless you are quite sure what you are signing for.

The Rations Officer was officially responsible for all the furniture in the open-air canteen at Arakan Barracks, so when Richard, my predecessor in this job, asked me to sign an inventory to prove that I had formally taken possession of every item, I added my name without fuss. I did not trouble to count the tables and stools before I signed the inventory. I assumed that the retiring Rations Officer would have done so, and that if he said there were 94 tables and 151 stools, that must be correct. In any case, I did not think that it would matter greatly if there were a few more or les than the list detailed, and as Richard was due to fly home to England in two days' time, at the end of his service, it seemed churlish to bother him when he was busy packing.

There were actually 63 tables and 95 stools...

This came to light when the Quartermaster made his first full inventory of Battalion property, after our move to the new barracks. The RSM said he thought some soldiers had been 'tiefing' furniture for their *gidas*, so he organised a search and recovered all but seven of the tables and quite a number of stools, but the rest were nowhere to be found. The RSM said they had probably been sold in Accra or used for firewood.

So there was a Court of Enquiry, at which Major Ives conveniently put most of the blame on the absent Richard, and the missing articles were written off. The incident should have knocked some of the arrogance out of me, since I might well have found myself in serious trouble. As it was, I was left virtually blameless, and the Enquiry procedure, with its quoting from Regulations and archaic phrasing, seemed rather amusing. Although I was shaken enough to vow that I would never again sign my name even on a letter without reading it through carefully, the mysterious disappearance of thirty stools and seven tables became yet another good story which would gain in the retelling.

The other jolt to my self-esteem I shared with all the other junior officers, when we first experienced a Battalion pay-parade. At the time it was alarming. The subalterns were expected to deal out the wages of their respective Companies. Headquarters was the largest of all – and as there were already enough officers to cope with 'A' Company, Mike was told to help me instead.

We drew from the Pay Office £1800 in Gold Coast currency, and for three hours without a break sat behind a table piled with notes and coins, frantically trying to balance our totals as the men came and went. Mike was already annoyed when we started, because he was not able to look after his own Company. Before long, we were both irritated and weary.

One by one we called the names and ticked the men off on the Company roll. Forty were still out on a jungle exercise, and this fact continually disrupted us, as their pay had to be kept back in special envelopes, to reach them later. There were others missing who were at the Military Hospital, and their pay also had to be kept aside.

Then Sergeant Alheri, the Carpenter, having collected his money, returned seconds later to say that he had been given £5, when he was entitled to £7. Mike and I dithered, wondering whether to be ruthless and tell the Sergeant that it was his own fault for not counting his money at the table and letting us know immediately he found he was short, or to pay him the extra £2 and hope the balance came right. Luckily for us, another Sergeant, who had just been paid, came up and declared that Alheri was 'one big humbug-man', who was always taking advantage of young officers who 'knew nothing'. He produced the £2 which the Carpenter had concealed under a stone less than fifty yards away.

At the end Mike and I found ourselves a few shillings down, and felt we were lucky. Simon was £4 *up* with 'A' Company, and slightly embarrassed about it, but the other subalterns had lost money. We all felt we had aged by several years.

As a postscript to our first paying-out, Mike and I took the envelopes to the four soldiers who were hospital patients.

"They're in Ward Five," said the clerk at Reception. "Except Corporal Yakubu."

"Oh?"

"Corporal Yakubu's back in his usual place. We'll have to keep a bed for him there, I think."

"And where's that?" We felt foolish at having to ask.

"The VD Ward."

That first pay-day was soon forgotten, and the complacency returned. If it was partly attributable to our youth and an overdose of power, it was certainly furthered by the sheer independence of our position. For when we were off duty there was no one at all to bother us, and with the 'tropical' timetable we worked – 6.30 a.m. until 1.30 p.m., usually – we had the entire evening off almost always, and on most days the afternoon as well.

Between our living-quarters and the Officers' Mess lay half a mile of rough ground, broken at intervals by plots of maize and cassava and sliced by the main road to the Camp. In the opposite direction Accra was three miles away. There were no telephone links, except in the immediate Camp area, so when we were at our quarters we had total privacy. If we were urgently required by the Colonel or the Adjutant, the message would have to come by land rover from the Camp offices, but this rarely happened. In any case we could always see the vehicle coming, so could quietly disappear until it had gone.

We were proud of the Junior Officers' Lines.

The green-and-cream dwellings were not luxury apartments, but they were quite comfortable, and we could do whatever we liked to decorate them. Our rooms quickly became cluttered with the picturesque bric-a-brac of Accra stores and Hausa salesmen: carved ornaments, wall-masks, tapestries, rush mats, curved Ashanti stools.

At the end of the veranda on my block was a large shack that housed baths, showers and toilets. Green moss grew up the walls from the constant drip and ooze, and the tin roof magnified the pitterpat of agama lizards chasing flies above. At night large bats flew in through a hole in the roof and hooked themselves like scruffy gargoyles in the corner above the showers. The bath-hut must have been a nightmare for the squeamish, but there was always plenty of running water, hot and cold, and after a day's sweating in the sun it seemed perfect luxury.

Fifty yards beyond this shack lay another double line of quarters, like ours but smaller, where the servants lived: one line for the batmen, another for mess-waiters and cooks. The area in front of their homes was a playground, and since few of the families living there had fewer than five children, many of them very young, all day a mass of fat, naked infants crawled and wriggled in the dust. When the Duty Land Rover drove by, very slowly, morning and evening, the mothers would swoop from their doorways to chivvy their own children out of the way, before returning to their cooking-pots.

Most of the servants came from the Northern Territories. They were happy, unambitious people. My own batman, Abongo Frafra, was methodical and reliable. He did nothing over and above what was needed, but his work was never inadequate. He had no wish to join an infantry platoon and gain a stripe. "I no fit be Corporal, be work too much," he always said, and meant it. His friend Kodjo Lorso, a tiny bird-faced man with very prominent eyes declared: "Dis be de best job. Plenty chop, plenty sleep…" but he was one of the few who might have liked promotion. I noticed him practising rifle-drill surreptitiously with a broom.

Abongo's wife was tiny and plump, with a wonderful smile. I asked him one day how long he had been married to her.

"Four year," he said. "I get plenty piccin."

He had indeed five tubby children, and the eldest boy looked to be well into his teens.

"I get my wife for four cow, four s'eep," Abongo reminisced. "She be fine one. Plenty time you get one wife one cow. Dat be fine cow, bad wife." He slapped his own wife on the buttocks to show how well-constructed she was. "How much you pay for wife in UK?" he asked.

"Well, we have to have a licence…" I said facetiously, "but we don't pay quite like you do."

"I tink," replied Abongo with scorn, "de time you no pay plenty money you no get fine wife attall…"

From our point of view it was convenient to have the batmen living so near. They made sure we were awake early, swept the whole area spotless each day and looked after our kit very carefully. In an emergency they were always on hand. From their point of view things were better still. We certainly did not overwork them. They were so far from Gifford Camp that they avoided virtually all parades, guard-duties and Battalion chores; and their houses were bigger and better than they would have had elsewhere.

Of course some of the batmen and Mess staff became lazy through having things so completely their own way, and we junior officers were so much lords of our own time that we often acted rashly. Unfortunately for our integrity as officers, authority invariably backed us, even when we were wrong.

One day a tall Mess servant named Awuni was arguing loudly with a stranger in the cassava plot just across the path from my *gida*. I was trying to write a letter, and yelled at them both to stop. Awuni was a surly man, who had often been in trouble previously, and when the arguing continued I strode forth, righteously indignant as I thought, Sanders of the River as usual.

"Come here," I demanded.

They ignored me, and continued to abuse each other.

"COME HERE!" I yelled. This time they came.

"Awuni, I tell you stop palaver. You palaver too much."

He looked down from a foot above my head. "Be my field," he said grumpily. "Be my cassava. I tell him go."

"I no fit work de time you make palaver," I declared. "Go away, both of you. I give you just one minute to go right away from here."

The other man walked away quietly, but Awuni refused to leave. He said he was staying to guard his cassava, as the other man would be back soon. My pride would not let me accept this. I had told Awuni to leave, and he had refused.

"If you no de go," I said, "I put you for guard-room."

This injustice was the inevitable junior officer's bluff, and nine times out of ten it worked. This time, however, Awuni refused to move.

"I no de go. Be my field. No be you tell me go. I *no* de go!"

Matters were out of my control. I sent for Allasan, the Mess Sergeant, and several others of the staff, and told them to take Awuni to the guard-room and lock him up. Alongside the giant they looked like dwarfs. He refused to budge: there was a struggle, but they overpowered him eventually, by sheer weight of numbers.

I hoped to be able to leave Awuni in a cell for a while to cool his heels, and then release him quietly. But no – he had been put in the guard-room, so he must be charged. The juggernaut was rolling.

I told the Adjutant that there was really nothing to charge him with, except refusing to obey an order that had been stupid anyway.

"He resisted arrest, didn't he?" said Major Ives. "We'll deal with him for that. The man's a trouble-maker. He needs punishing."

So Awuni was sentenced to ten days' hard labour, had his head shaved, and spent his time shifting rocks and weeding paths around the camp.

Chapter Five

THE WASTE GROUND

Beyond Awuni's ill-fated cassava patch and the 'fields' owned by the other servants, the waste ground opened onto virgin bush, which had become almost a small wildlife park. Even a casual observer, who followed the dusty path from our quarters through the cultivated plots, over a stream and out towards the Officers' Mess, would notice a great deal of colour and movement. Black-and-gold weaver birds chattered from big loofah-nests in the neem trees; barbets, like scarlet sparrows, fluttered clumsily among the tall grasses; dragonflies with blue bodies and whirring saffron wings hung above the herbage on invisible wires; and there were butterflies everywhere, of all sizes, shapes and colours. If you brushed a low shrub, grasshoppers would fizz and jump in all directions; if you jarred a branch accidentally, the red tailor ants that sewed leaves together to make nests a little above head-height would drop on you, biting like vitriol.

Care revealed much more, especially with the help of Abongo and Kodjo, who were skilful interpreters of the waste ground. A low branch would perhaps disclose a giant green caterpillar, perfectly camouflaged as a budding twig, even to the extent of a patch of white protuberances that looked just like a bird-dropping. Or a praying mantis, disguised as a folded leaf, would leap up if touched and sway like a pugilist. On a blue cascading vetch plant there might be a fat grasshopper with green wings and variegated legs, or perhaps a black-and-crimson spider poised in the centre of a flower. Near the stream was a clump of banana trees and beneath, in the shade, a pile of rotting leaves and fibres in which roamed eight-inch millipedes and vast black beetles. In holes along the pathway there were crickets that could tunnel like moles and at night flew whirring into our lighted rooms. And under almost every boulder were scorpions, ranging in size from inch-long fragile pink creatures to black, shiny giants resembling lobsters.

On one occasion Abongo discovered a female scorpion with dozens of tiny babies clinging to her back. I had just purchased some close-up lenses for my camera and was keen to photograph the whole brood, so we persuaded the mother scorpion into a cardboard box, still carrying her progeny. Back at the *gidas*, Jeremy volunteered to hold the creature by the tail, using a long pair of tweezers, while I photographed her against the pale green wall of the veranda. To start with, all went well: I took several shots while the scorpion hung obediently. Then she started to protest, bent her whole body round and began to climb back up the tweezers, clawing angrily and trying to release her sting. Not surprisingly, Jeremy dropped everything and jumped clear. The mother scorpion strutted on the veranda, sting waving furiously. With a broom we swept her into the cardboard box once more, then for the next twenty minutes we moved gingerly around the veranda scooping up dozens of baby scorpions in matchbox shovels.

There were also snakes in the waste ground.

In Hollywood Africa, pythons drape themselves from jungle trees and hiss as the intrepid explorer pushes aside the clinging creepers, while in the dry grasslands puff adders lie bloated and ostentatious. Snakes are everywhere. In reality, however, Europeans can spend years in West Africa and seldom see a snake; lizards and geckos by the thousand, certainly, but snakes, hardly ever. It requires someone like my batman, Abongo, to show how numerous they are.

I arrived in the dry season, and for weeks, saw very few snakes, and then only briefly. Abongo said: "Left small, rain come. Den you gettum plenty."

Jeremy and I were both keen to possess some snake-skins, not in the form of wallets, belts or moccasins as they appeared in Accra market, but complete skins so that we could relish their full colour and pattern – and preferably they should be poisonous ones, so that we could boast about their capture when we returned to England. Abongo said this would be quite easy, and proved his point soon after the first rains had fallen.

He had a 'snake-juju'. He did not boast about it, but the other servants vouched for its efficacy. If any snake was foolish enough to bite Abongo, it would be the snake that would die.

I never heard that the juju was put to the test, for he took sensible anti-serpent precautions like everybody else. On the one occasion I saw him face to face with a puff adder (a very small one) he killed it with multiple blows from a thick stick and left it in pulp on the road. Nonetheless he could locate snakes in the most unlikely places, and clearly his juju gave him a strong psychological advantage. Within a fortnight of the first rains, he had produced several corpses, almost undamaged, and on some half-dozen occasions had shown Jeremy and me live, slithering serpents. These were interesting for their variety, and alarming in that all resided within a short distance of our living quarters. The beautiful, blue-speckled sand snakes we did not mind, for they were quite harmless. But then we found that spitting cobras frequented the drain outside the shower room. There was one family of puff adders living in Awuni's cassava patch directly in front of my rooms; another near the road to the Officers' Mess; and Abongo captured a green mamba in the waste ground, where it had been twined around a branch about head height…

After this we thought we were prepared for anything, and when Jeremy and I discovered a small snake coiled in the rotting fibres of the banana grove, we called Abongo and Kodjo to prove to them that we too were skilful hunters. It was shaped like a puff adder, with the same evil diamond-head and bloated body, but the pattern was a vivid and beautiful chestnut-coloured latticework. The snake was very small, however, and as we saw Abongo and the other batmen all coming to examine our discovery, we were afraid they would be scornful of our 'piccin' reptile.

Instead, there was pandemonium. They gesticulated and yelled, declaring that it was 'bad pass all', and rushed off to find a stick 'for go beat um'. Fortunately, before they returned our tiny serpent had uncoiled and zigzagged away confidently into the undergrowth. We

found out later that this was a full-grown Carpet Viper, very poisonous, and feared as much for its brilliant warning-colours as for its bite.
Abongo assured me that it was the only snake against which his juju
was powerless. For several days he kept away not only from the banana
grove but from the cassava patch as well.

The Hausa salesmen first came to the *gidas* when I had been in Accra
five or six weeks. There were usually two of them, tall and very lean,
in long white robes and neat skull-caps, balancing on their heads big
ramshackle trunks, which they deposited carefully on the veranda.
 "Ehiiih, my friend, you come see."
 After much ritual sweeping of dust from the spotless floor they laid
out for inspection beautiful silks and laces and a wide array of ornaments in ivory, wood, metal and leather. Most of us bought trinkets
from them (I paid one-and-sixpence for a necklace made of greenish-
white stone that glowed in the dark) and with this encouragement the
Hausas returned a week later. Then they came every week, striding up
to the Lines in the late afternoon, balancing their heavy trunks as if
they contained thistledown, and sweeping the invisible dust from the
veranda before laying out their wares.
 After their first visit, we too developed a ritual, and for at least
ten minutes nobody would pay any attention to the visitors. This was
supposed to 'soften them up' and make them believe that no one was
interested, but Hausa patience was more than equal to our delaying
tactics, and before long we would all crowd round to see what they had
brought.
 The bargaining was enjoyed by both sides. We thought we had
shown cunning and ruthlessness if we made them quarter their prices,
only to find that the storekeepers in Accra, who themselves drove hard
bargains, were offering the same articles even more cheaply. We were
never badly swindled, however, because Tom's North-Country common sense only allowed him to buy small trinkets, and if the rest of us
looked like becoming extravagant, his scornful comments were enough
to dissuade us.
 Sometimes the Hausas produced surprising things from their
trunks. One week we had a shock when a row of small green-topped
jars appeared on the veranda and the elder of the two merchants whis-

pered: "Caviare, very fine, five silling for one."

We assumed he was joking. But it did look like caviare, and since none of us had ever tasted the real stuff, we could not judge. We bought three jars for two shillings each and as I was then in charge of the Mess food, I tentatively added 'caviare' to a dinner-night menu. The majors, who knew what was what, pronounced it excellent, and demanded that the next time 'those blighters' came we should buy up all their stock, but they never brought caviare again, and we could never discover how they had obtained it, or from where.

What the Hausas sold was mainly traditional material. Probably some of the cloth was made in Manchester, but the trinkets came mainly from the Northern Territories or, like the Hausas themselves, from Nigeria. From our arrival we had collected oddments from the Accra stores, but now our rooms began to look like alcoves in some garish museum of tribal art, with wall-masks leering through red-rimmed eyes, carved ivory elephants and ebony crocodiles, horn lamp-stands shaped into herons, shell amulets, horsetail fly-whisks, miniature Ashanti stools, and wide-brimmed hats from Bolgatanga in brilliant reds and yellows. The effect at night was stranger still, as giant moths and beetles blundered round the lights, casting huge, distorted shadows.

The Hausas also brought with them snake-skins, with elaborate wavy patterns, but Abongo was quite sure he could manage something equally fine. The first snake he skinned proved a miserable failure. It was a spitting cobra nearly four feet long and a fine purplish-black. He split it along the belly and carefully peeled off the skin, which he pegged out in the sun to dry. Impatiently we awaited the result. This proved to be a thin, brittle parchment, dull grey on the scaly side and almost transparent. A liberal application of black boot-polish to the 'inside' made it supple again, but this flimsy strip of snake bore little resemblance to a spitting cobra.

We examined more closely the skins that the Hausamen brought. These were thick, firm, but beautifully supple. So the next time that Abongo killed a snake, instead of peeling it like removing a stocking, he left plenty of flesh on the skin before pegging it out in the sun to dry. For a short while the smell was dreadful, but flies and ants quickly sucked out the juices and the hot sun did the rest. The result was a puff adder skin which maintained its colour perfectly.

My only text-book suggested that four foot was a record length for a puff adder. This specimen, even without its head, was several inches longer, which was exciting until someone pointed out that a pegged-out skin would surely stretch. Record or no record, when hung on my wall it made an impressive display, and before long several other *gidas* were similarly decorated. When next the Hausas produced their rolled snakeskins, we retaliated by laying ours out in a line along the veranda.

❖ ❖ ❖

If our rooms were colourful and interesting inside, the exterior remained unbroken green and cream, until with the first showers of the year orange lilies bloomed suddenly at the edge of the veranda, and the untidy green foliage twining up the supporting pillars opened trumpets of purple convolvulus.

Several pets joined us. Some green African Sparrows in a cage hanging from the roof were bright and entertaining for a while, but their bickering and shrill twitter soon became a nuisance, and no one was really sorry when they squeezed through the wicker-work and escaped.

The most noteworthy pet was Dai's Green Monkey, which was really yellowish-grey. It lived on a table outside his bedroom, fastened by a long chain to the catch on his shuttered window. It was at first a friendly beast, and the chain allowed it the freedom of much of the veranda. If anyone passed by unawares, it would leap onto his shoulder and tug affectionately at his hair or gnaw the buttons off his shirt. The batmen hated all monkeys and this one in particular – "Be like smallsmall man *too* much" – while the rest of us tried to treat it as a joke and avoided that part of the veranda when we remembered.

Sometimes when Dai went to bathe at Labadi Beach the monkey rode too, tied to the rear seat of his Lambretta scooter, clinging small and terrified to his shirt.

At Labadi it would frisk on the shore, tethered loosely to a palm trunk but for a few hours believing that it was a wild monkey again. Then one day it fell off the scooter. Witnesses said that some way from Labadi Dai had flashed by them at about forty miles an hour, with the monkey racing behind at the end of its chain, its feet a blur. Dai assured us that this was exaggeration, and declared that he had noticed when the animal fell off, and had stopped almost at once. Nonetheless a very morose monkey glowered on the veranda that evening. Physically it seemed little harmed, but mentally it was shattered.

It became vicious, liable to bite, and the servants were terrified of it. It escaped once, smashed an expensive electric iron by throwing it onto the floor, and tried to eat a watch. It was recaptured, but for a small animal that monkey had amazing strength. Soon it broke free once more, and this time careered systematically through the *gidas*, leaving a trail of smashed property. Its end was mysterious: sold, burnt or eaten. We never saw it again.

We had a variety of short-term pets. There was an African Grey Parrot that hissed but never spoke a word, which eventually found a better home with one of the warrant-officers at Brigade. There was a bush-baby that by night was marvellously agile as it leapt around the spare room like a giant flea, but never moved by day and smelt horrible. And there was a chameleon named Fred. I found him in the Shai Hills, and for a time he lived on a large pawpaw tree outside my bedroom window. One of the first tasks each morning was to 'find Fred'. He was obviously somewhere on the tree, but with his wonderful camouflage he sometimes remained undiscovered for several minutes. We used to release small insects on the branches near him and watch the miraculous whiplash of his tongue. When we offered him a giant millipede, however, he backed away with eyes rolling, the fastest we ever saw him move. Normally he never shifted one clawed foot until the other three were securely anchored.

We experimented for hours with Fred's ability to change colour, and probably did his metabolism no good. Green and brown, dull yellowish and dark grey he could achieve easily, and he could quickly assume a fine green-brown mottle if the background required it. Brick-red he could just manage, but on a scarlet rug he was uncomfortable and conspicuous. Blues were quite beyond him and he invariably turned greenish-brown instead, while black made him change to grey with apoplectic purplish blotches. On a white paper he turned pale green and looked so ill that we swiftly transferred him to some green leaves.

For three weeks and more Fred lived on the pawpaw tree; then one morning he had disappeared. Perhaps he had been picked off by some predatory bird. More probably he had finally tired of his limited fruit-tree home, and during the night had moved slowly down the trunk, across the path and into the waste ground, where there were plenty of trees.

These were the main pets, but unsurprisingly I also kept large numbers of insects in my rooms in a variety of cages. Usually these were caterpillars. The majority I found by myself, but via the batmen word soon spread of my interest, and several soldiers from the Battalion and a few officers also contributed creatures they had found. I reared huge silk-moths and several kinds of hawk-moth. Silver-striped Hawk caterpillars, with spectacular eye-spots, were particularly numerous, and instead of caging the larvae, I released them in the flower-beds outside our own quarters and at the Mess, where they fed on various convolvulus and vine plants. For a while I also kept several kinds of stick insect and praying mantis, including an extraordinary small greenish species with wonderful black and orange eye-circles on its wing-cases, which the batmen named 'the Gold Coast Flag'. Best of all were the fireflies, which flickered at night among the cassava plants. Ten or a dozen put into a net bag and hung in my window made a wonderful fairy illumination that I could watch from my bed.

I wrote to my friend Hugh Newman, who had a Butterfly Farm in Kent, to tell him of my experiences, and mentioned the insects I had seen; also how, although I had no light trap, I could find numbers of exciting moths every morning, around the electric bulbs on our veranda and, above all, by the strip-lighting at the Military Hospital and our own Headquarters Office. I received a letter from Hugh asking me to obtain for him 'a gross each of *nerii, celerio* and *livornica,* and 100 Praying Mantis' for his sales-list at the Butterfly Farm. I explained that such vast numbers were entirely out of the question, but I did send half a dozen each of Oleander, Silver-striped and Striped Hawk-moths, and a few mantids (including one 'Gold Coast Flag') and typically he wrote back offering profuse thanks, but also sending a fine kite-net. Later, I was able to send him eggs of the beautiful Oleander Hawk-moth, and he managed to rear several generations of moths from them. He said they were a big attraction on 'Children's Days' at the Farm.

Chapter 6

CHOPMASTER

For just under a month I was responsible for the food provided for the Officers' Mess. In some ways it was a thankless task, for good catering was taken for granted and seldom acknowledged, while everyone was ready to criticize a single bad meal. The funds available were constant, and while overspending was a crime, if there was too much money left over it was assumed that the 'Chopmaster' had been miserly. He was bound to lose, either way.

I enjoyed the job, however, and particularly the challenge of working with two very temperamental cooks. They made a wonderful Laurel-and-Hardy partnership. Cook-Sergeant Kofi was Hardy, an enormous, rather pale-skinned man with sad eyes and a wilting moustache. His normal speaking voice was an apologetic whisper, incongruous from such a giant. Cook-Corporal Atongo was Laurel, a short, very earnest fellow whose chief job was to purchase the fresh food from Accra. Each day he shuffled from stall to stall in the market on extremely flat feet, buying provisions from the mammies at reasonable prices without having to argue. He could neither read nor write, but always remembered exactly what each item had cost, and how much he had spent altogether.

Kofi and Atongo were good friends, but at least once a week they would have a blazing row. This usually started from something trivial. Atongo might have bought seven pounds of bananas instead of six, or perhaps Kofi had omitted one of the ingredients of a curry. It always ended in ferocious shadow-boxing with the big kitchen table between the two combatants, while the rest of the cook-staff and the Mess waiters watched in awe. What made their antics even more amusing was that, each being ignorant of the other's tribal language, they had to converse in pidgin-English. The Sergeant screamed and swore and tears ran down his cheeks, while the otherwise imperturbable Atongo would shake his fists and jump up and down with rage. Then both would subside, and laugh together.

The first time I witnessed such an explosion, I treated the cooks like infants. I said they were silly men pass-all, piccins and bloody fools, and if they did it again I would have them both dismissed. They stopped quarrelling and glared at me. For two days they did whatever I asked them, just about adequately, so that I could not complain. Cold war was declared. Then there was another fit of temper from Sergeant Kofi. He came screaming out of the kitchen waving a paper wrapping that had contained a loaf of bread, but now held an apologetic crust, like a battered barrel. The whole of the inside had been scooped out, and there were rodent teeth-marks and droppings on what was left.

"You bloo'y Corporal-man!" Kofi yelled. "You go lef' hopen bloo'y bled cubber! Bloo'y lat go tiefum!"

In seconds there was another ding-dong battle, which I left to its peaceful conclusions. After that, all was well again.

With ingenuity it was possible to prepare an exciting menu quite cheaply, although with so many British officers present, 'experimental' food had to be disguised. Everyone would eat strange ingredients in stews and curries, with no questions asked, but for other dishes more care was needed. Once, some very delicate meat that everybody enjoyed was called veal, but was really 'Grass Cutter' or giant cane-rat. And the huge prawns served as 'lobster' pleased everyone, but might not have done so if the junior officers had been observed at Labadi Beach, bargaining with the market-women for a basin-full of smelly red crustaceans covered in flies.

Kofi and Atongo were excellent cooks and good organisers, but if anything went wrong they would panic dreadfully. We had wonderful rice dishes and groundnut stews, and straightforward European food was always very satisfactorily cooked, but occasionally some small item would cause trouble. Ice cream produced one crisis.

Atongo bought a tin of ice-cream powder in Accra in mistake for powdered milk. Ice cream seemed an excellent idea anyway, so I told the cooks to go ahead and make some. With our help they followed the instructions on the label and put the mixture in the refrigerator. Unfortunately, the concoction refused to set, but as Kofi was not really sure what they had been trying to make, the white frothy cream was served at a meal – and politely rejected. There were angry tears from the Cook-Sergeant. It was explained tactfully that ice cream should be firm; you should eat it, not drink it. Perhaps the mixture needed whipping-up more. The cooks set to work.

Ice cream was served again at lunch next day. This time it was a square block of white ice so hard that we could not even cut it. Mike broke the block eventually by dropping it on the floor, and we used pieces to cool glasses of beer, but the sweetness and the cloudy effect were unpleasant. No one wanted to offend the cooks again, so we wrapped the rest of the 'ice cream' in a newspaper and smuggled it out to a dust-bin.

That same afternoon, as we were leaving the Mess, we met Sergeant Kofi in his smartest clothes, just setting out for Accra.

"Ice cleam be hall light?"

"Yes, fine," everyone agreed.

Kofi beamed and went on his way. As we feared, another block of solid ice appeared for lunch next day.

Regimental guest-nights were Sergeant Kofi's joy. At all times he liked decorating the simplest dishes, arranging fruit by colours and inscribing sugar-patterns on cakes and jellies. On dinner-nights he found real scope for his artistry, and often a course would arrive so beautifully arranged that it seemed a crime to eat it. Sometimes, however, the first stages of preparation were less refined. The turkey that was served for our New Year's dinner was delicious when we ate it at 8.30 p.m. Twelve hours earlier, however, when it arrived at the Mess, it was a very lively turkey. The servants grabbed the bird and poured three tots of whisky down its throat. They allowed an hour for the drink to 'soak in', then held the turkey with its neck stretched over a log. One blow from a machete severed its head.

The two cooks were Northerners, and so was Sergeant Allasan, who was in charge of the Mess staff. Most of the other servants were Southerners, but they were all able to talk together in barrack-Hausa and pidgin-English, and the Sergeant had little difficulty in making himself understood – except to Henry Irem.

Henry had recently come from Nigeria. He was a round-faced, pale-skinned man with protruding eyes that reminded us of a bush-baby's, giving him an expression of perpetual surprise. He knew no Hausa, and had to speak English all the time, even to the Mess staff, because no one understood his own dialect. His English was good: he spoke very, very slowly, with pedantic over-emphasis of unimportant words, but the officers found everything he said both easy to follow and sensible. Unfortunately, his fellow-servants could not understand his English at all.

Once we had a magnificent apple flan for lunch.

"Henry," Jeremy demanded at tea, "go and tell the cooks to bring us what's left of that pie we had for lunch. The apple one."

"I will tell them immediately, sir." We sat back and waited.

"Sir," said Henry, reappearing, "the cooks are saying they do not have the pie at all."

"They must have eaten it," said Jeremy. "Ask them instead, Henry, to make us a big, big plate of tomato sandwiches." Henry went.

Nearly twenty minutes later he came back with a big, big plate, as requested, but there was no tomato in the sandwiches – just butter.

"What on earth did you tell the cooks?"

"I am telling them," Henry said. "I am telling them to put tomato inside the bread. They have not done what I told them."

Jeremy went to investigate for himself.

"Sargy Kofi," he said, "be so Henry come for say we want sandwich-chop with plenty tomato?"

"Henry come, sah…" the Sergeant looked worried. "He come, sah, de time we no savvy de ting he say. We go haskim for say um so we savvy proper, den *he* no savvy de ting we say attall!"

As an afterthought Jeremy opened the refrigerator. There lay more than half of an apple flan.

We had two kittens at the Officers' Mess, one black, one white. They were named by the staff 'Africa Cat' and 'UK Cat', and were much pampered, but Sergeant Allasan had to keep a perpetual watch over them.

"De time I no lookum," he said, "somebody tiefum, takeum for chop."

The Colonel owned a small, leggy puppy of no known breed, and apparently paid the Mess sixpence a day to feed it on scraps of meat. I had been Chopmaster for over a week when he mentioned to me that the scraps were not being provided. I had heard nothing about these arrangements, so consulted the cooks.

"Be so, sah," said Kofi. "Long time we feedum. But now we get two cat, dey better pass piccin dog."

Kofi and Atongo were sometimes a pantomime, sometimes irritating, but they were very capable cooks and before long the food in the Mess really had reached a high standard. Everyone said so. I was beginning to congratulate myself on the excellent work I was doing – with some help from the cooks, of course – when one morning Major Ives sent for me.

"You're to hand over all your food duties," he said, in his usual abrupt manner. "You can have three or four days to teach young Browne how to organise the cooks, so he can take over. All right?"

'Young Browne' had joined the Battalion some ten days previously, so the switch in jobs was a natural succession. I wondered what Company I would be sent to as a Platoon Commander, and whether I should now have more time to work at the Education Department.

"Well, what are you waiting for?" said Ives. "Go and find young Browne. I haven't got all day, even if you have."

As I was going out, he added: "From next week you will be working for me, in this office…"

Abongo with a puff adder

Dakota Dagarti with the 'mad monkey'

Labadi Lagoon

Labadi Beach

Fishing boats

One of Accra's markets

Snake charmer

...and his cobras

Guard duty

57

Chapter Seven

POLITICS

In England we had been brainwashed thoroughly into thinking ourselves future Officers of the Empire. Our training had nurtured a belief in our own eventual superiority, and the brainwashing had included much two-faced lauding of our potential rank. If we had accused our superiors of racism, many of them would have been appalled. Nonetheless, the NCOs at Eaton Hall frequently launched into xenophobic tirades to boost self-belief, particularly in those of us who had ambitions to serve in Africa or Asia.

"Call yourself a leader (SIR)! In two or three months (SIR) you'll prob'ly find yourself in the jungle with twenty black soldiers depending on you (SIR) licking your arse and following you like bastard black sheep."

This unattractive caricature suggested that all nations would apparently bow down to us. Even the Welsh were proved by military logic to be an inferior race. I recall our company commander's reaction, after that humiliating evening in the pub at Trawsfynnydd, when the locals, who had been chatting in English when we arrived, apparently now understood only Welsh. The very next day he managed to magnify the incident to illustrate another of his homilies on the English Fighting Man's Superiority, much to the disgust of the Scots, Irish, Malayan, Gurkha – and Welsh – members of our unit.

Those of us who joined the Accra Battalion of the Gold Coast Regiment found, however, perhaps to our surprise, that racism would play no part in our service. Colonel Quinn was too gentle to lead a Battalion with distinction, but he had a genuine affection for his soldiers, and probably never even noticed their colour. Most of his senior officers were equally lacking in racist views (as the affable Major Willis said to me "There's not much point in coming out here, otherwise, is there?") and we were especially lucky in having some very helpful African officers, who quickly became friends and advisers. At first, Emmanuel Kotoka was our role-model. Before joining the army, he had been a schoolmaster, which enabled him to communicate easily with African soldiers of all ranks – and with European second lieutenants. He was the first African officer we had met; he obviously liked us, and we listened to him.

About five o'clock one afternoon Jeremy, Mike and I were returning from the beach at Labadi and stopped at the Mess. A new batch of newspapers had arrived from England, and we wanted to catch up on what was happening at home.

Two officers were in the lounge, sitting together, talking. One was Emmanuel Kotoka, the other an English captain none of us had seen before, a thin-faced man with a fair, watery moustache. We discovered later that he was from Brigade Headquarters, exercising his right to a drink as an honorary member of the Second Battalion Officers' Mess. The three of us collected our newspapers and retired to the other side of the lounge.

It was impossible not to listen. They were discussing the move to Arakan Barracks, their voices friendly but rather loud. Wasn't it a shambles, the Captain wanted to know, to have the barracks and the Battalion offices so far from the Mess? It must be all of two miles. Emmanuel replied that it was better that way, since it gave the soldiers a feeling of privacy.

Suddenly: "What was the matter with the old barracks?" the moustached officer asked. "The place seemed perfectly good to me. Good enough for the soldiers, anyway. Isn't it unwise to give them too much privacy?"

Emmanuel said nothing. The other pressed on, recklessly.

"If you leave them all by themselves at Arakan Barracks, there'll be mass drunkenness and worse, within weeks, I bet."

There was a long silence. We read our newspapers very seriously.

Then, "Why do you think that?" asked Emmanuel quietly.

The Englishman looked uncomfortable. The three of us kept reading. There was another long silence, broken eventually by Emmanuel himself.

"May I say how I think you see it?" he asked coolly. "You can tell me if I'm wrong."

"Do," said the Captain, looking puzzled. He was aware that he had offended, but seemed unsure how. "Yes, go on."

"I think you say to yourself 'these African soldiers are good enough chaps and mean well and all that, but they're bushmen. All they want is to have their chop and their drink and their women.' Isn't that about it?"

The Captain was trying to look bored, but seemed embarrassed.

"Well, don't you?" Kotoka asked. "Don't you think to yourself quite often, and sometimes out loud, 'If nobody keeps an eye on these people they'll go back to the jungle'?" For a moment his voice had become a wicked mimicry of the Colonel's.

"I... didn't..." Unease was defeating the affected boredom. "It's not... I'm not..."

"You said 'What's the matter with the old barracks'? That's not what you meant. You meant 'What's the good of giving these bush people new concrete houses with proper roofs, and special cooking rooms, and drainage, and washing huts with toilets?' You meant 'They were perfectly happy with their mud huts, cooking on charcoal in the open, and whatever you do for them they'll still use the gutters for latrines and keep goats and chickens in the back porch.' Not so?"

The Englishman said nothing, but he looked alarmed, unwillingly angry, like a child who has been scratched by a pet kitten. Emmanuel went on and on remorselessly, cutting quietly through pretensions and misconceptions, slicing through accepted illogic. The belief that because an African soldier could not speak English well, he therefore would not understand English, so you could be as rude to him as you liked... And paradoxically, that if you spoke to an African loudly enough he would eventually understand you... Africans, he said, were people, not possessions or 'things'.

"I'm an African," Emmanuel said, "or have you forgotten that? I'm not getting at you in particular – or at Michael or David or Jeremy over there who've been pretending to read their newspapers but have been listening hard all the time!"

The Captain from Brigade had to go. He was sorry, but he had been invited to dinner with the Brigadier, and must get washed and changed before he and his wife went along. He was sorry, he had to rush. It transpired that Lieutenant and Mrs Emmanuel Kotoka would be at the dinner, too. The Captain looked stunned, almost hunted. He walked out through the wrong door, into the dining-room, came back and said "Sorry. Thanks," and walked out down the Mess steps.

"Stop me next time I talk too much," Emmanuel said. "I'm supposed to be a soldier, not a politician."

One of the things Emmanuel tried to teach us, however, was indeed Gold Coast politics. In this respect my colleagues and I were naïve. We meant well, but perhaps if we had arrived on the Coast a little earlier, soon enough to have witnessed the July elections, we might have been less ignorant, less patronising. If, instead of reading about it later, we had seen and heard the violent clash between the Convention People's Party and the National Liberation Movement, the party parades and canvassing to drum accompaniment, the bribery, the thuggery – the deaths – we might have taken more seriously the sheer toughness of Gold Coast politics. The fact that the country was shortly to gain its Independence interested us to the extent that we would be there when it happened, but at first we made little effort to understand the true significance of the event.

Our view of the Government and its Prime Minister was certainly patronising. We tended to think of the Cabinet of the Gold Coast as a Lilliputian band, lorded over by Gulliver in the person of Sir Charles Arden-Clarke, the Governor. Kwame Nkrumah was Flimnap, the minister-clown dancing on his tightrope.

We saw Nkrumah sometimes on the cinema newsreels, opening fetes and show-rooms. We occasionally saw him in person in Accra, a big, beaming man with receding hair, who waved as he was driven about the town in a large black car with a motor-cycle escort, just as if he were the Governor, or rather how we had imagined a Governor should be. For we all knew that our real Governor was quite different, a nice old boy, not at all flamboyant. On our days as Orderly Officer, when we were inspecting the guard at Christiansborg Castle or Flagstaff House, we would sometimes see him, either in the courtyard or driving out towards Accra. He was an unassuming man, usually in a dark suit. When we saluted, he waved back or took off his trilby: a dignified, quiet man, the reverse of the Prime Minister.

We had all seen Nkrumah informally at a big Military Demonstration in the Shai Hills. We had all laughed at him.

That Demonstration had been the culmination of a massive exercise involving most of the Gold Coast military forces, and whereas Alec and Geoff had been out in the Hills with their platoons for the full time, I was only able to see the final phase.

The Shai Hills rise from a wide grassy plain some twenty miles North-East of Accra, and provide a wonderful site for military manoeuvres. The exercise spread far afield, but there was a permanent headquarters in the foothills, with rows of corrugated-iron-roofed huts. At night hyenas laughed, and reputedly leopards frequented the area. Certainly there were baboons, which stayed by day in the grassland but at dusk congregated in family parties above the army huts and, with simian humour, rolled boulders down the corrugated roofs.

Nkrumah came out with most of his Cabinet to watch the spectacular climax, Demonstration Day. He cut a tape to start things off, and everybody applauded. Then the Army went briskly to work. Smoke-grenades swirled dense clouds across the plain and thunder-flashes boomed; then, in a rumbustious attack with blank ammunition, black bodies died realistically all around, to the accompaniment of delighted screams of agony. Nkrumah beamed happily. The Cabinet clapped and yelled.

There was a Signals Exercise, followed by a Mortar Demonstration; then the Engineers swept into action flinging Bailey bridges rapidly over non-existent ravines. Every platoon and section seemed to be doing something. It was all an unqualified success.

In the next few days there were lengthy press accounts of this 'wonderful demonstration', with pictures of the Cabinet 'joining in'. In particular there was a photograph of Nkrumah chatting to the G.O.C., General Paley, with the Governor in the background. The Prime Minister of the Gold Coast was wearing an army tin-helmet, complete with camouflage-netting, and on his face was an expression of utter delight. I imagine that if the Governor had been wearing the tin hat we would have admired his sporting nature. As it was, "Silly kid," was the only comment when the photograph of Nkrumah appeared in the Mess.

Three or four days later there was a full radio account of the Shai Hills Demonstration, conveniently broadcast soon after lunch so that many of the officers heard it. The commentator spared little. It was, he assured us, 'an example of the Army's new, ruthless efficiency' (applause, especially from Alec and Geoff) 'and versatility' (more applause.) He pictured the various demonstrations colourfully and dramatically, then came to what was, for him, the day's highlight.

"Finally," he said, "there was a quite remarkable display of virtuosity given by the Signals Platoon, commanded by an African officer, Captain Crabbe" (applause for Alex's promotion.) "In fact, it was so breathtaking that I will play you an extract."

Voice of commentator, muzzy, on tape: Good afternoon, Captain Crabbe. What are your men going to demonstrate for us?

Alex, even muzzier: Signalling.

Commentator: Good. Now, what can they do?

Alex: You see that man on the hill up there?

Commentator: Yes. He's about two hundred yards away, silhouetted against the sky.

Alex: I'm going to speak to him, using this set and, you'll see, he'll do what I say.

Commentator: Well, that's very interesting.

Alex: Hello One, jump twice, over. Hello One, I say again, jump twice, over. *Long pause.* Go on. Go on! *Longer Pause.* Hullo One, JUMP TWICE, over...

Commentator: And he HAS! I saw him jump, quite clearly! Would you believe it! Captain Crabbe, that really was breathtaking!

We had belittled Nkrumah's enthusiasm, yet the naivety of the *English* commentator had been seen as a good joke. It needed the common sense of Emmanuel, but also of Sam Lartey and Alex Crabbe himself, to show us a more balanced attitude, and soon after I had listened to

Emmanuel's put-down of the Brigade officer, I had a chance to test my own new-found maturity.

It was my turn as Orderly Officer again, and I was determined to enjoy even that. I would learn from everything. I would not interfere, but would offer help only where it was needed. I would be smart and enthusiastic. I would work really hard.

I put my *Hausa Grammar* in the back of the land rover as a reminder, and drove to Flagstaff House to inspect the Guard.

They were very smart, as usual: khaki starched and spotless, zouave jackets red as a sunset, boots mirror-bright, rifles gleaming.

"Turnout be fine," I said to Corporal Salifu. "I likeum plenty."

The Corporal beamed. I stayed to watch him giving his men their instructions for night sentry duty. They were new soldiers, on guard for the first time, and stood in a line in front of him, listening earnestly. The ebullient Corporal was enjoying himself.

"You-all be sentry one-one," he said. "Be Kwaku firs', left small be John, den be Abompata. You-all. You savvy?"

"Yessah, Corp'l sah, we savvy!"

"Dis be de ting you do. Sometime Ordry Off'cer come. Tonight be dis Off'cer. You seeum?"

All the Guard turned to look at me, grinning. "Yessah, Corp'l sah, be so we seeum!"

"Dis be de ting you do. You hear dis lorry come," (pointing to the land rover) "an' you say youself 'Ahaaah, be Ordry Off'cer!' Den you go wake dis odder men, dey-all be ready. You savvy?"

"Yessah!"

"Mebbe sometime no be Ordry Off'cer attall. Alldesame, you de say youself 'Who dis man done come?' You de wake dis odder guard jusdesame, dey ready. You savvy?"

"Yessah!"

"De time anyone done come, dis be de nexting you de do. Be dark, you no fit see proper, you lettum come small small for dis place." Corporal Salifu paced forward fifteen yards or so from the sentry-post at the gates, and gestured with both arms wide. "For dis place, you savvy?"

They did.

"Den you de shout: 'Halt! Who – is – going – dey ?'

The men nodded.

"You liff yous rifle like dis." The men followed him, bayonets held rigidly before them.

"What ting you de shout?"

"HALT! – Who – is – going – DEY!" They pointed their bayonets ferociously.

"Fine," said the Corporal. "Now I tell you de nexting. Be dark like I de say, you no seeum proper, be too much far. Thasswhy you de say: 'Hadvance – one – to – de – firs' – crocodile.' Ebrybody hear?"

The men understood at once. I thought I must have heard incorrectly.

"What ting you de say?"

"HADVANCE – ONE – TO – DE – FIRSSS' – CLOCO-DILE!!"

Previously, I would have interrupted, trying officiously to get Corporal Salifu to give the correct orders from the Manual. Now, I was prepared to listen. When he had gone through his instruction to his own satisfaction, I asked him why he did not teach the Guard to say 'Advance one and be recognised'?

The Corporal was very patient, feeling no doubt that I was as raw and ignorant as his young soldiers. He explained that no one would understand this 'lecognise palaver' (and in any case why not say "Come to me, so I fit see you?") whereas everyone would know a crocodile. The words sounded much the same, didn't they? The challenging-area, where he had spread his arms wide and expected the sentry to shout, was the edge of the river. The first bayonet was the first crocodile, and there were plenty more in the guard-room, all with fine teeth for chopping with. It was very simple, really.

My new, listening self agreed with him entirely. As I left, he was explaining to the Guard, with chilling directness, what they were to do to any person who failed to halt when challenged.

Chapter Eight

INTELLIGENCE PALAVER

Major Ives's large work-table was placed diagonally across one corner of the office, so that he had an uninterrupted view of the Orderly Room and the other two doorways, and could tell who went to and fro on the veranda outside. My table was opposite, between two doors. When anyone came in from the veranda, my papers blew onto the floor, until I was given a dummy grenade to use as a paper-weight. The other door behind me was usually shut, and led to the Colonel's office. It opened soundlessly, and without a through-draught, but I always knew when the Colonel was emerging, because Major Ives would be halfway out of his seat before the door was fully open.

There were three trays on the Adjutant's table, stencilled *IN*, *OUT* and *PENDIN*, the painter having come to the edge of the third box without managing to complete his work. There was also a plaque which said *ADJUTANT, MAJOR D. H. IVES Royal Artillery* and was dusted each morning by the Chief Clerk.

I had merely an *IN* and an *OUT* tray on my table, but I had two plaques. The first said *ASST ADJT* and showed me to be Ives's deputy; the second said *INTELLIGENCE OFFICER*. I was proud of both, so left them prominently in view all the time.

More important than anything else in that office were Major Ives's two telephones, the vital part of his Adjutant's equipment. On these he kept up a remarkable one-way communication with all parts of the Battalion, organising, chivvying, rebuking, occasionally praising. It must have been a nightmare for the operators, for often both 'phones were in use at once, as Ives checked and relayed details to different departments simultaneously. The spoken word, he argued, was always better than the written message. He had been six years on the Coast, and He Knew. All soldiers were fine as long as you kept them up to the mark. As long as you made them think you were watching them. If you wanted something done and sent them a written notification, ten to one they'd lose it, or put it away and forget it until it was too late. You had to keep watching them. So he watched them with the telephone. This enabled him to keep his *IN* tray almost empty, while the *PENDIN* one was never used. Colour-Sergeant Annobil, the tiny Chief Clerk, used to make sure that every message he handed to the Adjutant was marked at the top with the sender's telephone number in red. If it was something that could not be attended to by 'phone, in my capacity as Assistant Adjutant I usually had to draft the written reply.

I also had a telephone in our office, although I used it far less often. Initially it had the same extension-number as one of Ives's 'phones, but this proved disastrous.

"Ring the Quartermaster for me," the Adjutant would bark, "and ask if he's done anything about those new blankets for 'A' Company. I'm just going to 'phone Brigade about the Signals Exercise."

We would pick up our telephones and dial the required numbers.

"Hello? Hello?"

"Hello. Who's speaking?"

"This is the Assistant Adjutant. Is that the Quartermaster?"

"No it's not. Does it *sound* like the bloody QM? It's me, and I'm all of four yards from you. Get off the line!"

So I was given a separate extension-number.

There was no telephone in the Orderly Room next door, although one was certainly needed. Ives declared that the clerks were safer without one – there was no knowing what they'd be up to with a 'phone, inviting wives and girl-friends along, or ringing Flagstaff House or what-have-you – and the European clerks would be worse than the African ones. So they managed without. If it was vital for them to learn something very quickly, details from the Military Hospital, perhaps, or Pay Records, Annobil would pad quietly in and borrow my 'phone, first making sure that Ives was safely engaged in conversation on his own double network or, better still, absent. Otherwise the younger clerks went on foot as message carriers.

The Intelligence Officer was supposed to know about everything that was happening in his whole Battalion area. Since the district was roughly the size of Wales, this knowledge was merely theoretical, but I hoped that, as IO, I would be encouraged to travel around and learn as much as I could about 'my' area. When I took over the job, however, Ives quickly put paid to such enthusiasm.

"Good God, man," he said, "there's only six weeks till Independence, and you expect to go gallivanting about in a land rover. There'll be more than enough here to keep you fully occupied. So my initial 'Intelligence' experience was largely obtained at my office table, struggling with the mysteries of *HERCULES*, *BLITHE* and *DOTAGE*.

These were Internal Security code-names, the explanation of which could be found in several thick files in the Intelligence Safe, beside the Adjutant's table. Ives held the key, of course, in both senses.

To my distant recollection, *HERCULES* was the security scheme covering the whole of the Gold Coast, with details of mobilization of troops in the event of 'trouble' anywhere in the country. There was nothing to explain what 'trouble' might mean: 'Little men with blow-pipes creeping in from the Ivory Coast,' was Major Watkin-Williams's suggestion.

DOTAGE, which seemed aptly named, was an exercise designed by Brigade Headquarters to see whether *HERCULES* would work (and, Ives added, to give Brigade HQ something to do.) *BLITHE* was the code-word meaning 'Degrees of Readiness: Stage 1'. We checked in the file and found an addition: 'Action, nil.' "Which means," said the Adjutant, "that you say 'I heard you,' but do damn-all."

The paper-work for all these Intelligence games was extraordinary. Dispatches came in duplicate and triplicate from Headquarters, and the procedure was an unvaried pantomime. A uniformed dispatch-rider would zoom up to the Orderly Room, parking his motor-cycle on the veranda before entering importantly with his dispatch-box. For a while, he and the clerks would greet each other with much back-slapping and many 'Ahaaahs'. He would come at last to our office. Now, from his box he would take an envelope marked *SECRET* or *TOP SECRET*, which he always handed over with the air of a conjurer showing his most exciting trick. Major Ives or I had to sign the receipt for it, and the dispatch-rider then departed with even greater ceremony of bowing and pirouetting, and zoomed back to Brigade Headquarters, a full two hundred yards away.

The document might contain a new security letter-code in which we were to correspond with Headquarters if secrecy was urged, or it might begin 'In the event of an emergency' and restate details of mobilization. More often, however, it proved to be merely a correction of some earlier letter: 'ref. ABC/22/581 third line, for <u>NOW </u>read <u>NOT</u>.' I would read it, sign it and hand it to the Adjutant, who would glance at it, tick it and sign his name in one corner. It went next to the Second-in-Command, who would say: "It makes sense, eh? Wrrrrwrrrr, I'm not signing my life away, eh?" and sign it. Then the Colonel would read it, say: "Glad everything seems to be under control. Hope you understand it," and sign it. After which I would add the document to its appropriate file.

Dai, as the previous Intelligence Officer, had never bothered much about letters from Brigade.

"At first I used to read them once through," he said, when explaining the job to me. "Then I filed them away, but so I could find them again if there was a flap on. Then, as nothing ever happened, I gave up reading them…"

Each month I was supposed to send an Intelligence Report to Headquarters, written in code (presumably for practice, mine and theirs) and Dai advised me to keep it short. I enjoyed the coding, however, and my first report, which took me hours to encrypt to my satisfaction, explained exactly what areas the Battalion could and could not cover for Intelligence purposes. I wrote in a joky style, which, after I had sent the document off, I feared might be considered in bad taste. In any case it was presumptuous of me, and it served me right when a long, enthusiastic letter came from Brigade, 'G 111 Int.', with detailed suggestions for reorganising our Intelligence set-up. It was written in code, and took me several hours to decipher.

"So, to get things back to normal," said Ives, "I suggest your next volume should explain to 'G 111 Int.', whoever he is, that *we* do not have a whole Intelligence Platoon with hours to waste, but a single very nosy Intelligence Officer who is also my Assistant Adjutant!"

Despite Ives's scepticism, there was a pleasant sequel to this Intelligence communication. At a drinks party given by our Battalion for the officers at Headquarters, I was surprised when a charming, bespectacled captain asked Colonel Quinn to introduce me to him.

"I'm Tony," he said. "G 111 Int.!"

He then went on to explain to the Colonel that I was the first officer ever to reply creatively to any of his encoded messages. "I think people usually just file them away," he said. "It's good for my morale to have someone prepared to make me work!"

"Douglas," the Colonel said to the Adjutant a few minutes later, deliberately in my hearing, "Brigade seem to be pleased with this young man, so I hope you'll give him time to meet them more often."

I had one chance for practical Intelligence work in those early days. It was not a success.

Friday night at the Officers' Mess was Regimental Guest Night, when we dressed in our white mess-kit to welcome two or three distinguished visitors, who had been invited to an especially elaborate meal. Afterwards, most of the senior officers stayed drinking and became maudlin, before some of them joined in foolish party-games. The junior officers were not supposed to leave until their superiors had gone home, which meant that often we were forced to stay at the Mess until three or four a.m. Fortunately, our fragile wages would not permit us to drink much, so we spent most of our time playing snooker with twisted cues on a cloth untrue, waiting to be allowed home.

Twice, when we returned to our quarters after a dinner-night, several of us found that sums of money were missing from our rooms. The first time, we felt we could have been mistaken. At four a.m. the problem did not seem to matter greatly, anyway, since we had lost only a few coppers and sixpences. Perhaps we had merely put our loose cash away carelessly. We forgot all about it. The second time was more serious, for several people were sure that they had lost one-pound or ten-shilling notes. It appeared to be an inside job, too, since on our return we had found our doors locked, and in any case only the batmen and Mess staff would have known when all the quarters would be empty.

Not everybody was convinced that money had been stolen. Geoff, for one, said that it was just imagination. He had lost nothing himself. After a dinner-night, he pronounced repeatedly, people were far too hazy to know whether they had lost money or not. So, to be quite sure of our facts, the following week we scattered coppers and sixpences in obvious places, on tables and shelves, making a note of what we had left, and where. The coins all disappeared while we were at dinner.

The Intelligence Officer swept into action.

Among my sleuthing possessions I had inherited a bottle of green powder, which I now had a chance to use. Apparently, anyone touching the stuff would quickly find a bright green stain spreading over his hands, and washing would only make it worse; so, in theory, anyone who picked up a coin on which a pinch of this dust had been deposited would be marked in vivid green for at least a day... Several subalterns tried it very gingerly. A tiny speck on the tip of a finger spread if it was rubbed even slightly, and transferred itself alarmingly wherever the finger touched. Unconscious scratching produced comic submarine patterns on faces, necks and bare legs. Emmanuel and Sam tried it, too, and the effect on black skins was even more surreal than on white. The detective powder certainly worked.

The next dinner-night we prepared our trap carefully. In several rooms coins were left out, liberally sprinkled with the almost-invisible green powder. All valuables were hidden away, all doors locked. We set off for the dinner in considerable excitement.

The meal ended early. Several of the senior officers were tired, and went home straight afterwards, and nobody stayed late, so that before one o'clock we were able to return to our quarters.

All the 'powdered' money had disappeared, as had several notes which had been hidden in locked drawers. So had Geoff's valuable camera and new telescopic lens, from a padlocked cupboard...

"Right," he said, "we'll get the bastard."

We went first to the batmen's quarters and banged on all the doors in the line.

"Outside! Come on, wake up! Everybody come outside!"

Slowly the families emerged, the men and children wearing towels, the women blankets, all rubbing the sleep out of their eyes. We made them stand in a line and dip their hands into a bucket of water. The women and children looked terrified.

They held out their hands. We examined each one minutely with a torch. There was not a sign of green.

"It must be one of the Mess-boys, then," Geoff said. "I might have guessed."

At the Mess-servants' quarters the same performance took place. Here, the men were very wide awake, since they had only just finished clearing up after the dinner. As before, the women and children were scared, and in the torchlight their wide eyes were unnerving. We woke up the cooks' families, too. There must have been more than fifty men, women and children standing in a line in the courtyard. And on none of the hands was there the faintest trace of green.

I explained rather lamely that a 'tief-man' had stolen some money and we wanted to find out who it was. Jeremy added sensibly that we did not think it could be a batman or a Mess-servant, and by checking now, we could be quite sure. We were glad we had been proved right. The servants retired to their huts very quietly. We went to bed ashamed and embarrassed. But strangely, no money ever disappeared from our quarters after that night.

Chapter Nine

CORPS OF DRUMS

As the Assistant Adjutant I had to attend Commanding Officer's Orders, "Because," said Major Ives, "after Independence I'm going on leave for a bit and you'll have to take over, God help you." 'Orders' was a squalid affair, necessary for the maintenance of authority, but degrading for all concerned.

The parade always began with a squad of offending soldiers being marched from the guard-room by a sergeant or warrant-officer, to the accompaniment of much shouting and abuse, and being made to sit ignominiously on a long bench outside the Orderly Room, in full view of the gleeful clerks. Meanwhile the Colonel and the Adjutant would be checking over the cases to be heard, discussing the reliability of witnesses and the type of punishment to be meted out: even whether it was really necessary to hear the evidence.

When the first name was called, the RSM would march the unfortunate man round to the Colonel's office at an impossibly rapid step: "Lefrighlefrighlefrigh – HALT! You-fool-man-why-you-no-de-halt-proper-lef-TURN – SALUTE! Uponetwo – downonetwoSTANSTILLLLL!!" Then the case against the man would be read out by the Adjutant. Perhaps the soldier had been fighting in the barracks, or had insulted a corporal, or had been in Accra when he should have been on parade. Most of the cases were straightforward, and the Colonel's punishments were severe, but just. Usually the convicted soldier had his head shaved, and joined a fatigue-party for several days, whitewashing walls or weeding paths. Hardly anyone complained.

The more unusual cases were often heard – and settled 'out of court' - by Major Ives, with the RSM as interpreter and even guide. Regimental Sergeant-Major Kramo Wongara was an imposing figure, tall and gaunt, with a scraggy moustache and bulging eyes. He had a distinguished war record, and on important occasions paraded with an impressive array of medals. In some ways he was the most powerful man in the Battalion, with influence even greater than Ives's, for the discipline of Arakan Barracks was his direct responsibility, and he ruled with severity and strict Muslim ideas about right and wrong. He lived in a big house, with purple bougainvillea trailing over the fence, and to ensure that everyone entering the barracks knew how things stood, he had 'R-S-M' painted in huge black letters across his white front wall.

To most of the soldiers, RSM Kramo was a more immediate and impressive figure than any of the officers. Although his English was not strong, he could read and write Hausa and Arabic fluently. What marked him out above all, however, was that he knew by name and face almost every soldier in the Battalion. When Ives was hearing complaints, the RSM would stand smartly at ease until asked a specific question.

"This soldier Seidu, who's on a charge for hitting Corporal Baz," Ives would say, "you know him, RSM?"

Kramo would crash to attention. "Yessah, he dey for 'A'Company, sah. He join 1955, at Takoradi. He good man, sah. For why he hit Corp'l, be him wife sick, he want take her for doctor. Corp'l say no, make he go for parade."

"So I punish him for hitting Corporal, but because he's a good soldier, I punish him smallsmall, OK?"

"Yessah. Fine, sah."

Sometimes the RSM was very shrewd. Once, a soldier called Alo returned from five weeks' leave and promptly asked for another week.

"Why so?" asked the Adjutant. "Your leave just finish."

"Be my wife, sah. She run away. I want leave for go chase her."

She had disappeared during his absence and had almost certainly gone home to her village in Northern Nigeria.

"You fit go and come again all in the one week?" asked Major Ives.

"Yessah."

Ives pondered. Then he turned to the gaunt giant beside him. "You're a man of the world, RSM. What do you think?"

I was expecting an uncomprehending 'What ting you say, sah?' but Ives knew his man. RSM Kramo understood, and spoke with feeling.

"I tink, sah, dis man he be fool-man. She bad wife. Ebrybody savvy she be bad – only dis man go marry um, he no savvy. She drink too plenty, she talk too plenty. De time dis man Alo no dey, she go for odder man dey-dey for Accra. Make he lef' her for Nigeria."

"Thank you, RSM. That sounds good advice. You agree, Alo?"

"Yessah."

Occasionally, however, RSM Kramo was let down by his own excess of zeal, particularly on religious questions. One extraordinary instance occurred, as ill-luck would have it, on a day when I had been left in charge, because Ives had gone to a conference at Brigade. Mike's batman, John Kanjarga, came in tears to say that the RSM had stolen his wife and given her to someone else. It was quite true: apparently Kramo considered that another soldier, a Muslim, had a better right to the girl than John, a Catholic.

I did not wish to offend the Sergeant-Major, who doubtless considered me a small-boy, anyway, and by taking sides with Mike's batman I would probably seem to be exerting undue pressure as an officer. Even more, I did not wish to be caught up in a long religious argument designed to make me look foolish. There seemed nothing illegal about John Kanjarga's marriage – and the girl was very attractive! – but I felt sure that the RSM would drag up obscure religious laws to prove his point. I stalled carefully and said that I would think about the matter and decide tomorrow. That evening I gratefully handed over the problem to Major Ives.

"If we argue with Kramo," said he, "he'll run rings round us with his Muslim rulings which I shan't understand and you won't either. I think it'd be best if I make him sort things out exactly as they were."

Sure enough, Ives simplified the problem in typical fashion, refusing even to hear the case. He summoned the RSM, then, talking in English instead of 'pidgin', he said:

"RSM, I hear that you have given John Kanjarga's wife to another soldier. That is wrong, and you know it. I will not argue with you. You will arrange for her to go back to John Kanjarga today. And don't do it again."

"Yessah," said the RSM.

Major Ives's other province, as Adjutant-diplomat, was the Corps of Drums, and he often used to say that it would be the death of him. Although he seldom supervised the drummers' work (although he could have done so, for he was musical) he was directly responsible for their well-being and conduct at all times, and for their turnout and performance at big parades.

"In fact I'm just about their damn Company Commander," he would say. "As if I hadn't got enough to do without that daft lot!"

Sometimes, after watching one of their practices, he would storm into the office, flinging his slouch-hat and cane onto his desk.

"God give me strength! I don't want to see or hear or know about another bloody bugle or fife or drum ever again. I can't stand any more. I'll resign. I'll collect my bowler hat and retire!"

But if anyone had seriously suggested that he should hand over the running of the Drums to another officer, he would not have countenanced the idea. Doubtless he would have blustered about the inability of anyone else to control such a rabble, or he would have declared nonchalantly that now he had got them properly organised at last, it was hardly worth altering his arrangements. In truth, Ives enjoyed being in charge of the Corps of Drums, and was proud of his success with the platoon. His periodic tantrums did not last, and when he next saw the soldiers he would laugh and say "Daft lot!" and forget the outburst. They would swear at him, silently in his presence and in a laughing chorus when he had gone. They liked him.

The Drums had a separate entity from the other Companies, with their own timetable, supervised by the Adjutant, their own accommodation, allocated by the Adjutant, and their own code of discipline and punishment, dealt out through a Drum-Major, who acted for the Adjutant. In addition, if a drum-skin cracked, or a fife was stamped on by mistake, or a bugle badly dented, the Adjutant had to order a replacement, since the Drum Major was almost illiterate. Major Ives tried to hand over this last task to the Band-Master at Giffard Camp – who refused the job, saying that he would be happy to incorporate some of the better musicians into the Regimental Band, as they were better than most of his own, but he had not the time to deal with their administration as well.

Then Ives said to me: "Since you're my assistant, you can help look after this Drums chaos," which seemed logical.

"You have most of them in your Education classes, don't you?"

"At least half of them, anyway."

"Well, you should be able to learn who's who pretty quickly, then. Between us we'll sort out the Drum-Major."

Ives left me to ponder this last cryptic remark. He seemed tired, unusually flustered. I wondered if he was cracking up. Adjutant sinks under strain – hands over office to inexperienced but able deputy… For the first time I realised I was not scared of him.

Akasusa Frafra, the Drum-Major, a skinny man from the North, was responsible for the musical training of the platoon. Probably he was very competent. Certainly, when the Drums were playing well, they seemed extremely proficient, smart and professional. I noticed, however, that if anything went wrong, Major Ives put the entire blame onto the Drum-Major. Several times the man had stood in front of the Adjutant's table to receive a fearful verbal drubbing. This had the justice of military logic, since the Colonel would doubtless have blamed Ives if the Drums had performed inadequately, but at first I could not believe that it was altogether fair on Akasusa Frafra.

"The man's up to something," Ives declared. "I don't know what it is, but I'm sure it's wrong. You watch him."

There were forty men in the Corps of Drums, and like any comparable unit this group included the occasional nonentity, but taken as a whole they were the liveliest, most creative soldiers in the Battalion, and also the most mischievous. This was apparent from the first. It was equally apparent that in the Corps there was just one slow-witted man, with no sense of humour… the Drum-Major.

This difference in temperament and intelligence did not fully account for the sudden fits of irresponsible behaviour to which the Drums

Platoon was subject. Skilled musicians, drilling stylishly, would suddenly become deliberately disruptive, or so it seemed to me. They would turn left when the Drum-Major screamed at them to turn right, then vice-versa; they would bump into each other. The buglers would start to blow, perfectly together, when they should have been silent. A bass-drummer would suddenly strike two or three fearsome BOOOOMs, exactly out of step. The anarchy was achieved skilfully: if it had been accidental, it would have seemed very funny.

It drove Akasusa frantic. He would yell at them in Hausa first, then in his appalling pidgin-English, and finally in Frafra, of which they genuinely understood not a word. He would wave his arms and whirl his mace, and sometimes it seemed he would fling it away altogether. From the edge of the parade-ground it was like watching a circus-finale, and any new-arrived spectator could be forgiven for blaming the Drum-Major, since it was obvious that no one could possibly understand the orders he was screaming out with increasing frenzy...

Then Major Ives would want to see him. Akasusa would appear limp and dishevelled in front of the Adjutant's table.

"A proper shambles today, wasn't it?"

"Sah."

"For why be so bad? You get any excuse?"

"Nosah."

I told Ives that to me it seemed the fault of the soldiers, not the Drum-Major. He was giving the right orders – they were simply doing the opposite.

"Maybe. But I think there's something behind it. They don't act like that for nothing."

"But how can you blame him alone?"

"I'm not having him wrecking my Corps of Drums," Ives said wryly. "Especially not just before Independence. Any way you look at it, there's something wrong. I know I shout at the Drums sometimes, but I like them. They're about the only soldiers in the Battalion who don't behave as if they're scared of me."

"So...?"

"Well, as Adjutant, I can't really ask the Drums whether their Drum-Major is a crook, can I? Well, can I?"

"Hardly, I suppose."

"But *you* can," said Ives.

The very next time Jeremy and I went to the Education Centre, we arrived just as one of the 'Advanced' classes was finishing. A group of Drummers came out together, as always, seven inseparables.

"Good morning!" they yelled in chorus. "Happy day!" And, as always, they stopped to gossip.

We were beginning to learn their names and mannerisms. There was Joseph Halm, tall and debonair, with the lazy smile; and James Ankumah was the one with the soft voice, who kept goal for the Battalion soccer team. The short, good-looking man with the zany grin and quick, chirpy speech was Godson Fiawatsror – and fun he had with that name, signing his full signature across every sheet of written work he handed in. These three had apparently been to the same school in Takoradi, as had William Stevens, a small copper-skinned man with a pixie's face and huge eyes. They were always sending each other up.

"Even now," William said, with a wonderfully solemn expression, "you see I cannot escape from these bushmen!"

"Bushman yourself!"

"Ehhh! How am I expected to work properly with silly people like these around me?"

"Poor Steve," replied Joseph, equally solemnly, "I am disturbed by the intensity of your emotion. You damfool man, how you tink we fit learn Englan' palaver de time we see you de work smallsmall, talk plenty?"

"*We* are trying to learn *Twi*," said Jeremy recklessly.

"Aieeee!" in unison. "May we hear you speak it?"

It was necessary to change the subject quickly, before Jeremy committed us both to making utter fools of ourselves.

"What went wrong with your parade yesterday?" I asked. "I don't believe it was the Drum-Major's fault at all. You all deliberately did the opposite of what he told you."

Righteous indignation, the high moral tone – we awaited a muttered excuse. But this group always surprised.

"It's a fact," said James. "We did. It was funny."

"But why? You got him punished."

"Yes, and we will do it again. It's a fact. He is a bad man. He takes money from the recruits. He says if they do not pay him he will punish them every day."

"And he is a bully," Joseph said. "He hits people he thinks will not hit him back. But God so good, we can make a big fool of him to get our own back."

"He will say anything, do anything for money. It's a fact."

"And he often borrows money from us and then does not pay us back…" This was Boadu Bekoe, always known as 'BB', a dashing man with a Clarke Gable moustache. "To speak true," he added, "he owes me one pound even now."

"But why let him have it?"

"Because I am too kind. No, to speak true, because if I do not lend him money he will find ways to ill-treat me. He will put me on a fatigue so that I cannot go home to my wife. But I will get it back from him."

"But why does nobody complain to the Adjutant?"

"Major Ives is a hard man," declared Joseph, "and the Drum-Major is afraid of him. But there is not a lot he can do. Like James and BB say, this Akasusa is bad, but it is not easy to prove bribery, is it? It is better to get him punished because he cannot make us drill well, than to accuse him of bribery."

"The Drum Major is not a good man," Godson chirped, "but when you know him he is really not so bad. He is a funny man because he does not know he is funny."

"When we go bush on parade he is very funny. He shouts and shouts, and the shouting of a fool is like the banging of an empty calabash," said Joseph, who was fond of proverbs.

"OK," said Ives, "so they make a fool of him, but that doesn't help me."

He spoke to the whole Corps of Drums next morning.

"Look, you daft lot. I have been hearing things about you that I do not like. You parade badly and now I know why. By Independence you must be bloody good. No humbug. No bad-on-purpose. And you, Drum-Major, I know about you, too. One more funny business and we have another Drum-Major, OK?"

"Yessah."

"I bet you told Major Ives," Joseph said, with the widest of grins.

"It's a fact," echoed James.

"It's a fact," Jeremy said, aware that with the Corps of Drums our dignity stood at zero, but not minding very much.

"And why not?" I said to our kindred spirits.

In addition to the two of us, most of the other junior officers became friendly with the Corps of Drums. We liked their outspokenness, their naturalness. Most of all we liked their refusal to think of us as officers: they were of our age and shared many of our interests. They regarded themselves as musicians, not soldiers. We fraternised with them more than our officers' rank should have permitted, as Geoff continually re-minded us, and probably his crude superiority made us more familiar still. Right to the end of his overseas service, Geoff refused to address any African by name: it was always 'you' or 'that fellow there'. He did not join us on our first expedition to Legon.

This began as a map-reading exercise for Stage 3 Education, but was in reality an excuse to take some of the Corps of Drums and their friends to the University for a day out. Alec, Mike and Jock came with Jeremy and me. We took a three-ton truck filled with maps, compasses and the Stage 3 soldiers, and left early in the afternoon, when official work was over for the day, so that none of the Company Commanders could complain about absentees from parade. The Colonel declared that we were using real initiative, and the Second-in-Command agreed that it was 'a wrrrrwrrrr damngood idea, young men.' Emmanuel Kotoka and Sam Lartey said they would come up by car and join us later. Major Ives purred happily to himself, because we had told him of our plans long enough in advance for him to claim a share of the credit.

From Legon Hill, high on an escarpment, there was a wonderful view far across the Accra Plain: every detail of the landscape was sharp and clear for many miles, roads, streams, buildings – even the indi-vidual termite hillocks.

We wore civilian clothes, so a startling variety of gaudy shirts, shorts, trousers and even togas emerged from the three-tonner at the top of Legon Hill.

"Gilbert and Sullivan," muttered Mike, oblivious of his own green shirt and shorts, red baseball cap and dark glasses.

It was a successful afternoon. We spent nearly two hours on the map-reading, and all of us learnt a great deal about the geography of the panorama in front of us. We worked in groups, and the officers learnt at least as much as the men. Then we explored the grounds of the University, undisturbed because the students were on vacation, and stopped to play football with a tennis ball along the main avenue, until this threatened to become too dangerous to the cultured surroundings. So we poked reeds at the myriads of tiny fish in the lily ponds, and threw pebbles at the agama lizards so that they raced up the library walls. We told the soldiers about London and the Queen and Manchester United, and about snow which had just fallen in Kent (and discovered how difficult it is to describe snow to people who have never seen or felt it) and they told us the *Ga, Twi* and *Fanti* names for the trees and flowering shrubs, the fish in the pools and the butterflies flitting around the hibiscus blossoms. Someone found an enormous black scorpion under a concrete slab, and the creature was prodded into the sunlight. I had momentary fears of its being ringed with cigarette-lighter fuel and made to perform the Dance of Death amidst the flames, but instead it was treated with great care, returned to its home and the slab placed back over it. Then Joseph Halm found a curled-up hedgehog, much like an English one but with large ears, which he placed on a stretch of grass, while everyone stood at a distance to watch it unroll. When it did so, to great applause, my fears returned, that one of the soldiers would take the beast home for chop, but no one did, and the hedgehog on its comic clockwork feet moved quickly away into a herbaceous border.

We played some more football, after which we collected up the maps and compasses and put them into the truck. Then Mike had to go back to where we had done the map-reading to collect his baseball cap which he had left there, or so he thought, but when he came back without it we discovered that Joseph Halm had picked it up and had actually been wearing it for the past hour without anyone noticing. Mike said he would have Joseph's guts for garters, and Joseph said it was a bushman's hat but he'd give sixpence for it. And Joseph's friend Godson Fiawatsror, who was keen on all sports, wanted to know what this baseball was, so Mike, who had never been to America or seen a baseball game, spent ten minutes explaining it quite incoherently, and then we played a game to our own rules, using the tennis ball and a tightly-rolled bundle of maps as the bat. Then we climbed into the truck and the Drummers sang all the way back to Accra. It was that sort of a day.

Teshie Range, CSM Binchiti

Teshie, Sam Osei

John Fynn, Ransford Adjei, Orderly Room

Mohamadu Gau and Medford Klutse, vehicle maintenance

**Eben Tawiah,
mechanic and boxer**

Eben's Band

Peter Kamerling, Joseph Halm, BB Bekoe, William Stevens

William, Maurice Essien, Godson Fiawatsror

Chapter Ten

INDEPENDENCE SNAPSHOTS

March 6th, 1957, when the Gold Coast became Ghana, was the most important and significant date during my term of service. On that day, not only did the country gain its Independence from Britain, but it was the first African nation to do so. I kept a diary at the time, and what follows draws heavily on it.

COUNTDOWN

Independence Day was drawing near. There was plenty of talk, but from the Army's point of view, remarkably little was actually done until some three weeks before the event. No new orders were issued; no schedule for parades or guards-of-honour. We learnt more about Independence from the radio and the Accra *Daily Graphic* than from official Army sources. The senior officers, both British and African, became irritable, and one could hardly blame them, since they knew that they would shortly find themselves with heavy responsibilities, but as yet had little idea what these would be. Colonel Quinn decided that whatever might be required, the officers needed to be fitter, so three times a week we went to Nicholson's Stadium at 6.45 a.m. in our shorts and singlets and jogged or raced around the track. 'Those under 35' was the Colonel's directive, and the first morning a few officers had aged several years overnight, but they turned out sheepishly the next time, on hearing that the Colonel and Second-in-Command had both been gallantly lumbering round the circuit.

Then the schedule of parades came at last, and rehearsals started. Glad to be given their targets, the soldiers drilled for hours in the sun on the square at Arakan Barracks, with obvious enjoyment, while beaming Warrant-Officers chided them, for show, but without need of abuse. Guards-of-honour, escorts, street-lining, even the big ceremonial parades in the Accra stadium would be easy enough, provided there was time to practise.

I joined the first few rehearsals, before Major Ives told me to stop.

"You and I," he said, "will have more important matters at Independence. All sorts of things are bound to break down, and we'll have to be spending hours on the 'phone trying to sort out cockups. You won't have time for a parade."

But I continued to join the other officers in practising street-lining drill, ready for the welcoming ceremony when the Duchess of Kent would arrive in the Gold Coast to begin the Independence Celebrations.

On an empty parade-ground, with plenty of willing troops, audible commands, and hours to spare, the soldiers seemed first-rate and the whole performance too easy for words. Then we had a dress rehearsal, with a 'crowd' consisting of many of the non-parading soldiers, their wives and families, all told to 'make plenty noise'. The lines wavered; officers and NCOs positioned themselves wrongly; the present-arms came too late when the Colonel drove by in the 'royal car'. So we went on practising.

The officers also had to learn sword-drill. Some of the Majors had their own ceremonial swords, which were polished beautifully by their batmen. The rest of us made do with the ten burnished museum-pieces from the Adjutant's office, and we practised enthusiastically with these. Unfortunately, they had obviously been made for officers well over six feet tall – or on horseback – and those of us of average height or less found it difficult even to draw our swords from their scabbards with the required smooth, nonchalant movement. As for saluting, the dramatic downward sweep, with the weapon-point checking a mere inch from the ground, was for days a laughable impossibility. The huge, heavy swords dug into the soil or struck embarrassing sparks from stones. Major Ives made sarcastic remarks about not needing fireworks on Independence night.

One week to go, and it seemed that already every nation must be represented in Accra for the celebrations. The VIPs poured in – royalty, statesmen, ambassadors, dignitaries: R.A. Butler representing Prime Minister Macmillan; Vice-President Nixon and the Russian delegates all together in the Ambassador Hotel… Among a host of black American celebrities, Martin Luther King and his wife received a particularly tumultuous welcome. The Embassies were filled to bursting, then the hotels and rest-houses, then the Government buildings, suitable and unsuitable. And from all over West Africa people were flooding in quietly on foot, staying with friends or 'brothers' in the town, sleeping rough in the porches, in the street, on the beach …

On Friday 1ˢᵗ March, the day before the Duchess's arrival in the Gold Coast, the Colonel was told that the Battalion would be helping to accommodate a detachment of the Royal Australian Air Force. According to the note from Headquarters, they would be arriving at 1400 hours. I was to meet them at the airport, the Colonel said. He would be there too.

14 Officers, 13 NCOs and 9 Other Ranks were supposed to be coming, so I arranged for two land rovers and a one-ton truck to meet them. We went to the airport.

Four Valiant aircraft arrived first, surprisingly quiet and unobtrusive. General Paley was there, smart in red braiding and white moustache, to greet the British RAF arrivals. An Air Vice-Marshall stepped out, and there was much saluting and handshaking before the whole party moved away in the charge of several senior officers from Brigade.

Soon after two o'clock the three little Australian Neptunes bustled noisily in, bright green craft with ugly bent wings. Men poured out of them: 36… 37… 38 altogether…

"More than we're expecting," said the General quietly, "but I'm sure we can fit them in somehow."

We walked to meet them.

"Wal, we mide it," said the Wing-Commander, who was stretching his legs vigorously. "Toucha cremp," he added. Then he noticed General Paley, and saluted.

"Pleesta meetcha, General," he said.

He introduced the men: 15 officers, 14 NCOs and 9 Other Ranks of the Royal Australian Air Force. They had just completed a ten-day 'world trip' to Accra and were tired. "Hopeya cen tike us all," said the Wing Commander.

"Oh… er… of course. Yes, delighted to see you," replied the General, still mentally adding and subtracting. "Of course. Colonel Quinn here is putting up five – no, six of your officers. This officer" (indicating me) "will take the others to 'B' Mess; then he will take the NCOs and Other Ranks to their respective quarters at the Garrison Sergeants' Mess and Commonwealth Camp…"

Fortunately the Sergeants' Mess had provided its own transport, so all the NCOs went off together, escorted by a very assured young Engineer Sergeant. To my relief, more transport then arrived for the Other Ranks. General Paley and the Colonel drove away together, leaving me responsible for the Australian Officers.

I took them to 'B' Mess at Headquarters, wondering how to explain to the Major-in-Charge about the one extra officer. I thought perhaps it would be best to say 'General's orders' and leave it to him to sort things out. Luckily there was no officer there. I managed to find an orderly, and we filled up one wing of the Mess with Australian airmen. The orderly muttered that several of the rooms were supposed to be occupied by a Pakistani detachment arriving later… I fled to our own Battalion with the other six Aussies.

I unloaded four Flight-Lieutenants at the Junior Officers' Lines, where Jock, Mike, Jeremy and Co immediately took charge, while I ferried the Wing-Commander and a Squadron-Leader to their more luxurious quarters, near our Mess. There, we unloaded their baggage…

"Hevya got me croc beg?" asked the Wing-Commander. The other officer had not seen it.

So a search began for one crocodile-skin briefcase containing valuable, irreplaceable documents. We tried the Junior Officers' Lines, the Sergeants' Mess, even the Commonwealth Camp on the outskirts of town. No 'croc beg'. The Wing-Commander finally concluded that it must have been left at one of their previous halts. "They'll send it on," he said.

Later in the afternoon one of the Flight-Lieutenants offered to show me over a Neptune 'plane. Jeremy and Mike came too. We climbed inside the first craft. It was horribly claustrophobic, strutted like the tunnelling in a mine.

"Holy fliming Jees!" exclaimed the Flight-Lieutenant.

On the back seat of all was a crocodile-skin briefcase.

Saturday, 2nd March 1957: *WELCOME QUEEN*

Eleven o'clock in the morning, and all along the airport-road the people were waiting for the arrival of Her Royal Highness, the Duchess of Kent. For days, weeks even, they had been crowding in from far and near, into Accra. Now, all along the four miles of roadway shiny with mirages they had been waiting for many hours already in the heat of the day.

The town was dressed happy-day, ablaze with colour. Flags festooned the specially erected stands along the roadway, twined around telegraph poles, fluttered from balconies of the big white paint-and-sunlight Government buildings. Streamers cascaded from the roadside trees, splashed in vivid kaleidoscope over the low bus-shelters. More streamers spun bright above the airport-way, branching off to where an avenue of waving pennants marked the Ambassador Hotel, sprawling in the suburbs like a toppled skyscraper. *WELCOME QUEEN*, proclaimed a banner hung between two trees outside the hotel, and *BIG DAY QUEEN COME* screamed an even larger banner suspended from the first floor.

Jeremy and I were perched on a wall by the approach to Giffard Road. From our vantage-point we could see right down the flag-decked avenue where, on posts high above the swirling crowd, gold-metal birds glinted in the sun, eagles with wings raised, symbol of Ghana-to-be. Somewhere far down the avenue, most of the other subalterns were street-lining, poor devils, waiting in the sun and the heat and the bedlam, set in position with their soldiers, waiting for the Duchess.

Everywhere colours dazzled. The women were sporting festive rainbow-shawls and cloths patterned with scarlet and yellow elephants. Freedom! The word was splashed in paint across the front of wooden shacks, ran riot on huge flags spread wide on the walls of the office-blocks. 'Freedom and Justice' was stamped on the mammy-cloths in the spaces between the scarlet and yellow elephants; many of the women were carrying on their backs tiny piccins wrapped in cocoons of 'Freedom' cloth. 'Freedom' stood out in white against the blue of a sagging tro-tro truck parked away from the road outside the Military Hospital.

It was best-clothes day, and the men also were dressed to outshine the sun. Some stood regally, loose-draped for free, excited gesticulation in flame-chequered togas of kente-silk; others were cardboard-stiff in new dark suits, formal, European, white shirt-fronts aglitter against black skins. In the shade of a row of flame-of-the-forest trees schoolchildren clustered tight-packed, boys and girls indistinguishable in purple and brown uniform. Policemen patrolled with red fezzes arrogantly aslant: abusive, ferocious they prowled on the roadway, pushing back the crowd.

Freedom!

For weeks every chop-bar gathering, every palaver in the markets, has discussed the advent of Freedom. The time is near, but the arguments are not yet resolved.

What is Freedom, my friend?

Iiiiih! It is many things, Kwaku. Some say that when it comes, all chop will be free and we shall not have to work. That I do not believe, for who, then, will pay the women who give us our chop?

Sunlight, laughter, and the tide of black faces at the roadside surged forward, expectant. In the midst of one cluster the Colonel's face appeared suddenly, pale and apprehensive. He had pushed his way through with his cine-camera, and was being jostled from side to side. The policemen were having difficulty in controlling the crowd.

"Freedom! Freedom! Freedom!"

"You are not permitted to stand on the roadway. If you persist in doing so, my friend, there will be trouble. So many cars are coming, you will see. Stand back there!"

"Yiiiiee! Allow me to stand where I am wishing, fool policeman, damfool man! Yiiieeee!"

A van-guard of motor cycles: then the first few cars of the procession crawled by, huge, black, important; inside, black sweating faces, pallid faces sweating less obviously.

"Heeiiii – YIIII – YIIIII – YIYIYIYIIIII!" the schoolchildren chanted in unison. The mammies waved flamboyant handkerchiefs.

The crowd beneath our wall was in wondrous confusion, leaping, waving arms, fighting to see, to see. There were suddenly twenty people on the wall with us.

"Aieeeiii! Yiiiiyiiii!"

"De Gobernor ibi him get de white febber dey for de hat!"

"God save the Queen!" Two very dark men in charcoal suits shouted loudly, precisely.

"Sabe de Queen!"

"SABE DE QUEEEEEN! YIIIII....!"

"God save the Duchess of Kent!" A fat businessman on the wall beside us, face alight with sweat and excitement, startled the crowd, shouted with both arms raised. Consternation. Delirious excitement and consternation.

"Heiii! What ting dis he de say?"

"I no savvy. Save de Queeeen!

"Aiyeeeiii! Gossabe de King!"

"Eh! Bushman, you no savvy she be Queen?"

The car was moving very, very slowly.

"Yiiiiyiiii!" The mammies tossed their handkerchiefs into the air. The Duchess turned her head and waved. She smiled at the schoolchildren, who squealed with delight. In spite of the hot day she looked relaxed, cool, and the car went by very slowly.

More cars...

But the cavalcade ended at last. The crowd began to disentangle itself and surged onto the roadway. The policemen vanished before the tide engulfed them.

The general conclusion was that the Duchess was beautiful and gracious: but there was one drawback to her beauty, by African standards. The Mess staff discussed her with us.

"Ahaaah! She be fine pass all,"

"She be *small* too much."

"I tink Europeans like smallsmall mammies, no be so?"
"Be so."

Tuesday, 5th March: *INDEPENDENCE EVE*

The Comet airliner soared from Accra Airport, flew low along the coast towards Takoradi. The passengers chattered excitedly, waving their arms. Few had been in an aeroplane before.

"Now you can see Winneba," said the intercom. Everyone craned to look. The fields were sharp and green, the sea deep, deep blue; even the lines of white surf were distinct.

"Yiii! Winneba!"

The chiefs in their golden kente-cloths tried hard to maintain their dignity, but with this wonderful view of their own country the excitement was too much. They chattered and clapped and pointed. The ministers and civil servants were less restrained, shouting and gesticulating gleefully.

Independence Air Cruise for VIPs...

And me? This morning the Colonel came into my office. "Put away those files," he said, "and go up in the Comet. Learn what the country looks like from the air."

Inland we flew towards Tarkwa, over grassy plains, over heavy, dark forests cut by silver snakes of rivers and red snakes of roads, with villages in tidy mosaic. In a huge arc, round Kumasi we were to go...

More than an hour; and now we were over Labadi again, and really low now, beating-up the beach. The palm trees directly beneath were near enough for us to see their swaying – and across the sand dark pygmy figures were dashing for shelter.

Towards Accra itself, and the new Freedom Arch showed white and glistening. Down below, in the dusty heat of the Stadium, Alec and Mike and Jeremy and Simon and Uncle Tom Cobbley and All were practising for the morrow's big parade, the 'Marching Procession' – lucky them...

OSAGYEFO

Raised on its pillars the Officers' Mess floated in the night like a huge, illuminated Galleon. Around in the moonlight, scattered far among the flower-beds and palm trees, the guests sat at tiny collapsible tables eating, drinking, nodding, chattering. Hundreds of guests had come to the Independence Ball, how many, no one seemed to know or care. Probably numbers of them had no invitations: it made not the least difference to this loud, numbing muddle of a party.

From inside the galleon the thumping beat of the Regimental Band sounded strangely muffled. It was a long way to the dance-floor. Between the tables couples came and went, came and went, shuttling in and out of the light. Most groups danced occasionally: the American party almost incessantly, leaping and whirling conspicuously, yippeeing, rushing back to their tables to find their glasses had been refilled. They were exhausting to watch, more exhausting to listen to: professional high-spirits, color by Technicolor.

The Africans wanted 'Highlife' music from the band, who were keen to play it, and since about ten o'clock we had even had 'highlifed' waltzes. It made little difference.

The young subalterns had each been allocated a table to look after. We were to see that our important guests were not left out of things. These VIPs were consuls and attachés and generals and admirals. I had an attaché and his wife at my table. They were not forbidding.

The attaché had white hair and a thin aristocratic face with mobile eyebrows, like Geoff's, which bobbed up and down independently. I had no idea where he was attaché to or from, or what his name or title might be. I did not care to ask. He went out of his way to be charming, speaking very fast in an accent that was too precise to be English. His wife was small and grey, with three chins. "I do not want to dance," was all she would say. She drank beer like a man and belched loudly. She was wearing green and purple, and it did not suit her.

It did suit Rose, who had been at our table until half an hour ago. She was a short, wiry girl, dark and beady-eyed like a stoat, who said she was from London and was a self-confessed gatecrasher. "Nobody asked if I was meant to be here," she said, "so I just came." The attaché had laughed at her jokes – particularly one about the Queen of Tarts, which from her winks and leers was presumably meant to be autobiographical

— but the attaché's wife was not amused, and her distaste was strengthened by the fact that Rose was wearing a dress very similar to her own, but with incomparably more dash. Rose had danced twice with the attaché and twice with me. She had told us both, very audibly, how marvellous we were; then she had disappeared with one of the Americans, and was probably now telling him the same, somewhere under the palm trees.

Rose had gone, but Sadie was still at our table. She was rather drunk. She poured a glass of gin into her beer and giggled weakly. Her beautiful pale face became ugly when the chin dissolved in silly laughter. Her husband took the glass before she could drink it. His name was Dan, or Don, or Tom. Dan, he said again. He was something to do with some army, not ours. Not American, either, although he talked with an American accent. He was long and angular, like a Gilray cartoon, with cropped ginger hair. He had hurt his leg and could not dance. Sadie said she wouldn't, and twice she declined to take the floor even with the attaché; but it was obvious that really she wanted to. Equally clearly she feared her husband, perhaps hated him.

The band thundered on. In our dysfunctional group I felt morosely sober. At the next table Mike looked caged, angry. His VIP guest, who seemed to be a naval officer, was saying that it was a Huge Gamble to let black people look after themselves. No disrespect and all that, but you Couldn't Be Sure. He spoke very loudly. Mike's glowering face took on a look of embarrassment. Our friendly attaché leant back in his chair and clasped the arm of the naval officer, declaring that he quite agreed, you had to remember that these chaps were Not Like Us. The two VIPs thumped each others' backs, and I awaited the slapstick of both chairs collapsing.

Mike moved across to my table.

"I can't stand any more," he muttered. "I'm going."

As if on cue, Jeremy, Simon and Alec appeared in a group.

"We're going to hear Nkrumah at the Polo Ground," Alec said.

The attaché decided to come too, saying that it would be 'an historical moment'. He persuaded his wife that it would be good for her. They offered me a lift in their chauffeur-driven limousine, but seemed relieved when I said I would go in Jeremy's Volkswagen. We left Dan at the table trying to pack Sadie off to bed. "She's had enough," he

97

said. She was attempting to balance her gin glass upside-down on the palm of her hand.

We reached the Polo Ground a few minutes before midnight. Never was there such a crowd, a vivid sea through which it was impossible to move, that rippled, swayed. Far out, like an island in the dark waters, isolated by lights, was the dais from which Nkrumah would speak. There seemed no way that he and his colleagues could wade to it through the crowd. We were only on the fringe, but even there the smell was rancid, strong, of sweat and excitement, heaving bodies swaying in orgiastic anticipation: Accra waiting in delirium for *Osagyefo*, the Redeemer, the Conqueror.

The siren at the Post Office wailed midnight, and there was a momentary hush in the rumble of chatter, a lull in the ripples on the sea of faces; and then quite near us a roar broke out loudening and loudening and we were buffeted back in a single surge as the crowd divided. Lights were flashing in the darkness, but we could see nothing of what was happening, hear only the growing roar and feel the single breathing of the crowd, leviathan panting. Then lights were moving towards the dais, and by standing on tiptoe we could see for a tiny second the waves dividing as Nkrumah made his way on dry land to his island, *Osagyefo* with his disciples.

They stood on the platform, sharp in the radiance of the lights, inviting worship: suave Kodjo Botsio; Casely-Hayford lean and bespectacled; Gbedemah beaming benevolence and mopping his brow; tiny Krobo Edusei leaping up and down in delight, his arms swinging; while Nkrumah stood quietly, accepting the adulation, biding his time...

They have all of them come through fire. All have been imprisoned for their faith, and now the 'Graduates' have emerged from their gaol-course to lead their land. See, they wear the smocks that show they are of the people, and the little white caps that proclaim their prison graduation. Aiyeeee! Here they stand in the lights that shine a halo of radiance about each head. See them and worship. When Nkrumah was in prison he flew out at night as a white dove to comfort his people: now he is Osagyefo; the Messiah has finally appeared...

Nkrumah's speech came muzzy across the distance and the breathing of a hundred thousand worshippers. His words were punctuated by waves of applause that set the crowd swaying anew, and buffeted the ears so that his next phrases were lost. What he said was not new, for he had been preparing the way in other speeches for weeks, for months. We had read it all in the newspapers, and heard it on the wireless. Ghana was free, and he congratulated the people on their part in winning the fight. Africa was emerging into the light. Africa could look after herself. All of Africa must be free.

He stood, one man in the radiance of the arc-lights, flanked by his disciples, while the flash-bulbs scattered their tiny sparks. He spoke like a god. It did not matter what he said. We were hearing a miracle. With him we had fought the battle and won. Above him the new Ghana flag hung limply in gorgeous red, gold, green, the colours of Freedom.

Aiyeeee...!

Cold reasoning departs. Common sense. Cynicism. The ability to think. We can just see Nkrumah, but he is minute in the distance. We can follow only part of what he says, but we hear his voice break. He seems to be weeping – and now he and his disciples are dancing, with joy. We are with him utterly, we sway and pant, we cheer and scream.

Aiyeeeee...!

As the crowd streamed out of the Polo Ground I was separated from Jeremy and the others, so I walked home. I felt exhilarated and shaken, both at the same time, as if I was floating a foot or so off the ground. Knots of Africans were talking excitedly on the roadway, but without the usual wild abandon and gesticulation. Some were dancing, the awed, silent dancing of people under a spell.

It was a very short-seeming three miles. I did not go to the Officers' Mess to see if the dance was ending. Instead, I returned to the Lines, and went to bed quietly. Most of the others were already back.

Wednesday 6th March: *INDEPENDENCE MORNING*

The first day of the new Ghana, Abongo woke me at 6.15 a.m., as if for a normal work-day, because I had forgotten to tell him that it was to be a holiday – except for those unlucky enough to be on parade in the Stadium, of which I was not one. The Mess Staff had not been told either, and anyway most of them had been at work for hours, clearing up after the dance, so I had an early breakfast before commandeering the Duty Land Rover and driving to Giffard Camp post office, for the first issue of Ghana stamps. There I met Colonel Rhys, the ebullient Brigade padre, who had the same aim in mind. We were the first to arrive and each bought several sets of the new edition. I addressed a number of envelopes to myself, so I should receive the stamps, postmarked, next day, together with some large blocks for my father's fine collection, and others for interested friends in England. Then Colonel Rhys asked the clerk at the counter if we could help him by franking our own letters and cards, 'to save him time' but in reality so that we could make sure that they were postmarked clearly.

The clerk was delighted, so the Padre and I joined him behind the counter, and carefully marked our letters and cards. It then occurred to me that if I postmarked an envelope *before* Independence, the stamps might one day gain in value – so a week or so later my father received a large envelope dated 4th March 1957.

Thursday, 7th March: *FLAGSTEAL*

The Duchess left Ghana in mid-afternoon, and this time Mike and I were on street-lining with the rest, as her motorcade moved to the airport. We went into Accra in a convoy of trucks at one o'clock, and it took us almost two hours to get into position properly. We had to wait another hour before the Duchess came by. All in all, it was more than four hours for one salute – however, this was the end of the Independence parades, and the prelude to four days' holiday.

After dinner that evening, Geoff said that he was going trophy-hunting in Accra. "It's a pity to waste all those beautiful flags," he said. We thought it an excellent idea. We were totally sober, and it is disquieting now to think that we had no qualms at all about what we were planning to do. We decided to set out sometime after midnight, when the chop-bars and street markets would be busy, but when there would be few people around the main 'display areas.'

Jeremy, Alec and Geoff went in one car, Mike and I with Jock in his. We drove first to Accra Stadium. Leaving the cars some distance away, we tiptoed into the arena, half expecting to be challenged by a guard or watchnight. For the whole circumference there were large flags of many nations hanging limply from their high poles, illuminated only by the moon. We walked along the outer row of seats, guiltily.

Eventually we plucked up courage and tried to pull down a flag. It was the Union Jack, but we chose it solely because it was at the point of the Stadium furthest from the main road, and in the shelter of the football stand. We had to lower it by a rope. The pulley creaked loudly, and the enormous flag flapped down like a vampire. We imagined eyes watching from all sides.

Then we lost our nerve. None of us felt capable of persuading a policeman, should one appear, that we were on legitimate business. In the vast Stadium we felt horribly exposed. We moved quietly back to the cars, where confidence returned and then an excess of valour. We drove fast along the almost empty Christiansborg Road, where the flags were magnificent but high out of reach. Then someone suggested the Ambassador Hotel.

We found a particularly fine crop there. They spread out from a dais in front of the hotel in a peacock's tail of national colours, and on either side of this another line of flags billowed on head-high poles.

We chose three each. Most of the countries of the world were represented, and we took some emblems for their importance, others for their hoped-for aesthetic value on the walls of our rooms. I had Canada, Australia and USA as my selection; Jock had France and of course his own Scotland; everyone found something that pleased him. Mike draped himself in an enormous Hammer-and-Sickle flag and pranced in front of the hotel, observing in a loud whisper that he was the Paramount Chief of Moscow.

As we were coming away with our trophies, we noticed two large bundles on the ground beside the dais. One was wrapped in sacking, the other in a faded Union Jack. When we looked closer we found these bundles were two night watchmen, fast asleep...

Friday, 8th March: *THE NEW LAND*

Everything looked much the same, but there was a fresh jauntiness, a new confidence.

"Welcome, my friend," said the man who sold cocacola at a stall by the Giffard Camp road. Usually he was a very humble fellow who called everybody 'sah' ingratiatingly and punctuated his sentences with 'please'. "Welcome. Today I give you special new Independence coke!"

"How much?"

"No be anyting. Today *I* dash *you*. I happy." His hair was newly greased and he was wearing a cherry-coloured T-shirt with a portrait of Nkrumah across the chest.

In the office, Corporal Adjei appeared with a pile of letters which he presented ceremoniously to Major Ives.

"Your special new Independence mail, sir," he said, and bowed like a courtier. Then Sergeant Christian entered with documents for the Adjutant's in-tray.

"May I wish you happiness with these, sir?"

"Thank you, Christian, but your leave does not start till tomorrow..."

We could hear Christian, Adjei and the other clerks talking loudly in the Orderly Room. Often roars of laughter interrupted them.

"I can't stand this excess of cheerfulness," said Ives, laughing himself. "We'll work to union hours this morning!"

Accra showed the same jauntiness. Most of the flags and bunting had disappeared from the streets (somewhat to our relief) but the gaiety was there in faces and clothes. In the market the mammies were wearing their special-day dresses and were selling fruit and vegetables at recklessly generous prices. One enormously fat woman gave me a bunch of twenty bananas for sixpence. Another, who was frying ugly brown fish in a pan over a charcoal fire, said "Freedom fiss!" and giggled. Her many chins shook, and her enormous bosom heaved. She speared a fish on a stick and held it out to me.

"You like," she said. "Freedom fiss be fine. One penny."

Crowds gathered to see the new traffic-lights. We saw no accidents, but apparently there had been several, as cars and trucks stopped suddenly, at sight of the altering colours, so that the drivers could signal excitedly to friends. Few had any knowledge as to why the lights should change as they did. Clearly, in their red-gold-green magnificence, exactly as on the Ghana flag, these 'traffic-lice' were part of the Independence celebrations…

Everywhere was the flag of the new land. Mammy-cloths, kente-cloths, shirts, curtains, parasols, *tro-tro* slogans were all in national colours. Even the snake-charmer by the lorry-station had added a topical touch to his programme. He had placed a calabash pot in the centre of a large Ghana flag, and as he swayed to and fro in time to the warbling of his pipe, four cobras reared up from the calabash and oozed out onto their red, gold, green stage.

The town was very crowded. Noticeable was the new African surge into European strongholds: in particular, crowds thronged the counters in Kingsway Stores, and hordes of small children shrieked excitedly as they jostled on the UTC escalators. As the people pushed and swayed in the new joys of the big stores, the leprous beggars sat outside, holding empty gourd bowls in fingerless hands. Nearby, a ragged cripple with smashed, dislocated feet ran like an animal on hands and knees among the pavement crowds. A sleek, very smart African in a dark suit held out sixpence. The cripple stopped and gawped at it, reaching out for the coin. The smart man flipped the sixpence into the deep drain, among raw sewage, and smirked. A pie-dog rushed to see if it was food. The cripple flung himself into the drain, snarled at the dog and grabbed the sixpence. The crowd guffawed.

PART TWO
THE GHANA
REGIMENT

Chapter One

IN THE MID-DAY SUN

The Trio and Albert arrived in the same week.

Subalterns were usually drafted out to the Regiment from England in twos and threes. Our batch in December had been an unusually big influx, and now, in the months immediately after Independence there came another rush of young officers. Amongst these the Trio, who arrived together, were bound to attract attention, if only because they were so astonishingly different one from another.

Rob looked like Victor Mature, and spoke in the same lazy drawl, but for all his deceptive casualness he was an extremely able officer. Only once did we see him lose his composure. It was in his first week in Accra, at a very dull barbecue late one night beside a Labadi swimming pool – a completely unmemorable occasion otherwise, and I forget even who was the host. The gramophone had broken down, so there could be no dancing, and the steaks we were supposed to 'grill for ourselves' kept falling in the sand... Rob had been drinking beer, bored and irritated: it was his first party in Africa, and he expected better of it.

Suddenly he poured himself a tumbler of whisky, brandy and gin in equal quantities, drained it at a gulp, leapt fully-clothed into the water and swam two lengths of the pool in fine style. Then he stretched himself out on the springboard and fell asleep...

With Rob on the same 'plane came Tim, small, pale and a muddled bundle of energy. He had rolling eyes and a high-pitched laugh, and we found him funny at first, even ludicrous, until we realised how much in earnest he always was, how intense about everything. In his enthusiasm he tilted at windmills with what seemed quixotic hopelessness, except that he often managed to bring them down by sheer tenacity – or sheer cheek. On one occasion he decided that the Army ought to supply an electric fan for his bedroom, and declared that in this heat it was bloody nonsense to have to live without one. Most of us had felt the same, had applied 'through the proper channels', and nothing had happened. Tim went into Accra and bought an electric fan from Kingsway Stores. He plugged it into his room, to test it. It was not powerful enough for him, so he went back and swapped it for another that produced a veritable gale and was nearly twice as expensive. This worked to his satisfaction, so he put in a claim to the Quartermaster. We all laughed knowingly and declared that Tim was up the creek and the QM would laugh, too. Not a bit of it. Captain Stan Goodman was a blunt Midlander who had come up through the ranks, and he admired Tim's directness. He refunded him straight away – so of course there was an immediate run on electric fans from Kingsway.

Tim hardly ever stopped talking: words tumbled over themselves in an extraordinary autobiographical patter, much of which was clearly untrue. Equally clearly, he saw fiction and fact as one, interchangeable, and everything he said, he believed implicitly. He had a remarkable rapport with the soldiers in his platoon, however, who enjoyed his loquacity and were keen to share his fantasy world.

Tim had another claim to fame: he learnt the words of the new Ghana National Anthem right through. We had all listened in the Mess to the various 'possible' tunes being played in succession, and were of the opinion that the correct choice had been made – the chosen anthem had the right jauntiness, and evocatively stressed details like the palm-fringed shore and the broad northern plains – but Tim went further. Within days he could recite and even sing it.

The third of the Trio was Richard, tall and scholarly, with a bumbling expression, as if he ought to have been wearing spectacles. He was full of erudite quotations, sometimes of his own fabrication, more often from famous writers. I actually heard him quote *Pilgrim's Progress* at Major Ives...

Richard had had to go to the Adjutant's office to collect some Company documents, and while he was there two duty buglers on the veranda outside had botched their performance badly.

"Go and practise it again!" Ives yelled, leaping to his feet. "Go round the block where I no fit hear you, and don't come back till you fine pass-all."

Richard murmured about crossing over and all the trumpets sounding on the other side. Ives snapped: "Talk English when you're in here, young man!" and concluded that Richard was just an over-sophisticated buffoon. This was unfortunate, for he was certainly not the caricature he seemed. His soldiers and NCOs worshipped him because, however eccentric his manner, he always ensured that his platoon was treated better than anyone else's. In his ability to plan a training programme efficiently, he was very like Ives himself.

We needed the Trio for their unpredictability, as well as their enthusiasm. Dai had returned to England at the end of his service, which made the rest of us feel old, suddenly; and to hear us talk, anyone would have thought we were Old Coasters with twenty years' service in the White Man's Grave behind us – and Rob actually remarked on this, within minutes of his arrival. Apparently he had also dared to interrupt the Adjutant's first breathless Accra-Tamale-Takoradi monologue with "Would you mind going a little slower, sir? I didn't follow half of that." Very polite, but determined, and quietly mischievous.

"That young man," Ives admitted to Jeremy and me in the office, "will either be an asset, or he'll have to be Dealt With."

Needless to say, the Adjutant's expression had not reflected his surprise, and the Trio were as scared of him as we had been. But their natural resilience was remarkable. When Mike, Jeremy and I went to the Lines to meet the new arrivals – the first subalterns to do so, apart from Alec, who had fetched them from the airport – we heard from afar an extraordinary sound, as of Nebuchadnezzar's musick gone astray, held together by a firm drumming rhythm. There was an improvised band on the front veranda: Rob playing a clarinet hideously (he had brought it with him 'to learn'); Richard elegantly pinging a bucket with a stick; Tim buzzing through a comb-and-toilet-paper, his face creased in fierce concentration. Two of the batmen were drumming on a table-top with their bare hands.

"God alive!" was all Alec could say to greet us.

Albert Ocran arrived a few days later. He was a young African lieutenant, who had come to us from a Mortar course in Wiltshire, and our first impression was that in character he was very like Emmanuel Kotoka. This comparison was strengthened by their previous careers, for both were southerners, Emma from the Ewe tribe, towards Togo- land, Albert a Fanti from the Western Coastal region; and both had started their service as schoolmasters. But whereas Emma, for all his friendliness and genuine interest in people, appeared slightly detached from the young subalterns by age and experience, Albert seemed much more one of us. He took part in anything and everything. If you searched for him after work was over for the day, you were likely to find him in the Education Centre talking to the sergeants about new teaching ideas, or chatting to the soldiers in the barracks. He came to all dances, parties and entertainments, both at the Mess and at Giffard Camp; he played in many sports teams. He was older, and also much more worldly than we were, for not only had he already had five years' varied military service, but he had a beautiful young wife, Agnes, and two small children, Patricia and Francis, (later to be joined by five more children!) and whenever possible he brought his family with him. The Battalion was captivated by the charm of the Ocran household, and Ives, perpetual oracle, pronounced with his usual perceptiveness: "He'll run the Army, one day."

Through Albert's gregariousness we also became real friends with two of the other young African officers, Sam and Alex. We had known and liked them from our first arrival on the Coast, but until Albert joined us, they were merely pleasant fellow-officers.

Sam Lartey was a quiet, kind-hearted lieutenant whose face bore an expression of perpetual amusement. He was utterly phlegmatic, the African equivalent of Rob. In his routine work as a Battalion officer he did exactly as much as he had to, no more. If, however, you asked him to do something as a favour, he would set to it straight away. He was no intellectual, but was highly intelligent and was willing to try anything, although it was a surprise to hear, a few years later that, when the Armed Forces were expanded to include an Air Force section, and despite his total lack of experience, Sam had been transferred to a senior post in the new Ghana RAF.

Sam was a very private person, but Alex Crabbe, the Signals Officer, was a complete extrovert, with a lovely wife, Esther, who was as friendly and open as he. Alex was a broad, powerful man who spoke loudly in a laconic drawl, and laughed often, a deep belly rumble. He had a bushy moustache, with a swashbuckler's grin showing very white teeth, and one could imagine him sailing under the Jolly Roger. With his slouch-hat tilted over one ear, he seemed ideally suited to be a pirate captain, and his forthright manner was equally in character. If something bothered him, he would object with shouts and waving arms, but having made his protest he would dismiss the matter from his mind. He said exactly what he thought, and his views often had a useful cathartic effect. With Alex present, no one could remain tense for long.

Once when I was working in the office I heard him in the Orderly Room next door, completing his promotion forms with the help of the rather officious Scottish Colour-Sergeant Preston. It was a day when we were all feeling put-upon. The clerks had typed something wrong and were sulking. They had given Ives a broken pencil with which to correct their mistakes, which had irritated him. I had had a note from Brigade asking me to explain something trivial in my Intelligence report - and the Colour-Sergeant had had his departure-date for Scotland delayed. Then the following conversation filtered through.

"Misterrr Crrabbe, I need a few more details, if you pliss."

"Uhuh?"

"Name, all rrright... Rrrank, all rrright... Spoose?"

"Eh! What was that?"

"Yourr spoose, Misterr Crrabbe?"

"What do you mean, Sergeant?"

"Yourr spoose. Yourr wiff. Have ye got a wiff, Misterr Crrabbe?"

"Give me that form, you silly man. I'll fill it in myself. Ah, 'spouse'. S-P-O-U-S-E. Wife! Why the hell couldn't you say it in English, instead of wasting my time!"

Ives shook with laughter, and we could hear even the Colour-Sergeant sniggering.

"Hohoho!" came Alex's buccaneering guffaw and then, with his usual lack of tact: "and they told me you Scottishmen never laugh!"

Alex was captain of the Battalion hockey team, in which Jeremy, Mike, Albert and I played regularly. It was a successful team, and we enjoyed Alex's boisterous leadership, although at first he was undermined by the redoubtable Major Holdsworth, who was not keen to play under an African captain and assumed unofficial command. Fortunately for the team, Colonel Quinn watched one match, saw what was happening and suggested quietly to the newly promoted Captain Crabbe that Holdsworth 'wasn't much good anyway' and that he should be left out of the side. We then won eight matches in a row.

Almost all the junior officers, African and British, played some sport at Battalion level. After comments back in England about mad dogs and Englishmen, it was surprising to find that we really did play, if not in the mid-day sun, at any rate in the heat of the afternoon. Sport was a good 'mixer', in that on the field we could compete with people of all ranks, from all parts of the Battalion and from other units. Since the home pitches were near to Arakan Barracks, and Ghana is a nation of enthusiastic watchers, as well as participants, there was great interest in every team's progress, and often we had large crowds of soldiers, with their wives and children, applauding our games. It was good for morale, and especially good for the public image of the young officers who took part.

Some sports, of course, were never played at Battalion level. Only Rob tackled polo (which surprised no one) and only a few of us were reckless enough to play rugby for the Accra XV. This we did on a bone-hard pitch, with grass that when cut was like corn-stubble, and if left to grow, wound itself in steel-strong swathes about our ankles and tripped us up more surely than any tackle. Hefty people like Mike and Geoff gambolled about like gargantuan puppies, bouncing each other on the unyielding ground with every suggestion of enjoyment. The more fragile of us scampered in and out of the thickets of clawing grass, and if we found ourselves with the ball in an open space, ran like the devil in case we were tackled and mutilated. Rugby in Ghana did wonders for our speed, but I, for one, was delighted when the short season was over and the pitches were deemed too hard and dry even for Geoff and Mike. The only game I had really enjoyed was at Kumasi, where we defeated the town team in conditions of extraordinary humidity, but on a pitch soft and yielding.

Most of us played volley-ball, and also basket-ball, at which Albert was an artist, gliding about the court and making lithe six-foot opponents appear statuesque. Geoff was manager-cum-trainer-cum-star of the Athletics Team (his capitals) and led by example, hurling the discus twenty feet further than anyone else could manage. Rob shook everyone by proving a fine long-jumper and pole-vaulter.

We played cricket, too. There was some kit held by Headquarter Company, and several of the Brigade units played quite seriously. When told where the Camp pitch was, we were startled to find that it was a huge red-clay parade-ground, on part of which we had earlier played a hockey match. The green matting wicket was hauled out of its shed and unrolled, and the result was a picturesque and surprisingly true pitch.

I was put in charge of the boxing team, and was pleased by the keenness not only of those actually chosen to fight, but also of the many who came to train without hope of being more than sparring partners. I thought it was my enthusiasm that had encouraged them to come, until I learnt that the Battalion offered extra food-rations to the boxers, to build up their strength. I believe, however, that they genuinely enjoyed the sheer animal exertion of buffeting each other. Certainly their skill reached a high level, and soon after I left the country several of the boxers were training for the Empire Games in Cardiff. Inter-unit competitions were taken very seriously, and on one occasion Seidu, our star light-weight boxer, succumbed to a *juju* spell, apparently put on him by his opponent. The day before his bout he seemed perfectly fit, but his left arm was stiff as a board and he could not bend it. Seidu was a Grunshi, from the Northern Territories, an impressionable man who was now convinced that if he tried to box, his arm would shatter. Edmund Dadzie, the charming Roman Catholic who took his place, had no belief in *juju*, however. He knocked out his opponent in the first round – after which Seidu's arm was immediately back to normal.

The national preoccupation with gambling exhibited itself at many Battalion sports, and boxing was particularly suited, since although there were only two contestants at a time, the outcome of any bout was undecided until the final bell. Apparently a few 'punters' did well out of the Dadzie fight. On the whole, however, support for all Battalion teams was too loyal to permit wild gambling, and for this one had to go to race meetings or football matches in Accra.

I attended just one Race Day, to see if it was as entertaining as my friends had suggested. Whereas in England you had to be an expert to tell if a jockey had 'thrown' a race, apparently here it was obvious, and part of the game.

There was a continual hubbub and confusion around the course that made it difficult to tell what was going on, and when the first race started the din trebled. While the horses were running, people near me were betting among themselves not on the final outcome only, but on individual stages of the race, individual horses, individual jockeys: whether A would arrive at a particular part of the circuit before B, or whether C would manage to baulk D completely by swerving across (he did)... One race reached the final straight with the leading jockey, on what seemed almost a carthorse, a good five lengths clear, followed by a tiny black pony well ahead of the rest of the field. The carthorse's jockey was tugging hard, trying to slow down his huge, striding mount, and only just managed to let the black midget nose past the post in first place. As they came off the course both jockeys were grinning widely and most of the crowd seemed delighted. Obviously this was the intended result.

Football was less obviously 'staged', although in Sekondi the *Hasaakas* were notorious for the whole team walking off together whenever a penalty was given against them. Their style of play often meant that their games lasted less than fifteen minutes...

We did not attend soccer matches often, but one fixture at the Accra Stadium was watched by almost all the European officers, among a record crowd. We went to support Stanley Matthews, who was to play in the first game of an exhibition tour of Ghana. The press had billed him well in advance, in the screaming alliteration West Africans love, with headlines like 'Super Stanley Comes to Show Us His Sizzling Swerve and Sparkling Sidestep' and 'Marvellous Matthews, the Mighty Magician of Matchplay', and I imagine that every English man and woman in Accra was praying that he would play well. Poor Stanley cannot have enjoyed that first match, however. He had flown from England overnight into the steamy humidity of a storm-menaced Accra. As it was an exhibition match, he was expected to be continually 'in' the game, racing, chasing here, there, everywhere. In addition, the shoulder-shrug and body-swerve, that would make an English full-back go the wrong way and probably fall down, was strangely ineffective against the Ghanaian defenders. They often did start to fall, but with catlike agility they would be up again without touching the ground, ready to tackle again. Stanley was in his forties; he showed a lot of clever tricks and positioned himself skilfully, but it was not the virtuoso performance we had hoped for. Towards the end of the game the threatened rain fell. It was a short downpour, but with typical searing West African force. By the final whistle Stanley Matthews looked old and utterly exhausted.

We were afraid that his performance might seem an anti-climax, after all the ballyhoo preceding the game. The crowd had cheered mightily, but we thought this was probably because their own defenders had played so well. We need not have worried. For days afterwards, Accra streets were full of youths kicking tins and stones, and tiny black Matthewses dummied and sidestepped their way across the smooth sand of Labadi Beach. In Arakan Barracks it was just the same. Not only the members of the Battalion soccer team dribbled their way to work each morning, sidefooting stones along the road. Fat, elderly corporals and sergeants flung dignity away for the moment as they swayed and swerved past imaginary defenders and belted invisible goals into every doorway...

...Matthewses at Labadi...

Legon, the University of Ghana

Evening by the Volta River

Aburi (with Rob!)

Major Watkin-Williams at Huhunya

Myself, Abongo and Sam Lartey at Mamfe

Sam, Keith Hitchcock and Albert Ocran at Mampong

The Orderly Room at Larteh

Chapter Two

SENCHI

Shortly before Independence we had heard that there was unrest in British Togoland, just across the Volta River boundary. Now, soon after the celebrations had finished, we had further reports of trouble in that area. We learnt the 'facts' from the English newspapers, which we always received three or four days late, and the gist was that the people of Ho and Kpandu were objecting to Independence, because they were not gaining anything out of it. We did not trust the English press, and in any case it seemed strange that we should have heard nothing of what was happening in our own region. Nonetheless, Brigadier Hayward decided to investigate, probably because he wanted some 'live' action after a very peaceful tour in the Gold Coast, so on 8th March he took several units of Brigade to investigate the situation, and Major Watkin-Williams, our Second-in-Command, went out to join him. They returned, saying that the trouble was 'negligable', and the Brigadier was clearly disappointed.

We were shortly due to take part in a series of full-scale Battalion manoeuvres, and after Hayward's visit to Togoland, it was no great surprise to learn that the 'jungle training' we had been promised was to start with a Battalion Exercise near Senchi on the Volta River, just where the bridge to Togoland lay. We were told this less than a fortnight before the exercise was due, presumably to make it more of a test, and as Major Ives would be going on a week's leave at that time, I would have to act as Adjutant, with Jeremy as my official Intelligence Officer.

Colonel Quinn wanted to examine the area for himself, and decided that the two of us ought to go with him.

"While we're at it," he said, "we'll go right through to Ho as well, and show willing. Check that everything's still quiet there."

The Colonel had only one day free. "And I have to be back for a conference at six o'clock," he said, "so we must leave early."

'Early' meant that we set off from the Mess at 4 a.m. in the Colonel's land rover, with his orderly at the wheel, and hurtled through the darkness. Once we nearly hit a large fluffy nightjar that blundered across the windscreen, and as day broke we did hit a slow-moving kite, which had been feeding on a road-kill. It fell on our bonnet in a tangled mass of feathers and travelled there a mile before it was blown off. A little later a gigantic cobra whipped across the road and vanished into the bush. We reached Senchi well before seven o'clock.

From the centre of the Volta Bridge we could see several miles of the river, both up- and down-stream. The water was very still, and the reflections of the many small wooded islets were sharply defined. A single narrow fishing-boat was drifting slowly with the current. The only sounds came from a troupe of hornbills flapping and cackling in the trees near the Togoland end of the bridge. We examined the likely vantage-points for the coming exercise on both sides of the river, then drove along several firm laterite paths into the forest, recording where the main clearings were. I made a rough map in my notebook.

After that we went on through the Togoland Hills to Ho, an attractive township of red-mud houses surrounded by dense, steamy jungle. We had lunch there at a roadside chop-bar, and in the Colonel's report 'noted that all was quiet'. In fact, we spoke to numerous people in Ho and the outlying area, and not only was there no unrest, but one village chief was anxious to learn about Independence, as he had no idea that it had happened, or even what it was. So we drove back to Accra, arriving before four o'clock... The visit had been brief but, as the Colonel said, we had 'done our homework' for the Brigadier's Military Exercise.

Whenever the Battalion was to move out into the bush on any manoeuvres or tactical exercise, the Office Truck came into being. This vehicle was Major Ives's invention, a three-tonner fitted out to his own design as Adjutant's-office-cum-operations-room. It had compartments and pigeon-holes by the dozen, wall-boards with coloured pins for plotting the progress of the exercise, map-holders, wireless sets, a portable telephone, a typewriter... It was astonishing how much could be neatly stacked into one large truck. There were roof-hooks from which to hang tilly-lamps at night; sliding benches to seat the various clerks; folding tables to be used outside when the weather was suitable... After every exercise Ives modified his truck, moving a wall-bracket up a few inches or shifting a cupboard slightly, each small change designed to aid efficient, comfortable working, so that by now the Mobile Office approached perfection. Ives himself was not due to start his leave until the day after the Senchi exercise began, so he was able to supervise the loading of his precious vehicle. Since it was to be only a three-day scheme, big in scope but short in duration, the minimum of spare office equipment was needed. In a drawer that would otherwise have held extra message-pads, pencils, drawing-pins and the like, I put two butterfly nets and a number of empty boxes.

Four of the Orderly Room staff would be coming on the Exercise, with Sergeant Christian in charge of them, a tall, handsome man of few words but massive competence. Under him would be Corporal Adjei, dapper and something of a humorist, and the two dispatch clerks, John Finn, a chaotic but well-intentioned pseudo-intellectual, and Joseph Mensah, a highly intelligent and responsible Ashanti, to do the typing and keep us all sane.

"If you don't know what's going on, Christian and Mensah probably will," was Ives's parting shot.

There would also be two men from the Signals Platoon, "to fool about with the sets", Joseph remarked. And finally there would be Abongo and Seidu, my batman and Jeremy's. We would all be travelling in the one big truck.

The Senchi Exercise would have made an entertaining film. Apparently it was a success, militarily. From first to last I knew comparatively little of what was going on, and Jeremy even less, but much of what we witnessed was amusing, and we enjoyed the three days immensely. The praise we received afterwards for our 'efficiency' was undeserved, but gratifying.

Early on an April morning the Battalion moved slowly out of Accra, together with various attached sections from Brigade, and the 'Enemy Platoon', dressed in blue denims, who were known to be from the Takoradi Battalion although we pretended to keep it a secret. The long convoy of trucks and land rovers crawled across the Accra Plain and into the forest, and eventually we halted in a jungle clearing at a place called Kpong, not far from the Volta Bridge. The Colonel told Battalion Headquarters – including our Ops. Truck – to stay there and 'settle in', which we proceeded to do. 'A' Company was near us. 'C' Company was sent to 'hold the bridge'. The others were 'deployed tactically' somewhere in the forest. As soon as I had fixed a wall-board map of the area in the truck, the Colonel jammed coloured pins in it, to show where all the Companies ought to be. I also pinned up the sketch map of the bridge area, which I had made on our reconnaissance-trip and had improved since, at leisure.

Suddenly, to the surprise of Jeremy and myself, and I think of the Colonel, too, General Paley emerged from the jungle, whiffled his white moustache, said "First patrol had better go out about two o'clock" and disappeared again into the trees before the Colonel's "Very good, sir!" could reach him. A little later, the Brigadier drove up in his land rover, barked "Not a bad site you have here", and drove off again. We waited to see if there would be any more surprise appearances. No one else arrived, so Colonel Quinn wandered off to see how 'A' Company was faring. The four clerks relaxed.

We arranged the Office Truck neatly, under the guidance of Sergeant Christian, who had done this on numerous occasions. By the time we had allocated and labelled all the notice-boards and shelves, and found a space for Joseph to do his typing and more spaces for our two signallers to work, it was nearly noon. We all clambered out to examine the rest of Battalion Headquarters. Tents had mushroomed around the clearing, each with a neat notice pegged in front of it to explain what office it was meant to represent. Batmen and orderlies were scampering to and fro with kit-bags, haversacks, clothes, mosquito-nets. Abongo and Seidu had cleared a patch of undergrowth five yards square, not far from the truck. In the centre of this area they had spread a groundsheet, on which they had deposited all our kit and their own. The two of them were now having their lunch, mess-tins of pepper-soup into which they dipped hunks of bread.

"Lazy men!" said Christian.

"No be so, Sargy," Abongo replied indignantly, "we de work hard pass all for cut dis place!"

"What about all these other soldiers, then?" asked the Sergeant, indicating the orderlies going to and fro with their loads. "They are still working, but you are having your chop."

"Dey chop done finish," said Abongo. "I tink, Sargy, be time for youself chop."

Sure enough, at this moment a runner arrived, panting, from the Kitchen Department somewhere in the forest, to say that the clerks and signallers should go for their lunch at once. He would have told them sooner, he said, but he had got lost.

"What organisation!" said Christian.

"Quite chaotic!" Joseph declared.

"Chop nownow!" yelled Adjei to John and the signallers. The six went off together into the forest. Jeremy and I concluded that as the exercise did not officially start until two o'clock, it ought to be safe to leave Abongo and Seidu in charge of the truck, while we went for our own lunch. We would be at the Officers' Mess tent, we told them, and would be back in half an hour. If the VIPs were to arrive again, one or other of the batmen must come across to fetch us.

"Can you recognise the General and the Brigadier all right?" Jeremy asked. "You savvy um OK?"

"Yessah. Dey get fonny hat. Bligadier be him get glass for him face."

The Mess tent was at the far end of the big clearing, under a large tree. Creepers dangled over the entrance. Mike peered out.

"I was just going to call you," he whispered. "The Big Bugs are here."

"Good," I answered, relieved that neither Abongo nor Seidu would have to be cross-examined by red-tab officers.

We all sat at one long table. It was covered by a white cloth, and we were waited on by the Mess staff exactly as in Accra. There was canvas above, and the servants wore khaki; otherwise, apart from the fact that there were now many more officers, it seemed little different from a normal Mess lunch. We had curry, followed by fresh fruit, after which we adjourned for coffee to the 'lounge', under the back flap of the same huge tent. The General was there already, with a cup in his hand. He looked quite different with his braided cap off, his white hair and drooping moustache making him seem like a tidied-up version of Albert Sweitzer.

"Ready for the off?" he asked.

"Yes, sir," replied Colonel Quinn, checking his watch. "Another hour, almost exactly."

"Your last jungle jaunt, I believe, Neville?" the General said. "Good luck in your retirement. And you three," he turned to Jeremy, Mike and me, "didn't hear me say that!"

Jeremy and I drank our coffee hurriedly. As we were about to return to our truck, Abongo's face appeared at the entrance to the tent. He peered in, grinning at the assembled officers.

"Hey! What are you doing here?" Jeremy and I spoke almost together.

"I jus' want for see dis Officer Miss tent, sah," he said. "Be OK, I lef' Seidu for guard."

"But we told you both to stay."

"I tell you be hall right, sah," Abongo said cheerfully and very distinctly. "No you de worry, sah. No blorry General come attall!"

Somewhere in the forest were the Enemy. At two o'clock, Mike took out the first patrol. Others followed. Less than an hour later Mike returned with four prisoners, dressed in blue denims. They seemed happy to be captured. In his official capacity as Intelligence Officer, Jeremy went to interrogate them, to see if he could learn any details about 'enemy movement'.

In the Ops. Room truck there was pandemonium at first. The signallers were bleeping away in morse, while Adjei and I were manoeuvring companies with abandon on the wall-maps, as new situation-reports came in. The other clerks were collecting information together, so that Joseph could type out important data and record it officially. The Colonel rushed in two or three times to check our map and add new details, leaving a string of messages to be relayed to Company Commanders. Now and again, Sergeant Christian's voice would rise above the confusion: "Give it to *me*," he would say, "*I'll* set it out properly": or "this goes *here*."

Jeremy returned from his interrogation.

"They say they got lost," he said. "They were happy to be found by Mike's patrol. Apparently there's only one platoon of enemy, and only one officer in charge. They say they don't know anything else, and I believe them."

We made the most of Jeremy's investigations, and filled in what details we could on the wall-maps and report-boards. Mike showed us exactly where he had made his quadruple capture, and we marked this spot on the map with a special huge-headed red pin. The only thing we omitted to say in our detailed report was that the soldiers had been lost, and captured largely by accident.

When the Colonel next appeared, the Ops. Room was no longer bedlam, and we could point out proudly how much we had achieved. It did look quite impressive.

"Things are going well," the Colonel said.

Then General Paley came in. "Good," he said, "nice and orderly. Well done, young men. I can understand those maps."

Before sundown, ten more 'enemy' had been captured in various areas. Jock's platoon had claimed five of them. He said that 'C' Company was no longer at the near side of the Volta Bridge, but had crossed to the Togoland bank where the ground was less marshy. They had found a crocodile at their first camp-site… We recorded all the details meticulously, including the crocodile, and concluded that half the enemy must have been captured.

During the night, patrols went out occasionally into the forest, but news came in very slowly. We sat outside the truck watching the fireflies among the trees, and listening to the cicadas' shrilling and the rising wail of a hyrax, some way off in the jungle. We had to hang the tilly lamps several yards from the vehicle, to prevent our maps and documents, hair and faces being covered by the ever-growing cloud of insects that whirled around each light. Now and then, among the mass of small flies and beetles, bugs, moths and mantids, there would appear the enormous, blundering shape of a giant *saturnid* moth, with soft, furry wings carrying, in the centre of each, a transparent patch circled in black, like an enormous eye. They are aptly named 'moon moths'.

We slept a few hours at a time, always leaving two people on duty at the Ops. Room. Towards dawn, Mike's platoon brought in three more of the enemy. Mike also brought with him a haversack, which he handed to me. It was heavy.

"Something else for your bug-collection," he said.

I opened the haversack and gently tipped out onto the ground what at first seemed in the half-light remarkably like a shiny new football. We shone a torch on it.

"It's an ant-eater," said Christian excitedly. "A big one."

"A pangolin," said Joseph, precise as always.

Slowly the strange creature uncurled. It must have been the size of a short-legged cat, with a snakelike head, a long reptilian tail and its whole body covered with reddish-brown spiky scales. One of Mike's soldiers had found this chimaera beast clinging to a branch in the forest, about head-height. Apparently, with its strong claws and prehensile tail firmly hooked, it had been hard to dislodge.

John Finn wanted to keep the pangolin, saying that it would be easy enough to find ants to feed it on, but was over-ruled, and we released it in a particularly thick patch of forest nearby. In the official log of the exercise we recorded that on this particular patrol Mike's platoon had captured

En personnel (3)

Pangolin (1).

Around eleven o'clock the enemy leader was captured, with four more of his men.

"I suppose that means we've won," Jeremy observed, as he added yet more details to the notice-boards.

The officer proved to be Steve, who had arrived at Accra on the same 'plane as myself, and had since been with the Takoradi Battalion. We gave him some coffee and a chair to sit in, and he said he was bloody glad to be captured as he had been bitten by a bloody mosquito in the night and his bloody arm hurt. He said there were probably about a dozen enemy still left in the forest, and that as one of these was his Sergeant-Major, they would probably be capable of looking after themselves.

Unfortunately for Steve, before he had finished his coffee, three more enemy had been captured, including the Sergeant-Major. Steve agreed that the exercise was as good as over. The Colonel came to the truck to examine the maps and diagrams, and was pleased by how well everything had gone. Being a good naturalist, he was intrigued by the 'pangolin': "Isn't that a sort of ant-eater?" he asked. We told him it was, and he enjoyed the joke, saying that he wondered whether General Paley would understand it. Thus encouraged, we began to amuse ourselves by sending out ambiguous radio messages. One read: "Company Headquarters is surrounded by *akyenkyenas*, but is in no danger." This was quite true, for *akyenkyena* was the Twi dialect name for a bird, the huge black-and-white hornbill, and dozens of them were feeding noisily in the trees around the clearing. Joseph dutifully typed the details into his official record.

And then after lunch the General released all the prisoners.

"We've another whole day," he said. "We can't have all these men just sitting on their arses doing nothing."

So Steve and his troops-in-blue went off rather dispiritedly into the forest.

By nightfall, most of them had been recaptured, and the rest were brought in early the next morning after an uncomfortable night. This time it was accepted that the exercise was genuinely over. Half an hour or so later, I was shaving at the edge of the clearing when I noticed an enormous caterpillar chomping on the small bush from which I had suspended my mirror. Having seen one, I became aware of others… and still more. They were four or five inches long, fat and green, with brown and mauve markings and huge eye-spots – Oleander Hawk-moth larvae were in hundreds, probably thousands all around the clearing. Some were feeding on diminutive oleander saplings, and many on the bigger shrubs at the edge of the forest. Others were chewing their way through a varied range of plants. For such exotic and brilliantly-coloured creatures they were remarkably procryptic. With the help of Jeremy, Abongo and Joseph Mensah, however, I was able to gather a sample of the largest caterpillars, which we put into map-cases and pin-boxes in the Office-truck cupboards; others we hung in large paper-bags from the roof-hooks. We collected more than a hundred. Abongo declared that they were *nyama-nyama*, a phrase that denoted something unpleasant and mysterious – he was clearly more worried by hawk-moth larvae than by venomous snakes. One of the signallers joked that they would be fine chop, to which I replied that if he ate any of my caterpillars he would run all the way back to Accra, tied to the tailboard of the Office Truck.

Promptly at noon the convoy crawled out of Kpong, led by the two 'enemy' vehicles. A mile out from the camp the Officers' Mess truck broke down. As it was near the rear of the column, the breakdown van, travelling last, was soon there to help. The Mess vehicle limped home, about an hour late. But when Steve's 'enemy' three-tonner broke down two miles further on, truck after truck drove by, the occupants callously cheering and jeering, while the poor Enemy in their incongruous blue denims waited for the breakdown van to finish its first repair-job.

Major Ives returned from his week's leave boasting of the huge waves he had mastered on Winneba Beach. His descriptions left a vivid picture of Canute-in-reverse, lying on a surf-board and urging the waves to carry him far across the golden sand. He was full of new zest, and rushed about the office with disconcerting enthusiasm. He did not want to hear about the Senchi exercise – "The usual shambles, I expect" – or about how I had been faring as Adjutant while he had been away.

"I expect you have been quite brilliant," he said tartly, "and no doubt I'll soon be getting replies to all those letters you've signed promising that *I* will do this that and the other, and *I* will be here there and everywhere all at the same time..."

I reflected that his remark was not as facetious as it sounded. It was true that I had been handed an alarming number of letters and papers to sign, from all parts of the Battalion and from Giffard Camp. With the help of Jeremy and the Orderly Room staff I had done my best to decipher them, but if in doubt as to their relevance and urgency I had several times merely signed them, stamped 'p.p.Adjutant' on them, and hoped for the best...

Chapter Three

DREAMTIME

As an English officer serving in an African army I had been aware from my first day in the Battalion that there were remarkably few racial barriers, and after Independence it truly seemed there were none. At the time I had relations living in both South Africa and what was then Rhodesia, who simply could not believe that in the Army of the new Ghana black and white not only behaved as equals but felt equal and trusted each other. I realise now that it was not as simple as that, but in our relaxed society life was really enjoyable, and my post as Intelligence Officer became challenging and rewarding.

Colonel Quinn had by now returned home to well-deserved retirement. He had not been a dynamic Commanding Officer, and at a less joyous time he might have been found wanting as a leader, but with his trusting nature and innate worthiness he had been an ideal man to guide the Battalion through the euphoria of Independence. Colonel 'Kerry' Harding, who followed him as C.O., took over at exactly the right time. He was a hands-on soldier with a proud war-record, who came to us from a successful tour of bandit-hunting duty in Malaysia, where he had known my Uncle Kenneth well. He was a stronger, much more innovative leader than Quinn, but like him he respected Ghanaians, and was scrupulously fair. Fresh from his Malaysian experiences, he took my post of Intelligence Officer extremely seriously, and from the first I found him very supportive. I had taken part in the big Senchi Exercise with naïve enthusiasm, but Colonel Harding made it clear that he wanted me to aim higher.

He encouraged me, as I.O., to join the infantry Companies on their training exercises, in the plains and the jungle. "Learn everything," he said. "And see if you can improve our maps!" So I took part in Company schemes based on Larteh and Mamfeh, two pleasant forest villages, and enjoyed a Signals exercise at Huhunya, where the officers made their headquarters in a comfortable rest-house, between the forest and the village school. Then Colonel Harding suggested I should visit the local Regional Officers, which was when an already enjoyable life became idyllic.

Ostensibly I was to learn the geography of the area and also the political situation in the outlying districts – but the Colonel knew how to motivate his young officers.

"Your uncle tells me you're an even madder naturalist than he is – so enjoy yourself! Get me some decent information about our district and brief me when you're back, and you can watch as much wildlife as you like."

The Regional Officers, each with a unique knowledge of his own area, introduced me to the district and people they supervised, and enabled me to meet local dignitaries. The Colonel repaid their support by inviting them to a dinner-night at the Officers' Mess. I especially enjoyed my visits to George Levack, Regional Officer of Koforidua, who taught me about the life of a government official, and in particular explained the etiquette needed to keep on the right side of village head-men – advice which was to prove invaluable. George was a first-class naturalist, who was always interested in the birds and animals I had seen. He recorded his own observations carefully, and even kept a tame Black Duiker at his home. It was fascinating to see this small, famously shy forest antelope, gambolling in his garden like a pet dog. My driver, Amadu Fulani, was much taken with the duiker, which would nibble his fingers and permit him to stroke its back.

Before long, I was allowed to plan my own agenda. There was a big wall-map of Southern Ghana in the office I shared with Major Ives, composed of Ordnance Survey sheets, on which I used to record where I had been and when, marking each destination with a coloured pin and a label. Some of the OS maps were limited in detail, and there were tracts of countryside, mainly forest, with almost no recorded features, so it was a challenge to fill the gaps.

I now had a land rover available whenever I needed it, with Amadu as my regular driver, and on many week-ends I went out on 'official reconnaissance'. Often I was accompanied by one of the junior officers, usually Jeremy – and always I took at least one person who could speak the local language. For this the Education staff and the Corps of Drums proved ideal, since the men of these units spoke fluent English as well as the required dialect, and Jeremy and I knew them well.

Our first trip was to the Shai Hills, which I had visited on Battalion training. It was exciting to see large troops of baboons, and we also saw a hundred-strong herd of beautiful kob antelopes. We visited a cave inhabited by thousands of chattering bats. It was a wasted trip, however, in terms of learning about the country, for we discovered little that was new and could add nothing to our wall-map. So after that we concentrated on the forest-country, where we always 'lived rough'.

Looking back fifty years, it is strange to recall the rudimentary nature of our preparations for these trips. In our packs we each carried a groundsheet, both to keep off the rain and also to sleep on, a mess-tin with combined knife-fork-spoon set, and a torch. I always had with me a box of matches and a supply of paludrine tablets. Nowadays these are not considered a 'safe' anti-malaria precaution, but in the 1950s we Europeans trusted paludrine utterly, and seldom bothered even to take mosquito-nets. We were bitten countless times, yet none of us contracted malaria… We did take a few warm clothes for night-time – but no tooth-brush, since chewed twigs of the quinine-rich neem tree proved an excellent substitute. In addition I carried a camera, a notebook and pencil and, distributed among my 'team', maps and a small medicine-box.

We took with us in the land rover a large container of drinking water and a pack of army rations 'in case', although we seldom needed to use them. In addition we always carried a crate of bottled beer and another of cocacola, some to drink but mainly, as I had learned from George Levack, to 'dash' to local headmen as a goodwill offering, so that they would accept our presence in their area and allow us to camp nearby. The villagers invariably gave us food, which they would bring out to our camp in the evening in an earthenware pot: frequently chicken and yam, or some form of meat stew.

In the forest country our procedure was to park the land rover beside the road, as near as possible to our intended destination, then move into the jungle carrying only our packs, with a share of the bottles. Time and again we found that places marked on the map were either not shown accurately or were split-sites, with two or more tiny villages spread over quite a wide area, each having the same name. We recorded what we had discovered, usually after a discussion with the headman. Surprisingly often we passed through settlements where the inhabitants had no idea that within a few miles lived other forest dwellers whose villages shared the same nomenclature, and twice we came to places where the people looked at Jeremy and me in astonishment, saying they had not seen white men before – yet we were less than fifty miles from Accra.

The 'official' part of these expeditions was enjoyable and worthwhile, but a real bonus came from the wildlife we were enabled to see. In the savannah country we had done most of our watching from the land rover, but in the rain-forest the world around us was full of birdsong and animal cries, but the creatures stayed invisible unless we moved carefully and kept very quiet. Only the insects were perpetually in view: flies, wasps and dragonflies were all around, and in every forest clearing gaudy butterflies swarmed. If we came to a stream the mud beside it was often tight-packed with swallowtails, *pierids* and *charaxes*, sipping from the ooze. On my first few trips I endeavoured to collect butterflies, but gave up because firstly I could not cope with the astronomical number of species, and secondly, I made the disastrous mistake of enlisting the villagers to help. They enjoyed it enormously, especially the children, who rushed around swatting flying insects with palm fronds, and produced for me, with great delight, what had clearly once been beautiful creatures but were now smashed beyond recognition. It was difficult to offer the hoped-for praise… When I returned to England I gave the few boxes I did fill to an expert on African lepidoptera, who found several new and unclassified species among them. In Britain, we have fewer than 70 kinds of butterfly, whereas from the rain-forests of Southern Ghana more than 500 have already been recorded, and there must be many species still unknown to science…

When we began to live unobtrusively in the forest we realised that birds and animals were also all around us, and creatures that we would never have come across in a day-visit to search for them, proved numerous when a small group of us camped under the trees. The birds were beautiful and strange: multi-coloured doves, turacoes and parrots were particularly abundant in the high forest. I had friends back in England who had a pet African Grey parrot, which spoke (and swore) fluently, so it was a weird experience to watch dozens, perhaps hundreds of these birds squabbling over fruit high in the canopy.

The animals were even more wonderful. The sounds at night were enthralling: splutters and hoots, growls and howls, clicks and hiccups, chirrups and whistles, but at first, even for an enthusiast like me there was comfort in a fire and my companions. Soon, however, it became apparent that there was nothing to fear from these vocalists, and by degrees, because we kept quiet, we began to see the creatures that made the sounds, particularly at dusk and dawn. Some were birds, many were insects, but the excitement came from seeing the mammals. Often the most vocal proved to be primates, of which my favourites were the black-and-white Colobus monkeys, which we often saw leaping from tree to tree. At dawn and dusk they gathered in clans and sent their deep, rumbling cries rising and falling through the forest. There were many other kinds of monkey, but usually we glimpsed them high up, and briefly. Once as it grew light, however, we watched a party of chimpanzees. We had several times heard their incredible range of shrieks and yells, but actually to see them was unforgettable. This was in a dense area of Togoland jungle near to the spectacular Boti Falls, a place we visited several times. We used to swim in the crystal clear pool at the base of the hundred-foot waterfall, and while floating on our backs could sometimes watch birds and animals coming to drink at the edge. That lovely area has since become the Boti Forest Park, to preserve it for the nation, but sadly, the chimpanzees and monkeys have all disappeared.

On our trips we frequently saw bush-babies, sometimes jumping huge distances from branch to branch in the half-light; at other times late at night, caught in a torch-beam, when their eyes shone golden and enormous. Around the villages we came across various types of mongoose, which the inhabitants encouraged, because they ate snakes and rats. We also saw several kinds of small jungle cat, and one memorable morning, as we were leaving the forest near Mamfe to return to our land rover, we glimpsed a leopard in broad daylight, crossing the red laterite track. On many occasions tiny forest duikers skipped across paths in front of us, and in a stretch of dense, humid jungle near the Volta River, when we had stopped for a rest in a small clearing, a bongo, a rare and very secretive antelope with huge twisted horns and a chocolate coat with white stripes, came upon us unawares. The beautiful creature stood absolutely still for a few seconds, so that we all had a clear view, before vanishing silently back into the trees.

The strange tree hyraxes we seldom saw, but they were common in the forest and at night their weird rising wail sounded from the tops of trees all around us. Soldiers who were townsfolk or came from the North found the cry of the hyrax alarming, and it was difficult to convince them that a small, harmless animal could make such a noise. The Twi people call the beast *Owea,* an onomatopoeic three-syllable word with the stress on the '*e*', which aptly mimics the creature's call. Once, in the village of Aburi, we found a captured hyrax, tethered by the neck to a string held by a small boy. Seen in daylight it was a pathetic creature, the size of a rabbit but shaped like a bear. I bought it from the child for five shillings, and after photographing the animal we released it in the forest, where it disappeared up a tree, seemingly unharmed.

Perhaps the most surprising beast we saw was a Giant Forest Hog, which came to drink in the early morning at a stream by our camp-site near Huhunya. We had seen wart-hogs in the savannah country, and bush pigs many times at the edge of the jungle, and I had heard tell of the Giant Hog, but we were all completely unprepared for what we saw. On this particular morning we were quietly filling our packs, prior to setting off further into the forest, when someone whistled softly – our signal to pay attention. There by the stream, drinking its fill, was a huge beast, almost black, with prominent tusks. Most startling of all, along its back was a stiff mane of hair like a crest, that made the hog seem even more gigantic. We watched it for several minutes, before it trotted off. My companions were awestruck, and spoke little for the next mile or more. Strangely, no one at the village had ever seen such a creature, and when we mentioned it on our return to Accra, no one we questioned had come across one.

If the Forest Hog was remarkable, the most fascinating animals we encountered were the flying squirrels. They cannot 'fly' in the true sense, but can cover an astonishing distance by spreading a membrane that joins their fore and hind legs, as they leap from the canopy to glide from tree to tree. We saw two kinds, perhaps more. One, which we encountered several times, was a rat-sized creature that appeared at dusk and, if we managed to shine a torch beam on a 'glider', it was pure white underneath, but when it landed on a tree trunk disappeared from view, as its back was grey. The other kind seemed no bigger than a mouse, and unfortunately we only saw this species once, but in the forest-glade where we discovered them one evening, there were dozens of these enchanting creatures, scurrying along branches, gliding easily across the wide clearing, and sometimes, it seemed, able even to 'fly' *upwards,* to land quite high on another tree trunk. We watched them entranced, until the light faded.

In the game parks of East Africa I have seen spectacular thousands of exotic birds and animals, prey and predators. My delight in seeing myriads of flamingos, or a pride of lions, or a cheetah in pursuit of a Thompson's Gazelle, or huge rafts of hippos, or uncountable herds of wildebeest is real, although I know I am viewing them as part of a commercial venture. By contrast the creatures of the West African rain-forest are far less easily observed, and with few exceptions are smaller and less dramatic. They are beautiful, strange and shy, however, and cannot be found 'to order'. This period of my life, when I was exploring the jungles of Southern and Central Ghana with groups of friends, and helping to add detail to the area maps, was my 'dreamtime', which I can never revisit but will certainly not forget.

Chapter Four

THE COMING OF THE RAINS

Before he returned to England at the end of his final tour of duty the Governor, Sir Charles Arden-Clarke, presented the Second Battalion with a mascot, a large white ram. The animal was immediately christened Charles, out of respect for the Governor, and a soldier was detailed to be Corporal i/c Ram, with the sole job of looking after him. It was hoped to have the animal well-enough trained to march in the Queen's Birthday Parade on Easter Saturday, when for the last time Sir Charles would be inspecting the troops.

The ram was not an ideal pupil. He looked the part, for his long white hair was brushed till it gleamed, his white horns were made whiter still with enamel paint, and his hooves shone with black boot-polish. He was even fitted out with a coat of the same flame-coloured zouave material that the soldiers wore, ornamented with a gold palm-tree design. He marched badly at the head of a column, however. He kept stopping to look around, or to nose at pebbles to see if they were edible. Seidu Grumah, the Corporal i/c Ram, spent hours teaching him to keep in step, without success. Charles seemed to have no idea of the importance of his position. Sometimes the Corporal would have to haul him along by his lead; at other times it was all Seidu could do to stop himself being forced into a run.

Once, at a parade rehearsal the ram broke free and trotted alongside the Drum Major, nibbling at his puttees. The buglers shook with laughter and broke down; the drummers lost their rhythm and marched an unsteady course. Angrily the Drum Major swatted at Charles with his mace. The Corporal i/c Ram regathered the leather lead and tugged his charge out of the way, but all dignity had gone from the parade.

Several of the soldiers suggested to Seidu that perhaps the ram's waywardness was caused by frustration. Maybe if he had a wife, they said, or better still, two or three, he would sober down and behave as a responsible mascot should. Seidu agreed to the experiment. But when the news reached some of the senior officers that Charles had been seen frisking in the company of a shabby brown ewe with lop-ears, and outside the Colonel's office at that, there was colossal indignation. Someone even suggested putting the Corporal i/c Ram on a charge for deliberately prostituting the Battalion mascot.

Luckily, Charles's demeanour showed that he, at least, was grateful, and the next morning he behaved in exemplary fashion on the parade-ground. Seidu was not even reprimanded. The tatty brown sheep was banished but, instead, Charles was officially married to a beautiful white thoroughbred ewe, much nearer his own class.

Birthday Parade rehearsals took place almost every day. Once again the officers practised their sword-drill antics in the comparative privacy of the Mess gardens. Once again the Assistant Adjutant was excused both the sword-drill and the parades, as he was deemed to have far too much to do. It was pleasing to be told so, anyway, and more pleasing still was the prospect of being able to watch the Birthday Parade without feeling involved.

Rehearsals started to take place earlier and earlier in the mornings, and finally RSM Kramo Wongara came to Major Ives to say that the Mallam, the Mohammedan Priest at Arakan Barracks, had complained to him that it was wrong to parade during prayer-time.

"I suppose you agree with him?" the Adjutant asked.

"Yessah. Anyting Mallam say be good."

Ives consulted his diary.

"No," he said, "I'm sorry, but I can't change the time, not tomorrow anyway. There's a kit-issue to 'D' Company at ten o'clock. We'll have to get the parade over long before then. I no fit change um."

"I tink, sah, Mallam no be happy. He say Allah no like parade for prayer-time..."

"You tell Mallam," said Ives, "that Allah and Adjutant no agree, and this time Adjutant go win."

The Sergeant-Major went out in a huff, leaving Ives to wish that he had been less brusque. He said with mock jauntiness: "I wonder what he'll do about *that*..." but then confessed that he hated meddling with religious matters.

Next morning, when the troops lined up at the edge of the parade-ground, the sky was overcast, the air thick and oppressively warm. As the first platoons marched on, the grey clouds became black. The soldiers strode forward into a hot, murky twilight.

The wind, rain, thunder and lightning seemed to strike simultaneously. For nearly a minute the Battalion stood firm, until the Colonel gave the order to dismiss and double away. Somehow! Anyhow! Officers and men raced for shelter through the cutting rain. Jags of lightning split the sky apart, like a window smashed by a stone. The rain fell in scything torrents. Within two minutes the parade-ground was awash, an unbroken lake of red, muddy water.

We had had showers before, some heavy, but this was the first real storm of the year, the start of the Rains. After the astonishing deluge, grass and herbage everywhere sprang up threefold. Then prolonged showers began to come quite frequently, but almost always at night, so that the days showed little change apart from the added greenery. But snakes and scorpions came from their holes and prowled and slithered in the dusk and even sometimes by daylight; and out from their caves came the big monitor lizards. One huge creature lived somewhere at the back of the Mess; he was more than five feet long, grey and wrinkled like a mummy, and in the steamy sunshine he lay stretched on a big rock in the garden. The cooks said he was fine chop, but would not venture near him.

The insects multiplied incredibly. They had been numerous before, but now, with the rains, their numbers became immeasurable. In particular, crickets and grasshoppers swarmed everywhere in wonderful variety. The crickets ranged from tiny black creatures resembling ants, to chestnut monsters four inches long, which flew into lighted windows at night with frightening velocity, crashing unharmed against walls and furniture. The grasshoppers were even more varied. Some, with long antennae, lived quietly amongst bushes and trees and were patterned like leaves; others jumped and flew in thousands among the grasses, their mottled forewings and thoraxes revealing brilliant crimson, yellow or blue hindwings when they were in the air. A few locusts appeared, almost the size of sparrows, but they were not numerous enough to do any harm.

Moths and butterflies came out with the rains in similarly increased numbers. My Oleander caterpillars behaved exactly as if they were at large, and timed their metamorphosis perfectly. Within a week or so of our return from Senchi, the first few had pupated in flimsy cocoons spun up from dead leaves and banana bark. The others quickly followed. The afternoon of the big storm, the first moth appeared, just nine days after pupating. Then more and more emerged, bright green and shiny. Jeremy and I fixed a mosquito-net tent over some bushes near our quarters, and released the moths into it, half a dozen at a time. They would pair in the night, and the following evening the female moths would begin to lay their small round eggs all over the mesh. Some nights, wild Oleander Hawk-moths flew in from the waste ground, and we would find them in the morning clinging to the outside of the netting tent. Later, when the tiny caterpillars emerged from the eggs, we released them all around the area. They did not only eat oleander leaves and, as at Senchi, many low-growing plants seemed perfectly suitable.

Of all the creatures that the rains brought out, the most sudden and surprising in their arrival were the termites. During the dry season we hardly noticed them. Their hillocks were familiar enough, great russet castles eight to ten feet high, rising from every patch of bare ground, but the pinnacled structures seemed merely to be part of the landscape, like rocks or trees: we did not see the builders. The only time termites forced themselves upon our notice was when insidious mud-streaks appeared on a door-post or table-leg, encroaching a few inches more each night, until someone noticed at last and knocked off the mud cover, to reveal a termite army gnawing away at the wood beneath.

After a rainstorm, however, the winged ants emerged by night in millions from their red-mud hillocks, and whirled like a snowstorm in one short flight before shedding their wings and becoming earthbound again. I remember one termite-blizzard with especial clarity. It was only a few days before the Queen's Birthday Parade.

That evening Mike and I went to the Cameo, the small open-air cinema at Giffard Camp, with Angela and Jane, our current attachments. It was not a very successful foursome. Angela was tall and anaemic-looking: Mike said she had 'style' but to me it seemed pure affectation. He threw her over pretty smartly a few days later, anyway. Jane was, I thought, beautiful, with golden tresses like Tenniel's Alice, but already I was beginning to wish she would not giggle so foolishly at my attempts at wit. She did not last long, either.

At the Cameo you could pay various prices, from half-a-crown for the superior seats under cover at the back, to sixpence for the chairs right in front of the screen, which were mainly filled by the soldier-friends of the doorkeeper, smuggled in free. Slow-dying hierarchy: Europeans sat at the back. Officers likewise sat at the back, especially if they were Europeans; the done thing; expected. The subalterns usually went further forward, partly from sheer cussedness, but defensibly because the screen was so small that we had a much better view from there.

This time Jane said dutifully that she didn't mind where we sat. Angela wanted to sit at the back, as she said she felt everyone was looking at her when she had a seat in one of the front rows, and personally I felt she had a point, there. The dress she was wearing would have looked sexy, on Jane.

"Nonsense, girl," Mike whispered loudly. "I'll hold your hand and save you from the nasty men."

"Don't be bloody silly," Angela snapped. Swearing was an important part of her 'style'.

We got seats four rows from the front. The moon was bright, but there were big clouds overhead.

"Good evening, sirs; good evening, ladies," said a grin of white teeth further along the row. It was Corporal Stephen Adjei, smart in cream flannels and a flamboyant shirt patterned with Nkrumahs rampant. Beyond him, Mrs Adjei smiled. It was a sultry evening and the sweat prickled my back. Bats were flitting overhead, disconcertingly close, and moths hummed past. The moon went behind a cloud.

The screen shone silver and the loudspeaker spluttered. There was a buzz of anticipation. The projectionist did his warm-up exercises, and a series of grotesque numbers and patterns danced across the screen, applauded by the viewers.

There was always real audience-participation at the Cameo. War films were popular, and the Foe (Germans, Japanese or 'Indians') were jeered mercilessly. Occasionally a watcher would be so carried away by his hatred for a particular character that he would hurl a coca-cola bottle at the screen, which fortunately was painted onto a concrete wall, so the exploding glass merely added to the excitement.

This time the screen proclaimed *ABOVE US THE WAVES*, and the chatter grew louder. The Turpitz story unfolded. A big ship was torpedoed and a small boat was tossed by the waves; a surging sea towered high and thundered into plumes of driving spray. Men were struggling in the water. The rain poured down.

It was several seconds before anyone realised that the rain was not on the screen – it was deluging in the cinema. Then there was a rush for the covered space at the back, where the quicker ones found standing-room behind the expensive seats. Others scuttled to shelter beneath a row of neem trees by the exit. We were jammed in the middle of a row, too late to get to cover. The girls were struggling to escape, almost panicking. But then we noticed that Adjei and his wife were still sitting down. They had picked up empty chairs from the row in front, raising them above their heads like umbrellas – so we did the same. Other people near us followed. The chairs kept off at least some of the rain.

We sat there with the water dripping down our necks, running down our sleeves, soaking our feet. Adjei was enjoying himself. "The rain come!" he cried, rather unnecessarily. Mike was the first of us to see the funny side of the situation: he giggled, then guffawed. We all followed, and soon a dozen or so more of the drenched spectators were shrieking with laughter in the centre of the cinema, splashing each other, making faces through tangled hair.

"Aiyeee!" cried Adjei, delighted. "Rain be fonny pass all – but he no keep long."

And soon, indeed, the shower was over. We put down our 'umbrellas'. The people who had tried to shelter under the trees began to creep away, bedraggled. On the screen the sea was rising and falling endlessly, and the boat was still drifting at the mercy of the waves.

For perhaps twenty minutes we sat there. It was not cold, and we were less soaked than we had thought; and anyway, after withstanding the shower we did not want to give in now. But the tossing boat was becoming a bore.

"It's all done in a tank, anyway," Mike said. "That's not a real boat. I hope they'll soon send a helicopter to rescue those damn men and let us out. Or another submarine…" he added deliberately. Jane cooed happily. Her uncle had been Something in Submarines.

Then the termites arrived. Brought out by the rain, drawn to the lights of the cinema, they came flying from all directions, only a few at first, then dozens, then hundreds, thousands. They smacked into the screen; they whirled around the light from the projection-box. They whizzed into faces, eyes, mouths. Angela got one inside her low-cut dress and screamed.

The shower had been a challenge; the new torment was too much. There was a laughing stampede for the exit, and soon the cinema was deserted, except for the projectionist marooned in his box.

We 'borrowed' the duty land rover from the camp to take the girls home. Alec was Orderly Officer and came with us: 'a tour of duty', he called it. The air was alive with wings above the steaming roadway. It was only a short distance to the Cantonments, where Jane and Angela lived, two hundred yards apart.

"I'm going to have a bloody bath," Angela declared as she waved goodbye.

Then Alec drove Mike and me to our own quarters. Two weak electric bulbs shone on the veranda outside our block of *gidas*, and ants were dancing in the pale light, while the long cream wall wavered with dark blotches. I swished at the wall with my handkerchief, and the blotches dissolved and became more wings, whirling faster and faster.

"Hey!" Alec called, "Geoff's left his window open."

Sure enough, one room at the end of the block was illuminated and unshuttered. We peered in. There was a fine flurry of termites round the light, which Geoff must have left on by accident. Hundreds were crawling on his furniture and bed.

"If we turn off these veranda lights," said Mike, "they'll *all* go into his room…"

143

Most of the other subalterns had by now emerged from their shuttered *gidas* to see what was going on: school-kids coming to learn a secret.

"He's at the Ambassador Hotel," someone said. "He'll be back late."

Geoff arrived some time after midnight, surprisingly sober. We heard him whistle his way across the courtyard and wonder aloud why the veranda lights were not on. Then we heard him clattering and banging up the steps, bumping into the deck-chairs on the veranda. The uproar gave the rest of us an excuse to come out from our rooms, yawning exaggeratedly as if we had just been woken up.

Geoff was standing on the veranda, illuminated by his own bedroom window, searching through his pockets to find the key to his door.

"I've been daft," he said with gallant cheerfulness. "Left my damn light on, and look what's happened!"

We looked. Hardly any termites were fluttering in the room. The furniture was covered in wriggling bodies; the bed was black. He had forgotten to let down his mosquito-net, so the ants were all over his sheets. Dark streaks on the walls undulated unpleasantly.

He was practical, was Geoff. Having found his key, he switched on the veranda lights, rushed into his room and turned off his own illumination, then came out again to wait for the winged exodus.

"That'll get the sods out!" he said triumphantly.

The few flying termites in the room drifted out onto the veranda – perhaps a dozen. When Geoff opened his door again and we all looked more closely, we saw that the floor was covered by a thick layer of discarded, glassy wings, beneath which and in which an army of naked termites scuttled industriously. Geoff did not lose his composure. He called his batman from the staff quarters.

"Awuni, make you get brush one-time for sweep my *gida*."

"Yessah," replied the servant, smiling and unperturbed by the eccentricity of an officer who wished his house to be cleaned well after midnight. "I go bling um nownow."

Soon there was a big pile of wings and writhing bodies on the veranda in front of Geoff's door.

"You're not going to leave them there, are you?" said Geoff. "I don't want them crawling back."

"Wait small, sah," said the African.

From his own hut he brought a bucket and an enormous spoon. He ladled half the pile into the bucket, fetched a big cooking-basin and filled that, and finished by scooping the remnants into an empty baked-beans tin.

"Where you go put um?" someone asked, as Awuni balanced the bucket on his head, then picked up the basin in one hand and the jar and spoon in the other.

"I take um for chop, sah," he said with dignity. "I take um for my *gida*, den I go fly um."

Awuni and his breakfast disappeared into the night. We went back to bed.

A few days later the Battalion said farewell to Sir Charles Arden-Clarke at the Queen's Birthday Parade with a dance-of-the-rainbow in a perfect setting. The occasion was sentimental: so vivid as to be almost unreal.

The grass of the big Accra Stadium was green and lush from the recent rains; the stands shone white, and whiter still the Freedom Arch rose beyond the arena, gleaming and clear-cut against the dark blue sea and paler sky. Into the stadium in neat ruled lines the platoons marched, their zouave jackets red as fire. With them marched Charles the Ram proudly, quietly. Then in came the Regimental Band and the Corps of Drums, flavouring martial music with a jaunty Highlife gaiety. By the main stand the Ghana flag fluttered red-gold-green. The Battalion awaited His Excellency.

Then, from the seaward entrance towards the Freedom Arch, on gleaming chestnut horses the Escort Police trotted in, two by two across the grass, resplendent in crimson and black, with gold braiding and long white gloves, each man holding aloft a streaming red and white pennant. Finally the long, slow, black car crawled into the stadium. Out stepped the General, the Governor and their aides, in uniforms of purest white. While Sir Charles inspected the troops, the red-gold-green flag was lowered, and the deep blue Royal Standard rose instead.

Shortly afterwards the Governor left for England after eight significant years in West Africa. Shortly after his departure, Kwame Nkrumah took over Christiansborg Castle. Shortly after this, it was announced that the Earl of Listowel would be coming to Accra as the new Governor. As a Labour Peer, he would not need a Castle...

Chapter Five

THE PRIME MINISTER

"Whenever I get too confident," Alec declared, "one day as Orderly Officer sorts me out."

It was true for all of us: duty days provided a regular test, with occasions of fine comedy but always one or two unpleasant moments to survive. Alec had more than his share of these. One of the worst was when a soldier, just returned from Teshie Range, fired a sten-carbine bullet through another man's foot. It was a total accident, and the culprit was almost as terrified as his victim, since he believed the sten magazine to be empty, but the two soldiers belonged to tribes of lengthy and traditional enmity, and the bullet had made an unpleasant mess of the foot. It was difficult, therefore, for Alec to persuade the injured man's friends that the action had not been deliberate...

One day when it was my turn to be Orderly Officer, I drove to the barracks on my normal tour of duty, to be met by a crowd of soldiers shouting in a panic that a man, Yaw, was trying to kill himself.

He had jammed his head through the squatting-hole in the floor of one of the barrack latrines. It must have been an uncomfortable way to attempt suicide, by suffocation by noxious fumes, but apparently this Yaw was an unstable man who had already botched two suicide attempts. Now the large crowd had gathered to see if he would succeed this time.

The RSM and Sergeant-Major Binchity appeared, wearing their off-duty clothes. They chased away the onlookers. The RSM apologised for not being there earlier: he had just come from the town. What ought we to do, I asked, hack away at the concrete and try to make a bigger hole? He said some people had already attempted to pull the man's head out of the hole, but it was too firmly jammed, and the hole was too small. Binchity declared that if Yaw had got his head through, the hole must be wide enough to get him back...

The concrete floor was several inches thick, so it would take a long time to chip it away, and this might be dangerous. In any case, from the man's coughing it was apparent that the fumes were affecting him badly, so we had no time to lose. I told the RSM to get some soap. We lathered the soldier's head as best we could, reaching down into the filthy hole, and rubbing the concrete thickly with more soap. Then we tried again to manoeuvre him back into the fresh air. At the fourth or fifth attempt we succeeded.

A week later, Yaw tried again. This time the soldiers got him out unaided. Luckily, he was then given a discharge on medical grounds, before he succeeded in his suicide bid. It was rumoured in the barracks that he wanted so much to leave the Army that he had done everything as a trick to have himself discharged. Presumably he felt that the end justified the means.

Incidents like this were rare, but the duty officer often had more than his share of worries. He would be called out at the most awkward hours to settle disputes about property... to investigate a report that strangers had been seen in the darkness near Government House... to enquire into a food-shortage at the barracks... to hurry in the duty land rover to fetch a doctor or midwife – "I tink, sah, piccin he de come nownow." Alec even had to assist at a birth – nearly. "I didn't actually do much," he observed, white and shaken in his proud nonchalance, "I just stayed there and told them all not to panic, while the husband went with the driver to get this doctor-bloke. There were lots of people milling around. Said they were all part of the family. Pretty girl she was, too. I was glad when I heard the land rover coming back..."

One morning when I was Orderly Officer, the telephone rang in the duty office just before normal parade time.

"Is that the Orderly Officer?" came Major Ives's voice.

"Yes, sir."

"Well, I don't want *you*. I want you to fetch my Assistant Adjutant. Tell him to hurry up with his breakfast if he's still at it. It's important. Tell him he's to –"

"He's here, sir. I'm here, sir."

"You damn fool. Why didn't you say? You've got to go to Christiansborg Castle with a sten and some ammunition. The Brigadier's going too. I'll be at my office in twenty minutes. I'm 'phoning now, in case you'd planned to skate away to Aburi to catch butterflies…"

He rang off, leaving me to wonder what kind of insurrection the Brigadier was planning to lead. I collected from the armoury a Sten Machine Carbine '4', the most up-to-date model we had, and five magazines of ammunition, and arrived back at the office at the same time as Ives.

"Now, revelations," he said, flinging his slouch-hat across the room so that it hooked neatly onto a peg. "There's a job for you," he said, sitting down impassively, as if the hat-trick was nothing unusual.

"Nkrumah wants to see some automatic weapons in action," he declared, in his Adjutant's voice. "It's something to do with equipping the new Ghana Army. I'd have thought that was our job, but I suppose it's when we've all gone he's thinking about. His all-African Brigade."

"Why me?" I asked.

"It's intelligence work, isn't it? Well, actually," he admitted, "I was asked to go over myself… but the Brigadier's going to be there, and I don't get on all that well with him. Anyway, it's good training for you."

The Brigadier arrived just after me. He was carrying a Sten '5', a slightly more recent model than mine. We were shown into the Castle up a flight of stairs. Nkrumah met us outside a door with a 'DO NOT DISTURB' notice hung slantwise across it. He was wearing a smart dark suit, white shirt, sober tie, very European. Thick lips, receding hair, an attractive smile. Kwame Nkrumah, the Prime Minister. You are shaking hands with the Prime Minister. I wondered, is it 'Sir', or 'Prime Minister', or 'Your Excellency'? Behind him stood four or five other Africans, all in suits. If they were Ministers, none of them were the familiar faces of the Independence platform.

"Good of you to come," Nkrumah said. "I wanted to see some guns." A soft voice, slightly American: not a bit like the honeyed, seductive public voice.

"What about this?" he asked, handing the Brigadier a short, squat automatic. It looked very clumsy. The Brigadier passed it on to me: a stubby, ugly weapon. Some sort of adapted sten, perhaps?

"I'd hate to have to fire that, sir," I said brashly. Then I noticed an inscription which said that the gun was a present to the Right Honourable Kwame Nkrumah from the Israeli Government.

"We know what he thinks, anyway!" said Nkrumah. The satellite ministers laughed dutifully.

We went through the NOT-TO-BE-DISTURBED Cabinet Room. It had an enormous table littered with 'confidential' papers. We were joined by several of the Cabinet: Casely Hayford I recognised, Gbedemah, Krobo Edusei… We went onto a big white balcony overlooking the Atlantic.

"Where the slaves were lowered from," said Nkrumah, dead-pan. "All right, let's try the guns."

The Brigadier must have known exactly what we were supposed to be doing, and why. He looked quite composed. He fired a few single shots efficiently into the sea.

"These are live," he said. "We have no blanks."

I had live rounds as well. I fired my sten. There were no fishing boats in sight, and the few people on the beach far to our left did not seem even to notice. Then the Brigadier's gun jammed and refused to fire any more. We tried the correct remedies. The Brigadier shook it, banged it, kicked it, to no avail.

Several Cabinet Ministers took over my sten, each in turn blissfully squeezing the trigger a few times.

Then Krobo Edusei explained how on the films he had seen guns like this which fired not "DAH – DAH – DAH – DAH" slowly, like ours, but "DADADADADA!"

Why did not ours do the same?

I set the weapon on 'automatic' and fired a short burst into the ocean. Huge grins from everyone: this was the real thing.

Krobo Edusei was allowed to try it for himself. He squeezed the trigger, and five or six shots rattled out into the Atlantic. He squeezed again, and turned delightedly to show the Prime Minister and his colleagues how proficient he was... The Brigadier and I leapt forward and between us managed to wrench the sten round, just in time, so that the bullets hurtled harmlessly out to sea...

Nkrumah was very calm: "I guess you saved a big headline!" he said.

"Well," said Major Ives when I returned, "shot him successfully, did you?"

My driver, Amadu Fulani

Boti Falls

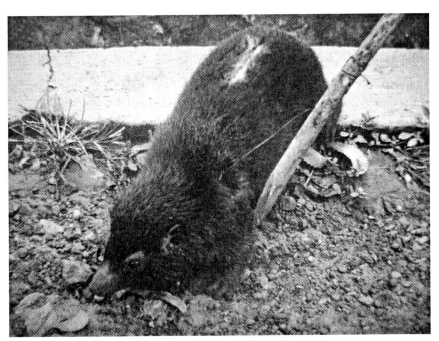

The hyrax we rescued at Aburi

River crossing near Adenkrebi

Douglas Ives, checking markers for the South Ghana Rally

Practising for the Queen's Birthday Parade

The Mallam, 'Charles',
Seidu, RSM Kramo

Christiansborg Castle,
'Where they lowered the
slaves...'

Chapter Six

ADENKREBI

Perhaps when you meet the witch-doctor off-duty he will be a wizened, fragile old man with a squint and a lame leg, and maybe you will laugh and think him barbarous when he professes to heal wounds by covering them with poultices of dung. And perhaps you will mock the incantations, and take aspirin for your headache and put elastoplast over your cuts, and spray your walls and floor with disinfectant. But you will be foolish to dismiss the *juju* man as a fraud, for he has real powers: and the psychologists who talk of 'induced auto-suggestion' realise that they have merely reached a starting-point.

I knew an English doctor who could charm away warts by speaking on the telephone to patients he had never seen. In the world of *juju*, where fact and inference and legend so often whirl together and become one, it is unwise to commit yourself too rashly with regard to what you believe and what you do not.

I learnt much about the subject from Joseph Halm, who was a naturally funny man, but also well-read and a deep thinker. When in a group with his friends his wit was light-hearted, even frivolous, but when on his own he told me things that I found surprising. I several times discussed religion with him. Like most of the Drummers he was a Roman Catholic, but he was very interested in comparative religion and, as he said several times, "There is no better place to study beliefs than Arakan Barracks. We have every religion there!" Joseph was full of admiration for the Muslim soldiers, for their strict adherence to their

156

creed and their absolute trustworthiness. "They never lie, and they always keep their promises," he said. "Christians are not so honest!" He was also intrigued by what he called 'Pagan people' and their beliefs. "Whatever you and I think, they work," he declared, "and anyway, you white people have plenty of *juju* of your own!"

To show what he meant, he jotted down for me some ideas on what he called '*juju* philosophy'. Jeremy and I later wrote these out more carefully, and added a few of our own:

When Nkrumah was imprisoned by the British, every night he became a white bird and flew out through the bars of the gaol to visit people loyal to him. Others say that he was not a white bird but a white horse...

In the back window of his car, Major Stevens has what looks like a smallsmall lion. It is made of wool, and he calls it 'Leo' which is a powerful juju *name, for lions are strong magic. It will guard his car on the roadway...*

Nkrumah is a Christian, but before he flies in an aeroplane a libation of gin is always poured on the airport runway to give him a safe journey...

Before Captain Charles flew home to UK a moon ago he dashed plenty money to a man called Insurance, who made a medicine to keep him safe...

Under his bush-shirt Lieutenant Mike wears about his neck a coin which has on it a picture of a god called Christopher, who is very strong but more strong on his left side, which is why Lieutenant Mike writes always with his left hand, and puts on always his left boot before his right, and when he plays football at the Stadium he kicks goals always with his left foot...

The lost child from Teshie who was found floating in the lagoon was reported drowned. But the body was not a whole body: parts were missing that no fish had stolen...

When Seidu refused to box against the First Battalion, it was because

157

his opponent had put a curse on him, that if he were to enter the ring his arm would break. Seidu's arm went numb: you could feel it like wood, hard, not bending, and he was the colour of dead ashes. So Edmund fought instead, and won by a knockout: the juju *was not for him. Then Seidu was well again…*

In his gida *Lieutenant Dave keeps in cages those bush animals he calls 'caterpillars', and gives them leaves to chop, and when he has had them a small time, for some reason known only to himself he turns them into small sticks or lumps of earth, and a little later he does a better magic and turns them into butterflies…*

If Amadu puts his hand on a scorpion it will sting him but he will not lift his hand…

When Captain Smith found a scorpion behind the pamphlets on his mantelshelf, he ran out of the office…

When the Europeans in Accra put up fine shining lights of red-gold-green like the new flag, they said it would stop accidents, so all the people with cars drove to see this magic, and the cars went "PHOOUM!" together at the crossroads right near the lights, and there were more accidents than ever…

Usually there were easy answers. Most things that were deemed 'magic' had perfectly rational, often amusing explanations, and even the less obvious cases could be explained without excessive mental gymnastics. Even after talking with Joseph I was sceptical about *juju* and its properties, although never to the extent of Geoff's vehement: "The whole thing's bloody rubbish."
And then Tim and I went to Adenkrebi…

❖ ❖ ❖

It began with Ambush Drill.
An exercise was to take place high on the Aburi Escarpment, in the dense forest. The plan was for an 'enemy' party of two officers and eight men to go out a day in advance and settle somewhere in the jungle

– only they would know exactly where. Then two Companies would be sent out to locate them, their aim being to ambush and destroy the 'bandits' as they moved into a village to get food. I was to be in charge of the 'enemy'.

"It'll be a test of your I.O. skills," Colonel Harding said. "You can choose your officer, but Major Ives is going to pick the soldiers. If you take your usual bright guys they'll probably never find you!"

Normally I would have chosen Jeremy – but he had recently been moved to Brigade Headquarters, to assist the Brigadier. So I asked Tim if he would like to come.

"Bloody fantastic!" he said, which was a good start.

Ives picked the eight men from different parts of the Battalion: he told us later that he did it with a pin. Whatever his method, he produced for us a team of formidable variety. There was a sergeant, skinny, bespectacled and earnest, and in total contrast a fat little corporal from the Upper Volta, who boasted that he had two wives and eleven piccins, and grinned eternally to show how much he enjoyed being the father of a big family. Then there were John and Kwabena, two slow, polite ex-fishermen; Kodjo, a clever, talkative youth who, like the sergeant could speak a version of the local dialect; a Northern Nigerian, inevitably called Amadu; Stephen, a rather pale man of mixed blood; and finally a quiet, nervous individual who knew virtually no English and looked like a dark version of President Eisenhower – so we called him 'Ike'.

We wore bright blue denims and forage-caps, to make us conspicuous. Tim and I carried stens, and the eight Africans had rifles, with a limited supply of blank ammunition. We would be sleeping rough, so took with us in our packs just the few essentials we always carried on my Intelligence 'recce' trips. I also took a compass.

"Is that all!" Tim exclaimed.

"You'll be able to get food in the villages?" Ives asked.

I told him I was sure of that. I had been to the Aburi area several times, and every village had been helpful and friendly.

We went by truck to the top of the escarpment. The driver left us at the road-fork south of Aburi, and we asked him to go home and report to Major Ives, but to be 'here for dis place' when the exercise was over. We followed a narrow pathway into the forest, with John and Kwabena carrying between them the usual crate containing bottles of beer and cocacola.

It was still early morning, and cool under the trees. Before long we came to a village of just five huts, and the inhabitants told us that it was named, as I recall it, Akwapon. There was no village marked there on the map: but then there was no track marked, either, in this particular area – just an expanse of virgin jungle. We presented the village headman with a bottle of beer, and he promised that if soldiers were to come that way, he and his people would know nothing of our whereabouts. Then we continued our route, with the excited trepidation of explorers in an uncharted sea. It was impossible to judge accurately, but we reckoned we must be moving parallel to the Aburi-Achimota road, perhaps not more than a mile and a half from it.

Our pathway grew rougher and less defined, and we reached another village overarched by orange trees and palm fronds. The Sergeant acted as our 'speechmaker', and in his own version of the local dialect asked where we were.

"Akwapon," said the inhabitants, saucer-eyed.

"Dis dam' people!" the Sergeant exploded. "Dey tink I be fool-man!"

Kodjo also tried, and received the same answer, which soothed the Sergeant a little. We went on again, leaving behind us another bottle of beer, although the Sergeant and Kodjo both declared it a waste, and undeserved. The roadway petered out, but the space between the trees remained clear, and before long we reached a third village. This, too, was apparently called Akwapon.

The Sergeant gesticulated helplessly, and mopped his misted glasses. Kodjo laughed. But the villagers were adamant that the place was Akwapon – and although they had heard that part of their 'town' lay back the way we had come, none of them had ever been there. In the opposite direction was Adjimenti, but that was far.

For the rest of the morning and much of the afternoon we followed our faint trail through the forest, along the ridge. We came to several more villages, each set in a haze of orange-trees, each containing five or six huts, and each thronged with goats and chickens. Always the people professed ignorance of more than two or three other villages. Every time we left our bottle of beer; and always we took careful note of our route, so as to be sure, eventually, of our way back.

Then the pathway improved again, and we reached Adenkrebi. This was a bigger place altogether, with more than a dozen huts, and was actually marked on the map. Here at last we were able to piece together some new coherent details, in addition to confirming some of which we were already aware. The rough track we were on led eventually to a bigger road on a mountain where trucks went *boooum* (back to the Aburi highway, presumably?) and not far ahead ahead was Ajimenti. Akwapon, said the headman, lay back the way we had come, but no one went there, because it was far, and the road was bad. Aburi was far, far back past Akwapon. He had been there himself, several times. It was a big town pass-all on the big road over the hills. In Aburi, he said, he had seen white men like Tim and me. We gave him his beer, after which he became all smiles and even consented to show us the illicit stills where the villagers made their *akpeteshie...*

By now it was late afternoon. We decided to camp for the night in this same area, and chose a site half a mile along the untried road, where the forest trees thinned into an attractive, flowered glade crossed by two streams. The inhabitants of Adenkrebi came out to our camp in the dusk with calabashes of goats' meat and maize, and wooden containers of palm wine. As I had foreseen, they would accept no money, but were delighted with our presents of cocacola. Kodjo was enjoying his job as interpreter. "They happy we here," he said. The ground under the trees was clear, so we put out our groundsheets and then lit a fire in haste, for there were mosquitoes about and the smoke would help to keep them away.

After a huge meal, we sat round the fire talking quietly and listening to the forest sounds, which seemed magnified by our hilltop position. Crickets and cicadas shrilled from the bushes and grass-tufts, and frogs belched and gurgled from the twin streams. At the edge of the clearing a crowd of big fruit-bats bickered in the tree-tops, before clattering off to search for food. Tim was ecstatic: "Bloody marvellous!" he kept whispering. The jungle hubbub unnerved the plump, normally cheerful Corporal Musa, however, who had apparently heard nothing to resemble it in the Northern grasslands.

"Dis place get palaver too much," he complained. As if to emphasise his words, a hyrax began its wailing in the forest towards Adenkrebi, faint at first, then growing loud and rising with a strange ventriloquial effect, as if the sound were right beside and all around us in the trees of the glade.

"What ting dis?" cried the Corporal. The others enjoyed his discomfort.

"*Owea*," said Kodjo, using the Ashanti name.

"Hyrax…?" Tim ventured.

"Be so, hy – rax…" Kodjo savoured the word approvingly.

"What ting dis hy – rax?" asked the Corporal belligerently, and with more confidence, since the weird howling had ceased for the moment. Answers came in a flurry.

"Be hanimal, Corp'l."

"Be small one, like dis" – hands held a foot apart.

"Igo for hup de tree" – pointing – " an igo Weaaaah… weaaaagh… weaaaagh…!" The imitation was uncanny, and the Corporal wilted.

"I tink, Corp'l Musa, you de fear dis smallsmall hanimal," said Kodjo with mock scorn.

"I no de fear!" Musa was furious. "I no de fear dis ting attall! Not line, not lept, not clocdile, not sanake. Notting! I no de fear notting!"

I had been asked to keep a journal-of-the-the-exercise, so improvised a table out of the beer-crate, with a sloping tree-trunk for a seat, and hung a torch from an aptly-placed branch. Then, rather complacently, I began to write, while the soldiers at first watched curiously. Sanders of the River again, filling in his log… Tim and Kodjo went down to the nearby stream, to see if they could see the frogs.

We appeared to have done well. We had made our way through hostile jungle with no real hitches. In retrospect, the well-tried beer gimmick seemed particularly successful and showed true initiative. My choice of Tim had been a good one. I was full of self-congratulation. Eight men under my command, independent in the middle of vast, unexplored realms of forest, looking to me for survival. As I wrote my account, with a smug feeling that I might be recording history, big furry moths blundered around the torch-bulb, and an enormous stick insect crashed onto the beer-crate, where it sat erect and goggle-eyed. It occurred to me that the insect bore a striking resemblance to Ike…

I filled several pages quite quickly.

Then I heard Tim returning, singing his own version of the current hit-tune that the Army had made its own:

"... If you mammy tell you come, Nebbah nebbah run away!" he warbled.

"For why - ? Because...   Fine-fine money no Fine-fine money no DEY!"

"My torch no good," declared Kodjo. "Battery die."

"We saw dozens of frogs, though," said Tim.

I switched my own torch off, and put away my log-book. Tim distributed bottles of cocacola to the men. It was beginning to grow chilly, and we sat close to the fire, but soon one by one the soldiers moved away, wrapped themselves in their groundsheets and settled down to sleep. Tim and I and the garrulous Kodjo stayed by the fire. In very fluent pidgin-English Kodjo told us stories about Kwaku Ananse, the Ashanti spider-man who is glutton, thief and general scoundrel. In the firelight glow the saga of the strange folk-hero took on a creepy, evil suggestiveness...

Suddenly the Sergeant appeared, wrapped in his groundsheet.

"One man sick, sah. Be Private Kwabena, sah."

"OK," Tim said, depositing his half-full cocacola bottle beside the fire. "I've got the medicine box."

Kodjo was fooling about with a giant millipede which had just crawled out of the log on which he was sitting. He jammed the creature into his own empty bottle, tail first. It filled the whole length, with an inch of waving legs sticking out through the top. Kodjo swapped the bottles round.

"When dis officer come back," he said, "I tell him be dis hanimal drink his cocacola..."

"You'd better come," Tim called.

"I tink you come, sah," echoed the Sergeant. "Dis man proper sick."

Kwabena lay on his back, motionless, his face grey and showing only the whites of his eyes.

"How long he like dis?" I asked. "Why you no tell us?"

"Be jus' now," said the Sergeant. "John say be sanake, sah."

John held his friend's limp arm and showed the tiny puncture-marks near the wrist. "Be sanake, sah," he said. "He done cut um." But no one had seen the snake.

It took only a few seconds for the competent young colonial officers to evaporate away, leaving two scared, ignorant subalterns. Tim looked calm, and later he said I appeared the same – but we both agreed that the reality was very different. There had been that lecture and various pamphlets about snakebite serum and tourniquets and gashing the wound with a razor-blade and sucking out the poison. But serum was laughable now, some joke! and the tourniquet, wasn't that out of date anyway? – and I for one had always known I would never be able to use the razor-blade on myself or anyone else and in any case it was too late for that. Thank God there were two of us, anyway.

The first-aid kit contained aspirin, our paludrine tablets, and ointment for treating burns. And a tin of elastoplast. And a small pair of scissors. And some insect repellent…

The African faces looked blank. No salvation there. The Sergeant spoke quietly.

"I tink dis man go die."

We stopped dithering. Quickly we decided that Tim and the Sergeant would go back into Adenkrebi to see if there was some form of transport there in which to get the sick man to hospital. Failing that, a message must be taken to Aburi. Kodjo and I would try the other track, to see whether it led to the main Accra-Aburi road. If it did, we might arrange for a truck to meet us at the junction. We told the Corporal to stay in the camp with the rest of the soldiers and to keep the fire burning, but under no circumstances to move the sick man.

"Yessah," said Corporal Musa, huddling into his groundsheet in grey funk.

It was a nightmare walk…

The winding track was treacherous with loose stones and sudden drops, of which the swinging torch-beam gave no warning. Shadowy figures seemed to sway in the darkness ahead, where fireflies beneath the trees flashed staccato green signals. The sounds of the forest built up

164

and drew near, and from above the hyrax laughed insanely, closer and closer it seemed, so that the whole forest grew tense, oppressive, claustro-phobic, and the light swung and the shadows danced and the thoughts whirled… Dis man go die. He will die, and you are responsible. An officer, and responsible. No proper precautions. He go die. You have ignored the pamphlets and the tourniquets and the razor-blades and the Court Martial will find you to blame. No precautions…

But then unbelievably we had reached a village of square red-clay huts, and Kodjo was fiercely abusing the one gaping drunkard still awake, and then by his vague guidance we had found the hut of the headman and were thundering on the door.

"Open the door, you stupid man!" I heard myself shout. "Open the door!" – but no answer came and we hammered again. And at last the door did open and the old headman appeared, clad only in a towel. In an anticlimax of stillness Kodjo asked about a truck. The chief nodded, then shook his head, and O God, I thought, what happens now? But there was a truck, further down on the main road: it was only that it was impossible to take it any nearer to the camp along the rough track.

The old man was still speaking, and Kodjo explained:

"He say mebbe dis soldier-man no fit go for dis place nownow. He say make he send doctor for Kwabena, den he fit go? Make I say be OK?"

Soon a strange party set off towards the camp. First went the old chief, barefoot, and behind him the medicine-man, carrying, incongru-ously, a BOAC bag. Kodjo and I brought up the rear – with the torches. This time the journey seemed much quicker.

Tim and the Sergeant met us, to say that they had arranged for a truck. A messenger had been sent to Aburi (at a cost of ten shillings) to tell a driver to meet us at a village 'smallsmall down'. It must be the place we had just visited.

The soldiers had kept the fire burning, and were huddled near it. The Corporal was very relieved to see us. The sick man had not moved.

The witch-doctor said something almost in a whisper, and produced from his bag what looked like several shiny stones and a ball of sticky clay. He placed the stones in a row beside the fire, and rubbed the clay over Kwabena's face and chest, muttering quietly all the while. Then he began to move in a slow, loping stride, circling the fire and the sick man. Nothing seemed to be very private. His simplicity was powerful – no weird garments or magic signs: just a tall, bony man in a loincloth, slowly loping. His voice rose slightly, and the watching soldiers murmured for a moment, then listened again.

"What is he saying?" I whispered to Kodjo.

"He say dis man no go die."

In the firelight shadows I could not follow closely what went on, but after perhaps five minutes I saw Kwabena stir and turn his head. Before long he was able to swallow something that the *juju* man gave him, and immediately vomited. This appeared to have the desired effect, for he seemed much better and could move his arms and legs a little. The witch-doctor loped round and round again, still chanting.

Next, to a gasp from the soldiers, the sick man rose to his feet and staggered a few steps. No one went to his aid, and the incantation did not cease. He sank to the ground again, but clearly the worst was over.

We carried him down the track without much difficulty. The truck was waiting. The driver demanded four pounds for his service, and between us Tim and I had four pounds ten shillings. We gave him three pounds, and he said that would do. The headman and the witch-doctor shared a pound between them, and we felt they had more than earned it. That left us with just ten shillings in case of further emergency.

Tim, John and the Sergeant went with the truck. They reached the Military Hospital at three a.m. Meanwhile Kodjo and I covered the distance between the village and our camp-site for the fourth time, and the path seemed quick and easy. It cannot have been as much as a mile.

Tim and John came out by land rover in mid-morning, having had several hours' sleep in Accra. They took the short-cut from the main road, and arrived in time for pepper-soup lunch-chop. Tim had brought more money and some torch batteries. The Sergeant had stayed behind: he had caught a chill, and was apparently also suffering from shock…

The men of Akwapon twice put 'A' Company right off our trail, but we were finally located by a soldier whose friends in Aburi sent drum-messages through the forest… and after two days the Exercise ended in a friendly charade as the 'enemy' were ambushed and annihilated on the roadway quite near their camp.

Then we all returned to Accra.

Tim and I asked Major Ives if we could have our money refunded.

"Call it 'First Aid and Ambulance'," he said, "and you'll get it back."

Then mischievously the Adjutant asked Tim: "I don't suppose you'll want to do that kind of jaunt again, will you?"

"Easily the best few days I've had in the Army!" replied Tim, to my delight.

As we were going out, Ives said: "It's all in the mind, you know. I don't suppose your witch-doctor friend could have cured *you?* Or me?"

We did not reply.

Private Kwabena left hospital three days later. A few weeks later, Private Kodjo became Lance-Corporal.

Chapter Seven

LOOK PEOPLE

The Adenkrebi experience might well have damaged our confidence, but in fact it boosted mine, and Tim's even more. I have no idea what version of the story travelled around the platoons, but the gist of it was that we had saved the life of a soldier. I am afraid that, although we never said anything to suggest it was true, we did nothing to deny it, either. As the Adjutant had picked our 'enemy troop' from all the companies, for a few days Tim and I found that soldiers we had never encountered before told us we had 'done a good thing'. At first we considered this embarrassing. We told our friends, both black and white, precisely what had happened, and Joseph Halm, as usual, made a wise comment:

"There will be plenty of times," he said, "when people think you have done worse than you really have, so let them enjoy thinking you are magic men!" So we did.

I soon found myself working with Tim on a more regular basis. Jeremy was now at Brigade HQ, shortly to be posted to Kumasi, so Tim moved from an infantry company to Headquarters, where he helped me in the Intelligence section, and took on the Education Centre himself. Indirectly, this meant that he came to know the Corps of Drums, and Joseph, James, BB, William and the rest quickly recognised in Tim someone who shared their views and enjoyed their company. Tim, in turn, realised that as the Corps of Drums was a separate unit, and only

168

indirectly part of the Battalion, he could say what he liked in return. "I see now where you get your 'inside information' from!" he said to me.

❖ ❖ ❖

There is no doubt that in the 1950s the young English officers in the Second Battalion were both clean-living and naïve. A decade later it might have been a different story, but as it was, we had comparatively few vices – and did not miss them. Almost none of us smoked. We did not take drugs (nor, for the most part, did we even know about them.) Although we drank, it was in moderation and socially, and our experiments with *akpeteshie* tended to consist not of imbibing the fire-water, but to see whether it would make holes in chairs and tables! We had girl-friends, but seldom for long at a time and seldom seriously, because often they were the daughters of senior officers at Brigade, and we sometimes felt that the girls had been foisted on us... Several novels that have attempted to depict West African life at this time and earlier give the impression that most young white men in colonial service lived in sexual abandon – I can only say that our group seemed to be remarkably chaste, and perhaps boring. Only Dai had had frequent liaisons with girls black, brown and white, and sometimes smuggled them home with him, but they had always vanished before dawn, and his batman could keep a secret. Others had long-term alliances with the daughters of senior officers but, Dai apart, none of us thought of making advances to African girls, however beautiful. We did not even know that Jock was already married, until his delightful Scottish wife flew out to join him, and he moved into married quarters!

Not only were we naïve, but with regard to morality we questioned little. Our senior officers were all married, happily we presumed. A few of them did drink too much, in the Mess and probably at home, but if they were living sinful lives in secret we did not know, nor did we worry about it.

It was Joseph Halm, once again, who told Tim that he was 'becoming an African' – like Jeremy and me! It was said (and taken) as a compliment, but it made us think. We knew we shared an enjoyment of African culture: we took pleasure in tribal art, and independently had begun collecting local paintings, carvings and wall-masks. We liked African food, and preferred eating at chop-bars rather than so-phisticated restaurants. We drank sparingly, but relished African beer and even palm wine, and we enjoyed our occasional visits to African night-clubs, where we found *highlife* music captivating, but never be-haved extravagantly. The other English subalterns liked these things as rare breaks from European company, whereas we found them our preferred way of life. Had we been by ourselves, we might have been treated patronisingly, but as we were always with African friends, this did not happen.

The main benefit for Tim and me of the episode at Adenkrebi lay in how it clarified our beliefs. I knew I loved Ghana, and that I had never felt happier anywhere, but until the affair of the witch-doctor in the forest, I had been confused in my mind about what I believed in, and what, as a colonial Englishman, I *ought* to believe, and by what standards I should order my life. I think Tim's confusion was less, al-though he shared some of my doubts. He once started to say "Suppose that soldier had died..." and tailed off. But he several times referred to Adenkrebi as his 'African baptism.'

In my own case I had been brought up as a Church of England Christian, by parents who worshipped regularly and with sincerity, but my boarding-school time, when I had had to attend services at least once a day with bored acceptance, made me distrust my religion. I think I wanted to 'believe', but then the British army, with its numer-ous church parades, perfunctory in length and substance, made my distrust stronger.

Now, in West Africa, we had few compulsory services, and those were for ceremonial occasions. Most of my English colleagues in Ghana were quietly agnostic. I had at first tried to be supportive of some African friends who were Christians, by occasionally attending their services, sometimes as the only white person present, but it was without conviction, although I much admired the intensity and involvement of the congregation. After Adenkrebi, however, I realised much more clearly where I stood. It was not that I believed in nothing – rather, that I was prepared to accept everything (albeit with reservations!) feeling that I could take or discard what suited me, without any sense of guilt, or even of involvement. Tim said he felt the same, and to my surprise,

Mike and Alec agreed, 'even without having met your *juju* man'.

So it was that we enjoyed talking about Islam with Muslims, whose enthusiasm was infectious and sincerity manifest, although we did feel sometimes that their views were dogmatic, or even simplistic – "But you can see why they make such bloody good soldiers," Mike said. "In my Company the Muslims are usually the best."

The fall-out from Adenkrebi helped us also to talk to 'those pagan people', as Joseph Halm called them, who, like my batman Abongo, believed in a host of spirits, and *juju* and fetishes – yet in many cases found the army an even bigger 'magic' – and, like the Muslims, were superb soldiers.

About this time two civilian acquaintances from Accra unveiled the start of a delightful pidgin-English version of the Old Testament. They had only managed to complete *Genesis*, and a few other picturesque stories, but their work showed such imagination and wit that we hoped they would do more. I have since come across several other dialect versions, but none as enjoyable or funny – and the fact that the authors of this one were non-Europeans made it all the more interesting. Later, in my teaching career, I sometimes read episodes of *De Book for Genesis,* to brighten school assembles. The picturesque start gripped immediately: *For de first time, nothing been be, only de Lawd He be, and He go work hard for make dis ting dey callum Earth...*

Many times I heard mature English sixth formers laugh out loud at the directness and political incorrectness of the argument between 'Hadam' and 'Heva': *Dat tree be white-man chop, he no be black-man chop. Why you go chop um?* – until they learnt that it was the work of a Lebanese (Joyce) and a black Ghanaian (Steve), whereupon laughter turned to awe. Many teachers asked me for a copy. In 1957, however, it was less the clever religious content that excited our admiration and amusement, than the topical references: for example Noah starting the Elder Dempster shipping line and ferrying his animals on board using surf-boats... To the best of my knowledge none of the devout Christians had anything but praise for *De Book for Genesis.*

It was soon after the pidgin-English bible stories appeared that Tim and I started to collect *tro-tro* slogans. It was his idea first, and unsurprisingly he got Joseph and some of the Drummers to help him, and then most of the other junior officers joined in. The slogans were everywhere in Accra, on shop-fronts, on white walls, on bus-shelters, but especially on *tro-tro* wagons.

There were hundreds of them, in many categories. There were enigmatic slogans: *Whatever You Do, Don't Forget Your Six Feet; Why Them?; It's a Lesson;* proverbial ones: *Poor No Friend; Waste No Time; Time is Money; The Wages of Sin is Death* (very common); and brash ones: *Black Boy; Sugar Boy; Big Boy* (many.) Then there were innumerable religious slogans, some very brief: *Noble; Glory; Blessing; Welcome; Harmony;* and others that were satisfyingly ambiguous: *Oh My Silent Saviour; Grace in Heaven; Abide With Me; All is God; God and Sin No Agree; Oh God!; Immortal Invincible* (sic). There was one truck that we always looked out for, which declared *Look People Like These They Talk What They Don't Know.* In another version this slogan was abbreviated to *Look People,* which we enjoyed even more, because we knew the missing words.

Written in huge letters, in brilliant colours and often decorated with vivid cartoon illustrations, these slogans brighten many West African cities, but Accra dazzled with them, and still does. After Independence they multiplied, often in the national colours of red-gold-green. *Show Boy,* Nkrumah's nickname, suddenly appeared, as did *Happy Day Come.*

"Only slightly-mad people would collect *tro-tro* slogans!" Joseph Halm declared to Tim and me, whereupon we told him that everyone at the Junior Officers' Lines was helping. "You see what I mean," he said.

[While I was writing these pages (May 2006) I looked up the subject on the internet and found that there is actually a competition running in Accra at present to find the best slogan and enter it on the web – with typical Ghanaian humour, the first prize offered is a ride in a *tro-tro* ! There are some brilliant new ones, but some have remained the same since 1957-8. I sent in a few slogans that seemed to have been lost – but clearly the spirit of *tro-tro* decoration is still healthy and well in Accra!]

Chapter Eight

VOYAGE TO TIMBUKTU

I was due a fortnight's leave in January 1958, and was anxious not to waste it. Most of my friends at Junior Officers' Lines who had had their leave already had headed west, to the beaches of Winneba, or to Cape Coast and beyond. Mike had gone east to Lome, which he had enjoyed: "The place doesn't seem to know whether it is Togo-African, French or German," he said, "but it's an exciting town." Emmanuel Kotoka agreed with him, but as he was from the Ewe tribe, and born nearby, he admitted he was biased.

I decided that I ought to go to the North.

In recent months I had explored many places within a 60-mile radius of Accra, and in addition I had spent a lot of time further east, in the mountainous rain-forest of Togoland. My visits to the Western Region had been more perfunctory, although I had played rugby at Takoradi, and had also been there with the boxing team. In addition I had joined Major Ives on an extraordinary motor-rally (as his navigator!) which had taken us, in his Riley Pathfinder, along the coast through Winneba, Elmina and Axim and right on, almost to the Cote d'Ivoire border. So I had 'seen the country' to the west, however fleetingly. In the Central Region I had several times visited Kumasi, always briefly, and usually in a sporting context. The exception was a week-end trip I had made with Mike and Alec, soon after Independence, to Lake Bosumtwi, a mysterious circular mere surrounded by thickly-forested mountains, some twenty miles south of the town.

My experience of the Eastern and Central Regions was therefore limited, but as I had as yet seen nothing at all of the Northern Territories, I was keen to visit those parts before I left Ghana. Of my young European friends, apart from those stationed at Tamale, only Simon had travelled north, into Upper Volta territory, and he had now returned to England at the end of his service. As usual, Emmanuel offered wise advice: "You have many African friends," he said. "If you are going north, travel with one of them. I think you will find it much easier that way."

There were plenty of suggestions as to where I should go. For over a year my batman, Abongo Frafra, had been telling me that I really ought to visit his home town, Bolgatanga, in the Northern Territories, while Oscar Songatua, one of the most erudite and articulate members of the Education staff, had said that I certainly *must* see Navrongo, his own home, which was even nearer to Ghana's northern border. I mentioned my proposed trip to my friends in the Corps of Drums.

"My leave is in January, too," said James Ankumah straight away. "I should like to come with you."

We had nearly a month to plan our journey. At first the idea was simply to travel north to Navrongo and perhaps cross the border into French Territory; then we obtained a map that included Haute Volta and the Soudan Francais (now Burkina Faso and Mali) – and decided to try to reach Timbuktu.

Until I had arrived in West Africa this had been for me an almost mythical place. When I was small I remember my father had avoided expletives by saying "Oh, go to Timbuktu!" The map showed the town definitely existed, but it was not somewhere people had actually *been* to – except Major Ives, of course! He had passed through, briefly, in a 'reconnaissance trip' after his service in Sierra Leone, before coming to the Gold Coast. When I was navigating for him on the Rally, he had told me about it, and the Niger towns became a reality

Our plans took shape. The first part of the journey was straightforward, for Joseph Halm had a friend who drove the *Daily Graphic* truck overnight to deliver newspapers in Kumasi, and if he could take James and me with him that would save a day. The First Battalion at Tamale could accommodate us on our outward or return journey, or both. From there we would head north through Bolgatanga and Navrongo, stopping overnight in one or the other, and then aim for Ouagadougou in Haute Volta. After that, everything was guesswork.

Major Ives and Colonel Harding were very supportive.

"They'll be pushed to get there and back in a fortnight," said Ives, "but if they're a few days late, we could call it 'Intelligence work'..."

"I don't think I heard that," replied the Colonel. "But – yes!"

Remembering George Levack's advice, about easing our way with 'presents', we asked the Quartermaster if he had anything in his stores that we could use – items that were both easy to carry and pleasing to look at, and also 'Regimental'. Stan Goodman's solution was brilliantly simple – "What about some buttons and cap-badges?" So we took a supply of these cheap but attractive items, each adorned with the Frontier Force palm tree. "Give them one of these and you'll feel like Doctor Livingstone," Stan said.

We obtained the requisite visas from the French Embassy. They were authorised quickly, stamped into our passports carefully, and the details overwritten in beautiful script in red and blue ink. Those visas were works of art, and I have kept that passport with pride, ever since.

On the evening of Friday 3rd January James and I left Accra, squashed into the back of the *Daily Graphic* truck. We piled up the bundles of newspapers to form a windbreak, for the vehicle was open at the sides and travelling fast. Soon the lights of the Capital lay far behind, and we were hurrying along the northbound road. Every few miles the truck shuddered to a halt at some wayside village, where we would crawl out to stretch our legs, while the driver hurled a bundle of *Graphics* into the porch of the local store. When we were not moving, it was pleasantly warm on the road, but as soon as we set off again an icy draught swirled around us and we cowered once more into the diminishing protection of the newspapers.

The vehicle swayed disconcertingly so that James and I were continually being thrown sideways onto each other. One especially violent

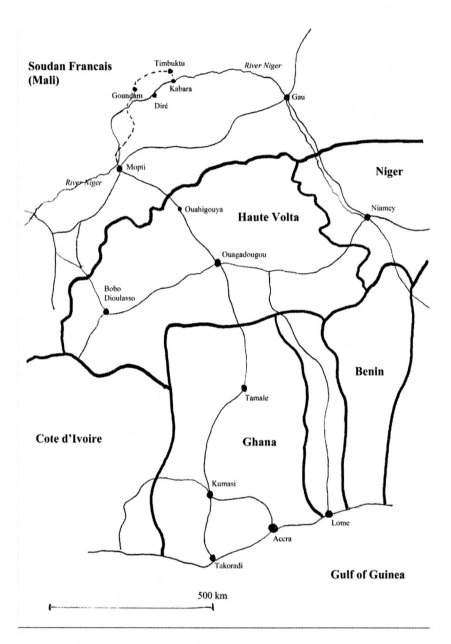

Map 2, from the Coast to the Niger, January 1958

jerk was followed by a rattling halt. The driver had stopped at the scene of an accident, where a *tro-tro* had missed the road and smashed into a tree. All the passengers had long since been helped from the wreckage and apparently there were no serious casualties, but the lorry was a total ruin, with debris scattered over a wide area. The front boarding had come to rest at the edge of the road, and on it in clear white letters was inscribed the slogan: THE LORD IS WITH ME. Quite a large crowd had gathered from nearby villages to examine with torches the remains of the mammy-truck.

Our driver pointed at the slogan. "Be lucky peoples," he said. "Be God be dem brother."

Shortly after two o'clock we reached Kumasi. The streets seemed deserted but when we stopped, three young men carrying empty beer bottles rushed up to greet the morrow's *Graphic* edition, crying "Welcome, welcome!" I received a specially honoured reception from the leader of the trio, who pumped my hand vigorously and observed with a bow that he wished to present me with some beer, but they had drunk it all. The truck-driver now had to set off on his delivery-round to various agents in the town, and the three youths insisted that they were good at delivering papers. They climbed into the back of the *Graphic* vehicle, where they began to sing loudly, and proved so difficult to dislodge that eventually the driver gave up the struggle and took them with him.

James and I walked to the transport yard, where several buses and trucks were parked. There was a dim light in the office porch, and an elderly watchnight emerged to tell us that two of the buses would be going to Tamale in the morning, so our best plan would be to get inside one and rest until it was light. We did as he suggested, and fell asleep almost at once, sprawled across the seats. After the *Graphic* truck, almost anything would have seemed comfortable.

When I awoke the yard was full of people but James had disappeared. He came back with the tickets to Tamale and an assortment of bread, peppery meat and fruit for our breakfast. We secured our luggage as carefully as we could, and watched as it was strapped firmly onto the roof of the bus, along with a mass of baggage that included pots and pans, baskets, bed-mats and bedding-rolls belonging to the other passengers. A large waterproof covering was stretched over the

entire pile. James remarked that he hoped we would not need anything
from our cases before we reached Tamale, and the same thought obviously occurred to a plump, rather pale-skinned girl with what seemed
twin boys aged two or three. She began to yell at the man roping the
tarpaulin onto the roof. To my surprise he unlashed a corner of the
covering and rummaged underneath. Then he threw down to the girl
a big pudding-shaped bundle wrapped in a red polka-dot cloth. This
was not right, and she threw it back. Another bundle came down, also
red, but smaller. The girl untied the cloth to reveal *keynkey* wrapped
in banana leaves. Without a word of thanks to the man on the roof,
she parcelled up her food supply again and climbed into the bus with
it, nudging the twins in front of her. The man shrugged his shoulders
and rolled his eyes expressively, then continued to heave at his rope. I
marvelled at his self-control.

"He's her husband," said James. "It is his food too."

A few minutes later the conductor began to call out the names of
the passengers, and we took our seats at the back of the bus. The driver
started the engine, but there was a delay because one man was still at
the other side of the transport-yard, buying food for the journey from
some very noisy market women.

"My friend," yelled the conductor, "dis lorry go for Tamale nownow,
you hear?" As the harassed man raced toward the bus shedding groundnuts and bananas as he ran, the conductor muttered: "Bushman!"

"He is anxious to show us that he can speak English!" said James.

In the early morning the route north through the forest-country is
dramatic and beautiful. Giant trees march in columns on both sides
of the way, soaring from the creepers and feathery palms to dwarf the
speeding coach. Pigeons flutter among the trees and bee-eaters hover
bejewelled in the shafts of sunlight. Black-and-white hornbills rise lazily
from the road and flap-glide-flap away as the wheels race near. Neat
cultivated strips, fields of maize and cassava and shady cocoa-farms
flicker at the roadside, and squat red-clay villages gallop past to be lost
in the enveloping green. Fat mammies skip nimbly into the shadows,
still balancing full water-pots on their heads. A bearded cyclist swerves
into the ditch and rises to shake an angry fist as the bus thunders by.
Stranded motorists signal desperately from the roadway and point in

vain at their offending cars before they too leap for safety. The big lorries and buses rule the road through the Forest Country.

At Mampong black goats scattered in front of us as we swooped to a brief halt, and women clamoured around the bus trying to sell oranges to the passengers. Three people got out and three others took their places. One was a wizened old lady who refused to pay her fare. The conductor explained that she was only being asked for the correct amount from Mampong to Tamale, and that she did not have to pay the full fare from Kumasi. She persisted that she was being 'humbugged', however, and became abusive. The driver looked worried, but his conductor solved the problem very simply. He lifted the old woman's large basket of belongings from the floor beside her, and while she gaped in amazement and fury he deposited it twenty yards away on the grass. She hobbled to fetch it, and the driver let in the clutch…

We stopped next at Ejura, a town of wide grassy spaces, where vultures were soaring in hundreds above the busy market. For lunch we had incredibly hot *chichinga*, strips of goats' meat wound onto thin sticks and fried in chilli sauce. Usually I had found this dish delicious, but now the first bite I took almost burnt the roof off my mouth. Sweat poured from me and tears streamed down my face; James laughed, and the market women stared in surprise at the white man who for no apparent reason was weeping in their market-place. Fortunately there were oranges and water-melons to soothe the burning.

Beyond Ejura the forest thinned out, giving way to low scrub with stretches of rolling grassland, and towards midday we reached Yeji, beside the Volta River, where we had to wait a short time for the ferry to take us across. Government Transport had priority over privately-owned vehicles, and we passed a line of cars and trucks waiting their turn. The drivers grinned and gestured at us. Most of them seemed in no hurry, and were taking the opportunity to gossip and buy food – black, greasy mudfish – from the inevitable group of market women beside the ferry. But one *tro-tro* driver was angry because our bus had usurped his position in the queue. He leapt out and ran alongside our vehicle, swiping at the driver's window with a length of flexible creeper.

"Bloddy man!" screamed our driver. "Why you trobble me? Why you no go 'way?"

But the tro-tro man would not go.

"I get hurry!" he yelled. "You tief my place! You drive dis big lorry pass me like I be notting. You tink you fit spit me!"

As usual our resourceful conductor had the answer. While our bus was gliding very slowly down the last yards of track towards the wooden planks of the ferry, he slipped out quietly behind the pestering man and with one heave lifted him clean into the river. The ensuing applause came not only from our bus but from the other watching drivers and passengers.

By mid-afternoon we were approaching Tamale. It was very hot and in several areas the grassland had been blackened by bush-fires, leaving wide, ugly scars on the yellow plain. We had left behind the square-walled Ashanti houses with their roofs of corrugated iron. Instead, the landscape was now thinly scattered with neat clusters of mud 'beehive' huts and the villagers wore either no clothes at all or loin-strings with leaves tied fore and aft.

Even in the scorched areas there were birds in great number in the grassland. Weavers had canopied the few trees with funnel-nests; tiny crimson barbets flickered like sparks at the roadside; and now and again rollers, crow-sized birds of clear electric blue appeared, perched always on the very top of the tallest anthills. Once our driver braked hard and stopped suddenly so that we could all see, quite near the road, fifty or more desert vultures hacking at what was probably the corpse of a cow. These scavenging birds were huge, far larger than the Hooded Vultures so familiar further south, and the largest of all was not grey like the rest, but strikingly piebald. We left the ghouls slashing and tugging away at their shapeless corpse, and drove on through the savannah, but within minutes the driver braked violently and stopped again. This time some of the women passengers cowered and a few hid their faces. Others gasped "Iiiiiiii!" and clung to their husbands as slowly, very slowly out onto the road strolled a big dog baboon trailed by his harem. With the authority of a policeman he stood in the middle of the track while his wives crossed over one by one, then he vanished after them into the long, yellow grass.

Tamale closed round us in a flurry of red dust, and our Government bus stopped in the transport-yard, for this was the end of the official route and the driver would return to Kumasi in the morning. Our choice lay between spending the night in Tamale with the First Battalion or continuing our journey at once. There were several trucks and vans that were going on to Bolgatanga before nightfall, but their starting time was uncertain. Then we were offered a lift in a large blue tro-tro that was just about to leave, and accepted at once.

We climbed into the back and held tightly to the wooden supports as the driver swerved out of the yard. His truck was already overloaded, but on the outskirts of the town he checked briefly four times to collect more passengers from the roadway. Then, to his cry of "Bol – iga, Bol – iga, Bol – igatan – GAH!" we finally headed north, packed like sardines yet clinging in panic to the wooden struts, as our driver set out to cover the eighty miles to Bolgatanga in the shortest possible time.

Abongo had told me that Bolga was a fine town pass-all. It was his tribe's Capital and he was very proud of it. The Frafras gained their tribal name because they were so friendly: "Frafra," they said to the first Europeans who came to their land. It was merely a greeting, a welcome to the white visitors, but they have been called Frafras ever since.

Bolgatanga proved to be a busy, straggling shanty-town of mud-shelters where vultures bickered in the roadway and mangy dogs fought each other in the doorways. Nkrumah's government was later to erect fine new buildings in Bolga, to prove that the North had not been forgotten utterly, but when James and I passed through, only a few solid houses along the main street stood out from the sea of shanty-dwellings. In addition to the dogs and vultures, goats and chickens wandered between the shacks, where fat, almost naked women bustled to and fro bearing on their heads yams in woven baskets, swinging their leaf-decorated buttocks seductively. James smiled: "These are the Drum-Major's people," was all he said.

Baskets dominated Bolgatanga. Beautifully woven in brilliant yellows, reds and greens, they flashed the colours that in the South were provided by *kente* and patterned cotton cloth – and the national flag. The main street shone with them, of all shapes and sizes; and hats too, wide-brimmed or conical, cunningly worked in the same vivid hues. The craftsmen sat with their handiwork displayed before them and hanging from the trees in splashes of colour. We decided to buy nothing until our return. Then a small child appeared and addressed me plaintively.

"Massah, you want fine-fine basket?"

"No," I said, "de time I come back I get um."

"You want fine-fine hat?"

"No thank you…"

A little later we decided that we did after all need something in which to carry our food and immediate requirements. In guilty haste we purchased a basket very cheaply from a pot-bellied man at the roadside.

Bolgatanga's small rest-house was full. Apparently there were some spare beds in the hospital, but we lacked the courage to ask if we could sleep there. At the police-station they suggested we should try the Government Agent. The duty-policeman spoke poor English, but more fluently than the friends with whom he was gossiping, and eventually we were directed to a café beside the main road. At the back of this building was a big, bare room where, it appeared, a dance was to start in less than an hour. Later in the evening the Government Agent would be there.

We sat at a table and ordered beer. The café boasted electric lighting and a kerosene refrigerator. From the fine display of bottles behind the counter it appeared that this was one of the town's chief places of entertainment, but for a social centre the décor was startling. Green chairs, tables topped in blue-green plastic, shuttered windows hung with tattered olive curtains, a riot of huge painted animals leering from pale green walls: it was like a submarine nightmare.

"I tink you Englishmans," the café-owner said effusively. "Mebbe you soldier for Tamale, no be so?"

"For Accra," said James, and the man looked delighted.

"Ahhhaaah!" he boomed. "Fine place, Accra. My daughter, she dey for Accra. You know her?"

Probably not, we concluded, amongst some quarter-million inhabitants, but the man was not in the least deterred.

"You go for France, no be so?" he queried. He lifted a circular rush-mat from the centre of our table and dabbed a pudgy finger on the cockroach that was uncovered. "You go for Paga?" he asked rhetorically, swishing the corpse onto the floor and grinding it into the green matting.

We admitted that we did have plans to go into French Territory, whereupon our host started to tell us of his own experiences across the border, followed this with much earnest advice on what to do when we arrived there, and warned us against countless evils that the French laid on especially to take advantage of inexperienced travellers from the Gold Coast. Apparently Independence had not yet reached Bolgatanga. To add proof to his own monologue, the café-owner introduced us to several of his friends, all charming and all exhausting, who duplicated his comments about 'Frenchmans'. Whenever they paused, we nodded or agreed monosyllabically.

Having exhausted that topic he proceeded to tell us all about his family, his relations, his distant relations, their distant relations... It was very hot, and the beer made me sweat profusely. The man's voice droned on and on... James was doodling in biro on the back of an envelope: his sketch of the café-owner was not an accurate portrait, but it caught well the earnestness of the man, his comic solemnity...

I was awoken by the band, which had started to tune up in the back room. Their music began softly as a discordant rumble, gradually swelling into an infectious, throbbing beat. The walls shook. The bottles and glasses quivered on the table. Someone outside in the street banged a loud, resonant gong. This was the invitation, and before long the townspeople began to arrive for the dance, shuffling through the room, hips swaying, feet tapping rhythmically. The café-owner and his plump wife stood, one each side of the 'ball-room' doorway, collecting the entrance money without difficulty at first, then having to struggle as the tide nearly swept them both onto the dance-floor.

"Dimidimi – dimidimi – dim – dimidimi – dimidimidimidimi – DIMMM!" The glasses danced on their green plastic sea.

"Dimidimidimi – dim – dimi – dim – dimi – DIMMM!" The drums stuttered and throbbed and the bottles swayed and the leering monsters writhed on the walls.

"What did he say when I fell asleep?" I shouted above the uproar.

"He never noticed!" James yelled back, beating time with a glass.

They came and they came, the aristocracy of Bolgatanga and the less well-to-do. The women wore long, flowing dresses mostly of red and gold. Tall, supple, shining, some wives seemed to be dragging unwilling husbands forcibly to the dance.

"DIMIDIMIDIMIDIMI – DIMM!" The tempo warmed: the drums crackled and rumbled. The red and the gold swirled.

A few of the men were immaculate in dark suits, formal, uncomfortable-looking in spite of their smartness; a few came swathed in flamboyant robes. The happy-go-lucky majority, however, arrived in shirt-sleeves and shapeless trousers, arguing, gesticulating as they swayed and jostled their way to the door.

At one point some of the crowd began to lose patience with the slow rate of entry. Two policemen were waiting in the street outside, and several times they intervened at a call for help from the proprietor, pushing their way through the mass and firmly ejecting anyone who showed signs of making trouble. Gradually, however, the rush slowed to a few unhurried groups, while from inside came the roar of the band and the gabble of several hundred sweating, chattering dancers.

The café-owner looked across at us and mopped his face.

"Dis fool peoples!" he exclaimed. "Dey come so plenty I no get time for look um!" Shouting at the top of his considerable voice, he explained above the din that the Government Agent was often late, but that we need not worry, he would arrive quite soon.

But at ten o'clock he had not appeared, and we had consumed a large amount of beer. "We should have stayed in Tamale!" James said. The two policemen were still in attendance and smiled at us sympathetically. One, who could speak some English, said that he would be happy for us to spend the night at his house. Unfortunately this was not possible, for he had to remain on duty until the dance ended, and without his help we should never be able to find where he lived. We thanked him as best we could, however, and were just about to ask the café-owner for the third time whether perhaps the Government Agent had already arrived, and might in fact be dancing at this very moment, when a car stopped outside and a group of men came in.

"Mafriend," said the educated policeman with relief, "be so dis Govimaygin com."

Perhaps we spoke to the wrong man. I wondered about this at the time. He was a short, very dark man whose face streamed with sweat, and for a Government Agent he seemed to have very little dignity. He was a Southerner, who spoke rapidly in excellent English, but with a whining intonation. He was sorry, he said; if the rest-house was full, there was nowhere else to stay. He blew his nose ostentatiously and scratched his neck with a carefully-preserved long fingernail. He pointed out that Bolga was in any case rather a bush town and he himself was not yet fully accustomed to the ways of its people. His friends, too, were from the South, and they also found Bolga a strange place. He was sorry we had been waiting for so long. He was sorry that he could not help. But then he could not, surely, be expected to help at such an hour? He stood on one leg, fidgeting with his coat-buttons like an abashed child. There was little point in arguing, so we collected up our baggage and went out into the lorry-station. The moon was high, showing row upon row of trucks filling the station-yard and overflowing onto the street. Between the trucks lay sleeping drivers and would-be passengers, and a number of drowsy goats. We peered under the canopy of a large, solid vehicle. Only one man lay stretched on the wooden floor, so we climbed in, spread our groundsheets at the opposite end, and settled down to an expected sleepless night. We were so tired, however, and so full of beer, that the hardness of the floor and the stink of the carry-all truck meant nothing. I slept well, and James even better. He did not wake until the driver of the vehicle banged two cooking-pots together near his ear and remarked that if James wanted to stay aboard that was all right, but the truck was going to Tamale...

This was about six o'clock. The morning sun was already warm: the basket-sellers had set out their work and the market women were arguing shrilly. At the well nearby a line of naked children stood waiting to fill calabash water-pots, which they carried away on their heads with inherited ease. We washed at this well, to the delight of a youthful audience, who found bubbles of soap a great entertainment.

The vehicle in which we hoped to travel to the French Border had seen better days. The roof was full of holes and hung down alarmingly. The wooden seats were loosely fitted, so that any sudden jerk would cause them to slide towards the back of the truck. Our driver said that he planned to start for Navrongo at nine o'clock, but long before this time his full quota of passengers had arrived and were muttering angrily

185

from their cramped seats, with their baskets of fruit and vegetables jammed into every space between feet and on laps. By half past the hour tempers were fast rising, and comments followed each other rapidly in a flood of Frafra invective that I did not need to understand.

"Aieee..." replied the poor man, obviously as ignorant of the language as I was. "No be me do dis ting. Lorry-owner say make I stay get two more passenger, den I fit go."

This was common practice, as the driver seldom owned the vehicle he drove, but worked for an owner under accepted rules; and as there was at that time no check on overloaded vehicles, a long-distance truck would seldom leave without at least five passengers over its intended maximum. We were already overloaded, however, and it did not seem as if anyone else was likely to arrive; nor would it have been easy to squeeze even one more passenger aboard.

James poked his head through the side of the truck and addressed the driver witheringly.

"Bushman," he said, "I tink you no fit go for Navrongo attall. Dis lorry spoil. Ino be good one. Left small, me and my friend go find 'nother truck. Ahuuuh?"

There was a murmur of agreement from the other passengers.

"I – I go hask lorry-owner," the driver muttered. He trotted off across the yard and disappeared into the shanty-town.

Meanwhile, within ten yards of our squashed seats a young Frafra, muscular in a pair of sky-blue shorts, his torso oiled and gleaming, began to execute a dynamic but obscene dance. We watched from our grandstand position, and a large audience quickly gathered from around the lorry park. The man pranced and leapt, squealing like a pig and slapping himself fiercely on the thighs. Then he crouched down and assumed a hideous expression. His eyes bulged and his tongue protruded, while the veins stood out on his straining forehead. At first I thought he must be an epileptic throwing a fit, but it was soon clear that all the grotesque movements were planned, and "Bushman!" I heard James mutter in disgust. Suddenly, to a shriek of delight from the spectators, the youth began to spin like a top, changed to a series of frog-leaps, and rounded off his performance with a demoniac fling that left him in a collapsed heap in the dust. Nobody offered to help him to his feet.

Here the driver reappeared with the cheering news that he had been given permission to start. He jumped into his seat and engaged the gears with an explosive sound, disturbing a cloud of vultures from the shanty roofs. The truck set off in a mad rush, accelerating so sharply that many seats leapt from their sockets and slid towards the back of the vehicle, trapping the legs of the passengers behind. For a while there was bedlam on board, with yelling and frantic struggling. Some fought to free themselves, others to avoid being pushed onto the road. Fists flailed, teeth were bared; baskets were tipped up and the road behind grew bright with peppers, bananas and rolling oranges. Amid the confusion our driver continued on his way, seeming not even to notice the uproar behind his back. And finally the seats were set in place once more, tempers cooled, and everyone settled down again for the short journey to Navrongo.

❖   ❖   ❖

Bolgatanga had seemed overcrowded, dirty and chaotic. Despite the vivacity of its basket-weavers and the friendliness of its people, it appeared a decadent town, heading nowhere. By contrast Navrongo was attractive, clean and well spaced-out, with neat blocks of whitewashed houses, and an especially smart police barracks. Even the primitive huts of mud and thatch looked meticulously spick and span. Avenues of trees stood outlined against yellow grassland. Even the trees were tidy. I could understand Oscar Songatua's pride in his home town.

Navrongo's friendliness is legendary. A month earler, Simon had visited the town on his way to the Upper Volta, and on his return spoke with awe of the hospitality he had found there. Apparently he had asked for the Navrongo rest-house, and was directed to a row of white-walled homes. He walked in through an open door.

"Can I help you?" asked a smiling African.

Said Simon: "I would like a large meal now, and a room for the night."

"Certainly," replied the man, and a few minutes later he came back with a big bowl of stew. While Simon ate, his host talked in friendly fashion ("and in better English than mine,") and half-way through his meal the Englishman realised that it was no rest-house he had wandered into, but the home of a member of the Navrongo Council. In great embarrassment he apologised for his mistake.

187

"Ahah!" said the Councillor, "the rest-house is over there, that house behind, but I should be very happy for you to stay in my home."

At Navrongo's Immigration Office the young man who stamped our passports proved to be an ex-soldier.

"Welcome," he said. "I hope you are liking Navrongo."

"Plenty, but we haven't had time to see much," answered James. "Perhaps on the way back –"

"On your way back I will show you our town. I expect now you are in a hurry to get to the Border?"

Unsurprisingly, he and James had common friends in the Army, although they had never served together. The conversation developed, as Ghanaian conversations do, into reminiscences of 'my brother this' and 'my brother that', for in Ghana all soldiers are brothers, but so too are all acquaintances, however slight. So I too was a brother and the conversation proceeded in a mixture of dialects, punctuated by Ahaaahs and Aieees from them and nods from me, and James and I found ourselves half committed to staying a week with our new friend on our return and to doing this and seeing that, and in the welter of words we did not manage to say that our leave was limited… And then the Passport Man suddenly drew breath and remembered where the conversation had started, and that we were trying to cross the Border.

"When you reach Paga," he said, "don't change money there, even if you are much needing French francs. The money-changers will humbug you. They will be giving you 500 francs for a twenty-shilling note on your way going, and on your return you will have to pay 700 francs to get back your twenty shillings!"

While we were talking, a little grey 'microbus' van stopped outside the office, and the driver walked in with his pass-visa.

"If he's going our way," James said, "let's change trucks. I've had enough of that other one."

Across the sides of the microbus was stencilled in white: 'Transporteur Touts Cercles'.

"Vous allez à Paga?" I asked tentatively.

"A Ouagadougou…" This was almost too good to be true, for Ouagadougou was where we hoped to spend the night. With relief we transferred our bags from the decrepit wagon in which we had travelled from Bolgatanga.

There were already six passengers in the microbus. On one side a policeman, who proved to be on leave from Kumasi, was sitting next to a shabbily-dressed half-caste with bloodshot eyes and several days' stubble. Four fat, glistening tradeswomen were seated opposite, discussing business shrilly. Three of them had close-cropped, masculine hairstyles, but the fourth wore hers long, dramatically shaped into three stiff points that stood straight out from her head. She was rocking a baby in her arms, waving it to and fro to accentuate her high-pitched argument. Now and again she would remember its presence and rock it more soothingly, encouraging it to sleep with soft cries of "Hiu… hiu… hiu…" before becoming involved in the argument again, conducting with the child as a baton.

In a very short time we reached Paga, where a treble-chinned official glanced with tiny pig-eyes at the passports of the three of us who had them, and was quite unperturbed about the market-women who had none. The half-caste held out what seemed to be an identity card from Kumasi Brewery, and the official nodded him on. Then we were allowed through the barrier into French Territory. Our driver explained that the microbus would have to be examined by the Customs: why, he did not know. He was not a smuggler, he declared indignantly.

We climbed out to explore the town, and were soon surrounded by the expected plague of money-changers who bore down on us with thick wads of notes held temptingly aloft. James and I could have done with some more francs, but we heeded the warning we had been given at Navrongo. There were several other trucks waiting to be examined before our vehicle had its turn, so we had time to visit the market. It was much like a Ghanaian one, except that every stall appeared to sell French-pattern shorts, scent, and oil for taking the kinks out of wiry hair. I wanted to buy a tin of condensed milk to put in our tea or coffee, and asked a very large woman if she would take English money. She nodded.

"Combien?"

"Sink sent franks – " she replied, in the anglicised French of the Border dialect. "Pound –" she added, in case I had not understood. I said she was trying to humbug me, and offered her a shilling. The argument lost all sense of money values, French or English, but eventually she agreed to take half-a-crown and handed me the tin. I tried hard to convince myself that I had come off best.

When we returned to the microbus, our fellow-passengers were sitting glumly on the ground and the policeman was muttering angrily to himself. Obviously something was amiss, but when I asked the driver his reply was puzzling.

"There is trouble, Monsieur, because today is Sunday."

Kwabena, the Kumasi policeman, explained. He was a tall, very black man, and drew himself up to his full height when speaking, as if public utterance required his most dignified manner.

"The fact is," he said, "that everybody has to be vaccinated by the doctor before the lorry can go on to Ouaga. Always it is so. The driver is already vaccinated, as I myself, and I expect you, too?" (We nodded.) "But the others, I think not so, and today the doctor refuses to vaccinate anyone at all. He is saying today is Sunday and he is wishing to rest – so all the lorries are here waiting."

James and I were not at all keen to spend the night in Paga. Nor was the policeman, for he had only a week left of his leave. So we decided to see the doctor and try to make him change his mind. We found him in his house nearby, a tall, angular Negro with tired eyes and a drooping moustache. As the three of us entered, he yawned vigorously. He was wearing only a pair of khaki shorts, and sat back in a canvas chair with his feet on a table.

He spoke in strange, heavily-accented English, interspersed with French words. He knew why we had come, he said. Always someone was in a hurry and could not wait till Monday. He was a busy man. Proper doctors were not many and all this examining and examining was very tiring, all these travellers who wished to go into the Haute Volta. Some he vaccinated, others he checked to see if they had been vaccinated. He assured us that he was very conscientious, but that at week-ends he always tried to finish early, because he was always tired; and this Sunday he was especially tired and did not wish to vaccinate anybody at all. Once before, not so long ago, when he had been really tired, *un anglais* had persuaded him to work on a Sunday afternoon... that was the trouble with *les anglais* – they were too impatient. We hesitated to say that Simon was a friend of ours...

I decided that flattery might succeed where anger would clearly fail.

"Mon ami," I began hypocritically, "I have heard that you are a very good doctor, and I quite understand that you must be tired. But I am in the Army, and my friend is in the Army also, and this our new friend, he is in the Police. We all have our documents correct – " (Here we flourished our passports with their elaborate visas for Upper Volta and Sudan, and proof that we had had 'jabs' for everything from TAB to yellow fever.) "If we have to remain in Paga until tomorrow, that will be one day gone from the leave we have been given, which already is too short for us to see the French lands properly. Besides, in Paga there is nowhere for us to sleep."

I felt proud of this oration, but the doctor just looked at the three of us and said nothing for a long time. Then he nodded his head, slowly.

"I tell you what I will do, Messieurs," he said at last, pulling on a filthy green shirt, "I will examine your vehicle, and then – *finis* – I will not examine any more. Tell your other passengers that I will be in the surgery."

We collected our disgruntled companions and Kwabena explained to them what was to happen. He spoke in the Mossi dialect, and the four women nodded their heads and smiled. The half-caste stared blankly in front of him, clearly not understanding a word. I tried my French, but still he showed no sign of comprehension. James spoke in Fante, Twi and barrack-Hausa, with no success.

"I think he cannot hear, cannot speak," said the policeman. "He is saying nothing at all on the way from Bolga."

We asked the driver, who said that a friend had paid for the man's ticket and that he had not heard him speak. So we resorted to signs and gesticulation, and the half-caste followed us to the 'surgery'. The doctor made no attempt to vaccinate anybody, nor did he even examine us. He signed the driver's pass and we walked back to the microbus, quietly as we had come, so that no one else should realise what was happening. Around us, the other drivers and their passengers drowsed in the sun, seemingly resigned to their fate, but as our vehicle came to life and swung out onto the road, a murmur arose from all sides, and a dozen or more people struggled to their feet and were racing towards the doctor's primitive surgery…

The little grey van was comfortable, and by African standards not overcrowded, and our road lay straight across a dry, dusty plain. It was a speed-fiend's paradise, and soon the speedometer was showing well over the hundred.

"Heh!" James exclaimed, and waved his arms delightedly, and it was disappointing to discover that it was marked in kilometres and not miles.

The soil of much of the Upper Volta Province is very poor, yet it supports a large population. The Mossi farmers are hard-working, and need to be. Most of the villages we passed were haphazard settlements of round mud huts with conical thatched roofs. Chickens ran every-where, scratching and pecking in the dust: apparently their owners do not feed them, but expect them to scrape enough food to live on. Often drifting piles of feathers around the houses indicated that in this almost barren land the meat of chickens is worth more than the few minute eggs they lay.

We crossed the Red Volta River, which runs through the most deso-late of landscapes, with not a village within miles of either bank. It was much later that I learned of the big area covered by the Volta in flood, and of the river-blindness near its banks brought on by the *simulium* fly, causing a wide strip of land to remain uninhabited. Beyond the fly-belt the plain grew less dusty, and in places yam fields stretched into the distance on both side of the road. Villages were here tight-packed and frequent, and the children waved and shouted as we passed. At length we could see, far off, the untidy outline of Ouagadougou.

❖   ❖   ❖

The town centre, when we reached it, was a surprise. We drove through dreary outskirts, sandy streets flanked by rows of old mud-brick houses of primitive, flat-roofed pattern, when suddenly we found our-selves in Ouagadougou's new quarter. Wide tree-bordered roads; fine modern shops; cars, and a throng of erratic cyclists: we seemed to have reached a mechanised fairyland in the midst of a desolate plain. We stopped at the lorry-station, which was huge and appeared to be used as a bicycle race-track, and the other passengers drifted away, except for our policeman friend, who asked us where we wanted to go.

I said I could do with a full night's sleep. James said he could sleep anywhere, but he did not really want to spend another night in a truck. The driver was confident that he knew an excellent *campement* that was not too expensive, and asked if he could take us there.

"I am now going home," said the policeman.

"Before you go, I would like to know one thing," I said. "Why are you called Kwabena?" This had intrigued me ever since he had told us his name, because although he was clearly a Mossi and had the distinctive ladder-like face-cuts of the tribe, he had a southern name. In the Twi language, Kwabena means 'Born-on-a-Tuesday'.

"My name is Allasan," he said, "but when I am joining the police in Kumasi they think I am some other person. I do not know how it happens, but some different person becomes Allasan and I am Kwabena. Nobody understand the palaver and nobody change the book. My passport says I am Kwabena. It is not troubling me at all: sometimes I am Kwabena, sometimes Allasan!"

We said goodbye, then went with the driver.

From the wide balcony of our lodging we watched the swift fall of night over Ouagadougou. There was no real dusk. One moment the great mosque, a proud turreted building far across the town, was gleaming golden in the light of the setting sun; and then, it seemed, Ouagadougou was suddenly wrapped in grey and already it was dark.

The hostelry was comfortable, although sparsely furnished. The accommodation was ridiculously cheap, but the cost of a meal was exorbitant, so we bought our evening food at a stall just outside the entrance, and took it back to the *campement*. It was wonderful, after the previous rough night, to be able to sit in comfort on our balcony enjoying delicious chicken and rice – with showers and real beds making for absolute luxury.

The next morning James and I made our way early to the lorry-station to find out what trucks were going to Mopti and the Niger, for we did not wish to be stranded later in the day with no means of leaving Ouagadougou. There were dozens of *tro-tros* and vans, and an old man in tattered khaki seemed to be the organiser and guide. He stood in the centre of the park, manoeuvring lorries into lines or through minute gaps between other vehicles. He was signalling methodically with a pointed grey flag and cursing loudly as children ran in front of moving trucks. We waited until he had dealt with the immediate traffic congestion, then asked if there would be anyone driving a truck to Mopti.

"Seulement Zuki…" He grabbed a small boy who was playing on the top of a *tro-tro*. "Va chercher Zuki –" and the child ran off. The old man had frosted hair and a chocolate, weathered face, very wrinkled. A row of medal-ribbons was pinned to his dirty smock. He saw I had noticed them, and pointed to the first. "Médaille militaire," he observed proudly. We told him we too were soldiers, from Accra, at which he became gracious and charming.

The child returned with Zuki, a rather surly youth who showed us his lorry and said that at midday it would depart for Mopti. He implied clearly that it would leave for Mopti then, whether or not James and I were in it. The Old Soldier presumably felt that Zuki was paying insufficient respect to the military, for he launched into a tirade that I could not follow, but which had the effect of making the youth much more deferential.

Around the lorry station were rows of ramshackle huts and dozens of tiny open-air stalls selling everything from aspirins to alarm clocks. There were rope sellers, with cord of every thickness and strength laid out on the ground. They were doing good business, for anyone who travels far in a market-truck or *tro-tro* likes his belongings to be securely lashed to the roof, but an even more profitable business seemed to be that of the Spare-Parts Man under his striped awning, who offered bolts, brackets, screws, nuts, tyres, inner tubes and all manner of essentials.

"I bet he tiefs them off the trucks and buses in the night and sells them back to the owners in the morning," James suggested, and the long queue outside the Spare Parts shelter implied the same.

It was by now breakfast time, and we decided once more that a meal at the *campement* would be extravagant, and probably insufficiently filling. We thought of returning to the stall we had enjoyed the night before, but instead discovered a small chop-bar quite near the lorry park. There were legions of flies buzzing inside, but the soup-smell was really appetising, so we took seats at a rickety bench that ran the whole length of the room. There were four other customers waiting, all Africans: a woman in a beautiful purple cloth and head-shawl; two tough-looking youths incongruously clad in indigo robes and berets; and a naked small boy aged three or four, who had captured a minute lizard and was trying to make it bite his finger.

The food came in huge, dirty bowls, a thick stew with lumps of meat and yam in it. It looked unpromising, but tasted delicious, as good as any meal we had on the entire trip. The men scooped out theirs in their fingers, swallowing rapidly and belching between mouthfuls. The woman, James and I tackled ours with spoons. The tiny boy discarded his lizard and staggered to the bench carrying a bowl half his own size. He dug both hands into the mixture, and plunged his head forward as if washing his face in it. After several ecstatic gulps, he raised his face with its tideline of stew, grinned widely at the rest of us and belched squeakily. He placed his still-nearly-full bowl carefully on the floor beside the bench and curled himself protectively round it. Then he fell asleep.

We returned to the *campement* by a roundabout route. We changed some money at a bank in the town centre and looked at numerous shops but did not go in. We watched two cyclists collide and then start fighting, and then embrace each other as the best of friends. We saw a pedestrian struck down by a *tro-tro* and wondered if he was seriously injured, but he leapt to his feet and seemed to be apologising to the driver for being in the way.

We had been told that if we reached Ouagadougou we must see the *Grand Marché*, the town's gigantic market. We only had time for a brief visit, but found it so fascinating that we determined, if possible, to stay longer on our way back. The *Marché* was like those of Accra and Kumasi in its bustle and noise, but much tidier and with a large covered area. Instead of the women staking claim to their own stands or patches of ground on which to spread their wares, here the market was divided into neat, white-panelled wooden stalls. It was also less obviously matriarchal, for there were numerous salesmen, although the majority were still women. The variety of goods sold was incredible, and we moved quickly past stall after stall of clothes, carpets, fresh vegetables, hats, leather goods, each worthy of closer examination – and then unfortunately we found ourselves in a covered meat-section, where huge red gashes of beef and complete skinned goats hung from hooks or lay in gobbets on the counters and even the floor. Flies buzzed in clouds and settled on the meat in black streaks. On one counter a grey kitten with runny eyes was licking up a pool of blood. We moved back into the fresh air.

Outside the market, a tall Hausa merchant was standing, a striking figure in white robes and neat skullcap. On the ground in front of him he had laid out a familiar assortment of 'Hausaware': metal ornaments, ivory necklaces, animals carved from ebony, sandalwood boxes, metal knives, hair blankets. There were also two huge python skins, far bigger than we had seen in Accra, and the scaly coats of several monitor lizards. To James's relish, the man realised immediately that I was English and not French.

"Massa like something nice?" An acquisitive ivory smile lit up the ebony face. "Fine box? Fine knife? You like?"

"Ouagadougou, Accra, all de same!" mocked James.

"How much dat big sanake?" I tried.

"Four-poun-ten, massa."

"Attall! You tink I be piccin?"

"Massa, I be poor man. You be big man, plenty money. I tell you de ting I do. For you I make special las' price four-poun."

"Look, my friend, I no go pay four-poun. Dat sanake ibi fine one but I no get dat plenty. Four silling be good price."

"Eh! Massa! You want humbug me too much! I make special last price – tree-poun-ten?"

It was a surreal feeling, to be haggling in pidgin-English – and in English currency – with a Hausa salesman in the capital of French-speaking Haute Volta territory. Eventually I did buy the python skin for ten shillings and the best of the monitors for five. The merchant was clearly disappointed by the price he had received for the python, but he probably considered he had done well out of the big lizard. James was speechless with laughter at the whole performance...

At midday we left Ouagadougou, on time and without mishap, squeezed into the front of Zuki's large *camion*, a dilapidated vehicle built to carry livestock. The back was piled high with rolled blankets and household utensils, and on top sat five Mohammedan passengers, their little white caps silhouetted against the sky like a neat row of chimneys

196

under snow. James and I were occupying the front compartment, the finest seats, as the driver pointed out, but our pleasure was short-lived, for a bearded tribesman in filthy turban and stinking robes also climbed into the front of the *camion* as it was about to start.

Zuki told us that Mopti was far indeed, and that we should not be there until the following night. This evening, he said, we would reach Ouahigouya, and in the morning early we would leave again for Mopti. We scanned our map to discover this new place: it *was* there, a small speck about half-way between Ouaga and Mopti.

The *camion* rolled into the semi-desert and the afternoon sun hammered through the glass of the windscreen till James and I felt sick with the heat, but the driver and the turbaned vagabond seemed quite at their ease. Luckily for us, the Mohammedans at the back were also finding the day very hot. No sunrise and sunset prayer-limit for them: we stopped at several bush-villages, and each time the Muslims extended the halt by facing Mecca and prostrating themselves in the dust. Then they would wash their feet with water from kettles carried especially for the purpose; and finally they would urinate beside the track, before climbing back to their seats. Their devotions took about ten minutes each time, giving James and me the chance to cool down and also stretch our legs at every halt.

It was dark when we reached Ouahigouya, which seemed a scattered settlement of few houses and many stunted trees, although Simon, whose trip north had ended there, had told me that it was actually a sizeable town. We were prepared to sleep in the open by the *camion*, but decided to search quickly around the town in case there was somewhere better to stay. We had said we would pay Zuki when we reached Mopti, not before, so felt confident that he would not leave without us.

The first house we tried was a tiny bungalow owned by a French couple, who said that they had visitors already, but there was a shed in the 'garden' – which was distinguishable from the surrounding scrubland only by virtue of a single-strand wire fence – where we would be welcome to stay. Then they had a better idea. Monsieur Lionne, the Education Officer, was at home. Apparently this was quite an event, since his job took him far afield, but when he did return to Ouahigouya he was hospitality itself, and welcomed company.

They took us to an even tinier bungalow, where a very sunburnt man with silver hair received us as if we had been long-awaited friends. Monsieur Lionne made us sit down to an enormous meal of cold meat, bread and cheese, and with pride produced beer from his kerosene refrigerator. While we ate, he told us in fluent English of his 'Education District' – an area of some thousands of square miles where schools were so far apart that he could only hope to visit each of them once in the year. He was away again in the morning, he told us. Would we mind looking after ourselves after breakfast, as he would be leaving early? There was no need to lock any doors. There were no thieves in Ouahigouya, he said with complete assurance.

Monsieur Lionne retired early. We, too, had a long journey ahead of us so it seemed wise to follow his example. Our host had one spare bed already made up; for the other he produced a camp bed, a 'Lilo' inflatable mattress, sheets and some beautiful camel-hair blankets. James was captivated by the 'Lilo', and having learnt how to blow it up he insisted on sleeping on it. He was surprised when I said that I far preferred the other bed.

At sunrise the Education Officer poked his head round the door to say that the 'boy' would give us breakfast when we were ready. He murmured goodbye and was gone, and a moment later we heard his old, battered jeep spluttering into the distance.

Fired by his example we rose at once, and had a chance to look round Monsieur Lionne's fascinating house by daylight. The main room was almost a museum, with walls, shelves, cabinets, book-cases all crowded with ornaments and curios: jade elephants walking in line up a green mountainside; ivory paper-cutters shaped like crocodiles; fans, glass, beautiful cloths; pottery and porcelain; ebony face-masks in profusion. There was even a barometer where, in a tall glass jar, abstract designs floated in colourless liquid – something that was to prove popular in Europe several years later.

We breakfasted on more bread, cheese and beer, then carried our cases to the *camion*, for which display of early-morning enthusiasm we were rewarded by a wait of more than an hour while the rest of the passengers assembled. There were nearly thirty of them. When we had joined it at Ouagadougou, the truck had been already loaded, but now we saw in detail what was taken on board. Each passenger (James and myself excepted) had a large bundle of bedding and several pots and pans. There were food baskets, clothes bags, coiled ropes, wicker baskets of live chickens, wooden staves, several rolls of thick matting, sacks of yams, and two bicycles. Also, there was a donkey. The passengers lifted everything into the back of the conveyance, and climbed in themselves. Even then there seemed to be plenty of room. The donkey was munching some thorn-twigs; it had obviously travelled in a *camion* before. James and I packed ourselves into the front of the vehicle, where the turbaned vagabond had already settled himself comfortably on a pile of rugs.

For hour after hour the roadway led across desolate country peopled by toiling small-farmers and by nomadic families who walked beside the road, their possessions tied to the backs of slow, sleepy oxen. Sometimes hunters strode by, carrying light spears, although what they could have hoped to hunt was a mystery. The sun rose high and beat into the front cabin of our *camion*, and a fiery breeze swept through the window, bringing clouds of red dust that made even the bearded patriarch cough. At every roadside village we had to stop for water to cool the engine. Nion, Sabe, Yako, Mako: neat, strangely prosperous settlements they seemed in such a forbidding landscape. Most of the huts were pumpkin-round with roofs curving to a point; there were miniature stalls where a small grilled chicken cost the equivalent of a shilling. Mischievous children peered from doorways or played hide-and-seek around the truck.

Our brief halts probably gave us a false picture of these bush-villages. The people seemed lively, friendly, even healthy. We saw few distorted bellies and ulcerated legs; there were plenty of old folk. But their life must be very hard. With the best will in the world and the greatest industry, you can grow little in such a dustscape.

In one remote outpost we met *Les Pères Blancs*, a group of French missionaries living in a long hut standing some way back from the road. There were five Fathers, all quite young, all bearded, and all wearing the long white garments that give their Order its name. They had almost no knowledge of recent events beyond their small community, but we soon discovered that their eagerness for news was very superficial, and they seemed to have given up caring what went on further afield than

Ouagadougou or Mopti. They laughed a great deal, with an emptiness that we found embarrassing. One of the five produced a bottle of *syrop de menthe*, and we joined them in a glass of the weak green liquid. When Zuki came to say that it was time to leave, our hosts proposed one-for-the-road so tepidly that we made our excuses and followed the driver. We returned to the *camion* to find the children still playing hide-and-seek around the wheels.

Each time a village appeared ahead of us, Zuki sounded his horn and the passengers at the back chattered and shouted excitedly. As the *camion* slowed, one man would leap out to collect water for the engine, landing skilfully on his feet near the village well. When the truck stopped, the Mohammedans climbed down slowly and debated exactly which way lay Mecca. Then the five of them would lie prostrate on the ground, after which would follow the ritual foot-washing and urination by the track, before they climbed aboard again.

So it came as a surprise when Zuki suddenly stepped on the accelerator as we drew near to one particular village, and all the passengers behind us were silent. As we passed, I glimpsed tall women standing at the doorways of some of the huts. They were the darkest people we had seen, wearing gold earrings and nose-ornaments. I saw no children, and no men. Zuki muttered something about 'bad people – always fighting' and would say no more. James suggested that they must be the Basares, as a lot of people were scared of them.

"Perhaps we can learn more about them when we reach Mopti," he said. In fact we never did find anyone to explain, and on our return to Accra the numerous Basare soldiers in the Battalion were adamant that their tribe was very peaceful...

Morning turned to afternoon and afternoon became cooler evening, and as night was falling we passed through a majestic gorge dividing the sudden ridges of the Bandiagara Scarp. For a while the sheer features were colourful in evening shades of red, brown and yellow, but very soon it was dark, and the truck was struggling in a black wilderness of undulating sand... Then an expanse of grey shimmering to the left of the roadway showed the limits of the Niger marshes. Zuki brought the *camion* to a halt at the last village before following a high causeway across the shallow water to Mopti. Everyone got out, and most of the passengers queued for peppery soup at a little chop-bar, lit by an oil-lamp. James and I set off down the incline towards the water, for our first proper view of the Niger.

"I think we are in Kardo country now," James said. "In which case there are cannibals in the hills. Sergeant-Major Kardo told me so, when I said I was coming this way."

We had not gone far when a weird cry echoed from the bush, an unnerving howl. We both stopped. My first thought was of the 'cannibals'.

"Wolf!" said James without hesitation. "I'm not going on!"

He started back towards the truck. I was about to yell that there were no wolves near Mopti and that it must have been a stray dog, when the howl came again. I followed James.

Zuki shared the conviction that a wolf, or some strange and ill-omened creature lived at the edge of the swamp. The owner of the chop-bar assured us that nobody from the village ever went near the water at night, for if they did, they would not return. He was not sure if the evil spirit would harm a white man: but I fully agreed with him that it would be foolish to meddle with the supernatural. When I asked him if he knew anything about people in the hills who 'chopped men', for a second he looked scared and frail. This was obviously a mistake, so with James's help the conversation was swiftly brought back to the subject of our travels and hopes of reaching Timbuktu. The chop-bar owner gave us a whole chicken, cooked without pepper, and we paid him double (but still not much over a shilling), so confidence was restored all round. One more mournful howl came from the swamp, but faint now, in the distance, and everybody laughed.

The causeway lay needle-straight over the marshes, a solid, well-surfaced road from the Ivory Coast, far superior to the dusty track we had been following from Ouagadougou. On both sides of the way low water glimmered, broken here and there by dark clumps of reeds, and from the flooded land a chorus of frogs swelled out. The sounds rose from far and near, easily audible above the throb of the engine: throaty bellows, hoarse rumbles, high-pitched flutings; aristocratic tenors emitting polite, regular croaks; whistling frogs piping strange liquid melodies;

vulgar frogs belching outrageously: a full amphibian concert.

"Fine – fine – money – no – dey!" sang James.

The comparison was inspired. In this exuberant frog-chorus I could picture exactly the Corps of Drums thumping out their music with the same wild improvisation: Boadu and William, Godson, Peter, Maurice and the rest, carried away by the zest of their hit-tune.

Before long a line of faint lights appeared across the water. The roadway curled to the right, so that the lights lay directly ahead. They grew brighter and more numerous, and finally Mopti emerged out of the marshland. Zuki kept his foot down hard, and the *camion* rattled over the last yards of the causeway, into the town.

It was past midnight.

We drew up outside a big house which had a high porchway decorated with climbing convolvulus plants. Zuki said that this was the *campement*, the rest-house where we could stay the night.

"Can we go in at this hour?"

"*Certainement!* They do not mind people arriving late."

We tiptoed to the door. The lights were still on.

We went in. There were about half a dozen Europeans and the same number of Africans in the room. Some were playing cards in groups, others looking at colourful magazines. The tables were piled with empty bottles and glasses, but everyone seemed very sober, very quiet. A few heads turned to look at us, before returning to their cards and magazines.

Monsieur Jormel and his wife greeted us more effusively. They were a strange pair. He was short and corpulent with flame-red whiskers and a face of deep mahogany hue. She was thin and pallid and her hair fell dark and straight. He insisted that we must be given a meal before retiring, and she hurried to prepare it

He told us he was not really the proprietor of the *campement*, but the owner was on holiday and he hoped that he and his wife would give satisfactory service. He asked about our journey, and while Madam clattered and banged away in the kitchen we told how we had arrived at Mopti and said that we hoped to reach Timbuktu. He explained that there was at present no way through to Timbuktu by road, and that even at the best of times any vehicle was likely to get bogged down in the sand every few miles. He spoke English fluently, but with odd pauses for head-shakings and sly winks.

"What about the river, then?" James asked.

"Ah… the river, yes; there is a *pinasse* leaves tomorrow for Kabara – this Tombouctou is *near* the river but first you must go to Kabara – I think four, maybe five days the journey. Also the little boats, they are going one or two every day… but they take very long."

He winked again so obviously that it was clear that he was holding something back. Sure enough: "Perhaps you are wanting to fly?" he said. "The aeroplane goes tomorrow to Goundam. I am one of the officials of *Air France*."

I had not realised that there was an airstrip at Mopti, or indeed anywhere among the Niger towns. Jormel promised to take us there at noon the next day.

Mopti stands at the meeting of two rivers, where the Bani joins the main Niger stream, and in time of flood the town becomes almost an island, insecurely linked by roads to the mainland through the far-spread marshes. Sometimes even the Ivory Coast causeway is flooded, or smashed by fierce waves.

The front of our *campement* faced onto the town; behind lay the river. I awoke late and lay back comfortably, listening to the sounds of slopping water and boatmen's cries. There was also a strange, whistling murmur. I looked out of the window onto what seemed an African Venice. Wide-sailed houseboats were drifting with the current; sharp-prowed fishing vessels tacking into deeper water; low punts propelled by muscular men in big coolie-hats. A tiny canoe splashed by, overflowing with small black children. They sang shrilly as they paddled, and the boat rocked and bobbed.

James was busy with his travelling bag, trying to replace all the things he had taken out on arrival. As usual, these were scattered about the room. He had been up for over an hour, he said.

"What's that noise?" I asked. 'The whistling seemed to be louder.

"There's a tree of birds in front of the house."

"A what?" It was too early for jokes.

"A tree of birds. You'll like them. Come and see."

It was exactly as he had said. In the front courtyard stood a great umbrella-shaped tree, thickly matted with what looked like loofahs. The whistling was coming from this canopy of grass and hair, and now and then a lime-and-black head would emerge from a hole in one of the loofahs, peer around and vanish inside once more. There must have been more than five hundred weaver-birds' homes in the one tree, an almost unbroken mass of nests from the lowest boughs, about head height, to the topmost twigs.

We found our breakfast by the river. A girl was grilling tiny blue-gold fish over a smoking fire. They tasted of mud and charcoal. The roadway was thronged with townsfolk all heading in one direction, and many bearing on their heads great loads of merchandise tied round with string. We followed the crowd along the road, through the town, and soon the river lay ahead as well as to the left of us, and the street ended in a kind of dockyard.

Here the water was crowded with boats. Some were short and squat, canopied in stout canvas and seemingly built to survive the fiercest gale. Others were long and elegant, double-tiered and fragile, each flying the *tricolor*. Ranged on the bank were enormous mounds of foodstuffs, bales of cloth, calabash water-pots, ironware, all waiting to be shipped up- or down-river to the desert towns. And there were loads of dried grass for transport into the barren lands, where nothing green will grow except stunted thorn-bushes. We watched these varied cargoes being stowed aboard. Surprisingly, it was the long, handsome boats that bore the heavy loads, while the sturdy, workaday craft carried little. The aristocratic, flag-flying vessels were the cargo-ships that would journey to Kabara and beyond, while their clumsy neighbours were fit only to ply to and fro in the vicinity of Mopti.

From the riverside bustle we walked towards the town-centre, but never reached it, for we came upon an open-fronted shop displaying colourful Ghana cloth patterned in spear-throwing hunters. It was no surprise to learn that the owner came from Kumasi, and he and James argued and gossiped together in *Twi*, and he gave us a second breakfast, fish again but more tasty this time, and said that on our return visit to Mopti we must stay at his home. He and James became magnificently sentimental, and although I was now beginning to understand the language quite well, I felt an outsider to the aieees and ahaaahs and swapping of relations – but I remembered that we were to meet Jormel at the *campement* at noon, and it was time to head back there.

At the stroke of twelve he drove up in his smart blue van with *AIR FRANCE* splashed in white across the sides. He took us through the town and back along the embanked roadway over the marshes. At my request Jormel stopped on the causeway for a while, so that I could watch the birds in the swampland: white herons and tiny egrets stalking the shallows; bitterns skulking in the reed-beds; jacanas tiptoeing over the water-lily leaves on outsize spider-feet; piebald kingfishers diving for minute fish in the stretches of clear water.

"No wonder the frogs come out at night!" James observed.

All too soon we had to leave the Niger floods, and the road ran once more through the familiar sandy scrub. I suggested that if we came to Mopti again on our way home, we might make a fuller expedition to the marshes to see the birds. James nodded, now fully converted to ornithology.

Jormel broke in, brutally destroying the romantic picture.

"Yes," he said. "It is true. We are having many birds, but they are not good ones. You cannot eat them."

❖   ❖   ❖

The airport was wide and very flat, and there were two runways marked in white paint. At the edge of the strip stood a large airport-office-cum-restaurant.

"Nearly every day we are having aeroplanes," Jormel declared, "and so the airport is become big."

The building was spacious and cool. There was a long food-and-drinks counter, but nobody was waiting to be served. A volatile gang of elderly black waitresses rushed to and fro laying places at tables for diners who, it seemed, would never come. Down one side of the hangar was a long bench, where sat a score of African women in dazzling dress. They were the only people in the hall apart from the airport staff and ourselves, and they were sitting in expectant silence. Their beautiful cloths were draped in loose folds: star-patterned silks shot with blue, green and gold, and topped with rainbow-tinted head-shawls. Heavy gold ornaments glittered about their necks, and more gold hung from their ears and noses.

Jormel explained that these women had come to give a rousing welcome to a Minister from Equatorial Africa, who was to arrive by this very 'plane. Soon, he said, a guard-of-honour formed by the soldiers would arrive also. He smiled proudly.

Then the quiet was shattered. A shout that the aircraft was in sight caused the officials to rush outside, straight into the path of the guard-of-honour, which had just arrived. Yells and curses from both parties were drowned by a shrill wail, as the sparkling women broke into their song of welcome. They moved outside, still singing. Everyone else – James and I, Jormel and the waitresses – followed them, and stood at the edge of the airstrip to watch events. Quite a large crowd had by now arrived from the town.

The soldiers were a shambles, bumping into each other, talking, arguing. They all wore khaki-drill, French pattern, with very short shorts. The white officers in their de Gaulle-type forage-caps were armed with pistols; the African soldiers wore squashed red fezzes and knee-high leather gaiters, and carried on their right shoulders rifles which looked to be of great age. Their turnout was slipshod, unpolished, and few of them seemed to know what they were supposed to be doing. By the time the 'plane had landed, they had formed themselves into two roughly-straight lines near the airport-building, but there was still a great deal of jostling and audible argument. Out on the runway the officials stood, white-coated and stiff, awaiting the Minister.

Most of the passengers had climbed down and were on their way to the building, when a tall, gangling African unfolded himself through the 'plane's low exit and stepped out into the sun. He was a full head taller than any of his entourage, and stood very straight, which made him appear taller still. He was wearing a grey suit and soft hat, and beside him trotted a tiny fellow in identical dress, who seemed to be his secretary or personal assistant. At sight of the giant, a plump captain, who was commanding the guard-of-honour, came to life.

"*Présentez... ARMES!*"

The soldiers sluggishly obeyed. In the back rank a squabble broke out as one man accidentally struck his neighbour with an ancient gun. Red caps jerked up and down and the whole line wavered. The Minister took one look at the slapdash assembly, and walked straight past. As he reached the airport building he swept off his hat, but still he had to duck to get through the doorway. The wailing anthem of welcome grew loud.

Then it was our turn, and as we walked towards the little green-and-silver aircraft the soldiers, ignored and unwanted, began to move back to the two trucks that had brought them from Mopti.

At first it seemed as if we were to be the only passengers, and James was chattering in his bushman's voice about 'big men pass all, fit get plenty soldier for seeum go', as if the ceremony had been provided for us; but just before we were due to leave, seven other passengers arrived in a *camion* and sauntered over to the aircraft as if time meant nothing. Even then, there were many empty seats, and we were worried that perhaps the pilot would operate like a *tro-tro* driver, and would wait indefinitely until he had a full complement. Fortunately this was not the case, and we took off on time.

We flew low and had a wonderful view now of the undulating desert, now of the wide river. From the air the Niger looked gigantic, and sometimes there was nothing but water to the farthest distance, but green strips patterning the silver showed that much of the width was marshland, with water barely covering the reeds. In one stretch, which from our map we reckoned to be Lake Débo, we saw a mass of dark blobs that from their commotion and splashing were probably hippos: there must have been more than fifty together. Shortly afterwards, on a small island, we had a much clearer view of another hippopotamus herd, but only about a dozen beasts, this time.

The round windows of the aircraft were awkwardly placed, and for a good view James and I had to lean forward at an uncomfortable angle. In addition the small aeroplane bucked and rolled clumsily in the shifting air-currents above the river, and when we were at last clear of the Niger, flying over Niafounké in its waste of yellow sands, the bucking and rolling intensified. Only the excitingly clear view of the strange landscape and the knowledge that we could not now be far from Goundam kept back my feeling of apprehension.

But James loved every moment of the flight. It was the first time he had been in an aeroplane, and to him it was a blissful experience that would have to end far too soon. He found his seat-belt an encumbrance, for he would have preferred to rush up and down the 'plane looking through each of the windows in turn. Imprisoned as he was, he peered intently through our small porthole, not wishing to miss anything. He pointed excitedly as we flew above a 'floating village' made of several boats bound together to form one giant raft, and "Look there!" he exclaimed, as our shadow and roar disturbed a flock of ibises from a stretch of reeds, so that they took flight in a pink cloud. In his keyed-up, observant mood James was able to point out details that I would never have noticed for myself: a houseboat aground on a sandbank, with tiny figures trying to push-and-pull it off; six ostriches looking from above remarkably like dark thorn-bushes; a flock of sheep near a small, isolated flood-lake.

Then the aeroplane began to lose height still more, and we were landing at Goundam Airport.

"Ah – it is Mopti all over again!" said James in feigned confusion, so that the smartly-dressed businessman sitting in front of us half-turned in a moment of worry, before regaining his composure and smiling. Indeed it was like Mopti: the same smooth red runway; the same dazzling-white airport building; the ever-present *camion*, ready to take passengers into the town. But Goundam airstrip it was, and we climbed into the truck feeling that at last, perhaps, Timbuktu lay not too far ahead.

The clumsy vehicle ploughed slowly along the track between the sand-dunes, past a nomad settlement of low tents, rounded like felt basins, their shape perfectly suited to the contours of the sand. Soon, a great plateau rose from the desert ahead of us, and nestling at its foot was Goundam, yellow and white in the afternoon glare. As we drew nearer it became a walled town of square, flat-roofed buildings dominated by a white castle with the *tricolor* flying from its battlements. Goundam is some way from the Niger, but an arm of the river reaches the town, and we drove across a solid structure, part dam and part causeway over the flood-stream, where children were hauling in big purple-and-gold fish on crude fibre lines. There must have been a sudden glut of these yard-long monsters, as four or five were being pulled in even as we passed. In the shallows the old laundry-women stood, thumping sodden garments on sunbaked rocks and stretching them out to dry on the wooden supports of the causeway. They worked to a swaying rhythm, bare breasts flapping loosely.

We went on into the town itself, through dusty alleys between high mud walls, till we reached the centre, an open square acting as a general market. Here the driver parked his *camion,* and all the passengers got out, except for James and me. He asked us where we wanted to go, and we told him, to the *campement.* He spat very deliberately, snorted, and said that it was back across the river and quite near the airport… however, he agreed to take us there.

The *campement* was a long, low building standing alone, and from it there was a clear view across the water to Goundam. We were the only people staying there, apart from the old couple who looked after the place. The rooms were ill-furnished and the beds hard, but the extreme friendliness of the caretaker and his wife more than compensated. Soon, we had been shown all over the *campement,* had met a cat, some geese and a donkey foal, and had climbed a ladder onto the flat roof of the building, which gave us a panoramic view well beyond the airport in one direction and as far as the plateau in the other.

From the rooftop Goundam became a beautiful impressionist-painting. A half-mile stretch of water, bright blue, reflected the sky, with deep purple and mauve wind-shadows. This was broken by clumps of vivid green reeds rising from yellow sand-spits; then beyond the flood-lake a double line of brown and chestnut mud houses, their doors and windows picked out sharply by black and indigo shadows, reached right down to the water, with a patch of dark green thorn bushes beyond. Rising from this greenery the white battlements of the 'castle', Goundam Palace, gleamed bright as a lighthouse in the sunshine, and beyond again, sweeping far round to the left, the plateau, high and rising sheer, was dark purplish-grey, flecked with orange, sharp against the final azure of the sky.

"Fine-fine Africa…" gushed James, in unusually sentimental mood, then, reasserting himself, "let's try and get that boat."

It was a small rowing-boat, aground on a strip of sand only about fifty yards from the *campement* walls. We came down from the roof and waded out to it through water barely ankle-deep. Slabs of rock had been placed around the vessel to stop it floating away if the flood-level rose, and as an extra precaution it was tied to a thorn-bush growing out of the sand-spit. There were no oars. We went back.

Two men had left the boat a year ago, the caretaker told us. They had used it to row across to Goundam. Then, in the night, the oars had been carried away by the water.

"Americans, were they?"

"No. I think they were English. They said they wanted to see the birds in the water, but why, I cannot tell. You cannot eat those birds."

"The English are like that," said James.

We floated the boat. It leaked only a little, so with a clothes-line pole we punted out into the flood-lake, slowly, very clumsily, but without much splashing. Fifty yards out, the water was still very shallow and we kept running aground. Another hundred yards and it was only a little deeper. By now there were birds all around us in the water, and it was remarkable how little attention they paid to the boat. When we had walked by the *campement* they had flown away noisily, but now they returned, and allowed our craft to drift to within a few yards of them. We kept very low in the boat, and tried not to make any sudden movements. Most of the birds were small waders, brown-patterned stints and sandpipers, interspersed with larger, brighter plovers. They skittered in the shallowest patches, weaving in and out of the reed-stems on legs slim as pencil leads, tracing swift arabesques in the water, their thin beaks probing ceaselessly. With them were several Black-winged Stilts, with snowy chests and jet backs. They strode gracefully on astonishing telescopic legs, as if in a slow-motion film. We managed to drift the boat towards them, and they seemed to regard us as a slightly mobile but unobtrusive natural feature of the flood-lake. James was by now thoroughly enjoying this stalking game, and sat in tensed silence as the birds strode elegantly around us. Then suddenly the whole flock, stilts, sandpipers, plovers and all, whirred up from the water and dispersed rapidly towards Goundam.

"Allo! Allo! Allo!"

From the roof of the *campement,* the caretaker and his wife waved happily.

We returned to the lake in the darkness. It was a still night. The stars were sharp in the sky and equally sharp in the water, where they vied in brilliance with the reflected lights of Goundam. We disturbed a heron, which jerked up suddenly and winged away without a sound. Near the water, strange pale shapes were darting between the reed-

210

clumps. They came nearer, goblin-figures flitting across the sand in a series of effortless glides.

"Bush-mice," James whispered. "The jumping kind."

When one paused on a little hillock, very close, I had my first real view of a jerboah. Most of all I noticed its bat-ears and huge eyes, and the springiness with which it bounced on its long hind-legs.

There must have been hundreds of the jumping mice, for in the morning their small footprints were all around the *campement* in the sand. We found a dead one, too: it was larger than an ordinary mouse, with a thin puckish face and those enormous ears; its fur was pale yellow, and the long tail was like a miniature ostrich-plume.

Later in the morning we walked into Goundam to see if we could find transport to take us the remaining way to Timbuktu. At one big store, which seemed to be the town's transport-office as well as the *Air France* headquarters, I tried out my French on a beautiful olive-skinned girl who was sitting behind a counter, flipping through a Paris brochure. She flashed me a dazzling smile, and answered in English.

James stopped laughing when it transpired that no truck was likely to visit Timbuktu in the immediate future, nor was any transport going to Diré, the nearest riverside town. Indeed, the number of vehicles of any kind in Goundam – she fluttered her eyelashes pityingly – could be counted on the fingers of one hand. We were frantically discussing the possibilities of assistance from the French Army, going by camel, or even walking, when the door opened abruptly and in came the Minister we had seen at Mopti Airport... He had flown from there, and had come to the office to make arrangements for another flight to Gau, further down the river, in two days' time. From his rapid conversation with the girl, I gathered that he was leaving immediately on a brief visit to Timbuktu. She explained our predicament.

"Messieurs," said the Minister, "I am happy to convey you to Tombouctou. I am leaving at once, if you wish to come."

A tall servant took our cases and we followed him to where a dusty but almost-new jeep was parked. He deposited our luggage at the back, beside a couple of shot-guns and several coils of rope. We found it surprising to find such a vehicle in Goundam, but the Minister said there were really far more in the Niger towns than one might expect.

They were the only vehicles that could cross the sands. Except camels, of course. We smiled dutifully. He had been lent this jeep by a friend here in Goundam, to use during his stay in the town.

James and I were directed into the front, while the Minister and his secretary sat behind us on seats covered in white linen embroidered with blue camels. The servant took the wheel.

The presence of such an important visitor had already attracted a crowd, and we drove through streets where excited families shouted and waved as we passed. When James and I had entered the office, half an hour earlier, these same streets had been almost empty. Somehow, word had gone round that a Big Man was in Goundam.

Shortly after we left the town, the roadway, which had never been very distinct, almost disappeared into a wilderness of sand and scrub. A line of telegraph-poles ran unbroken into the distance, marking what was presumably a proper road, although most of it was now deep-buried in sand. Here the driver's skill really began to be needed, for he had to zigzag between drifts and follow an invisible trail over shifting ridges and through a tangle of thorn-bushes, a route that could be learnt only by experience. His name was Salifu, and apparently he was not the Minister's servant, but a local man who had journeyed this way often, for several years. He was tall and thin, almost as tall as the Minister, with a smile that showed very white teeth, and he was wearing what resembled an indigo track-suit, with baggy trousers, crimson socks and white gym-shoes. He wore this attire with a composure that made it seem perfectly usual.

It was an eerie sensation, pursuing an invisible road through the bush. There were occasional shrubs and bent trees, grey and withered, and clumps of hardy reeds and leathery small plants stood out above the sand, but few landmarks showed among the wind-made furrows and curving dunes. Yet Salifu never hesitated, and followed his erratic course at astonishing speed.

We passed a chain of lakes, offshoots of the Niger, where flocks of sheep and goats grazed in the less barren land around the water. Big pie-bald ground-squirrels hopped beside our path, and often scores of guinea-fowl, grey-freckled with comic red helmets, would scatter in alarm as our jeep appeared at the top of a sandy ridge and hurried down towards them.

The Minister muttered to his secretary each time he saw a flock of these birds. At last he signalled to Salifu to stop, and I saw that he was holding one of the shot-guns. The driver pulled up on a level stretch, from where we could see several dozen guinea-fowl that had been lying in the shade of some thorn-bushes. Now they began to move off in a dense throng, jostling and bumping. They were about forty yards away. The Minister took aim and fired once. Birds scattered in cackling disorder, and when the smoke had cleared several heaps of grey feathers lay on the sand.

"Salifu – " said the Minister, pointing.

The driver strode over to the spot, and returned with seven dead guinea-fowl. The Minister smiled, but said nothing more, and replaced his gun at the back of the jeep. Salifu threw in the birds. Then we set off once more over the sand.

So we continued in state, James and I sitting importantly in front, the Minister and his diminutive companion nodding behind us. We had passed no villages, but now turbaned tribesmen began to ride by on great loose-limbed camels. The way became smoother, and soon we joined a clear track indicated by a white-arrowed signboard proclaiming the one word *TOMBOUCTOU.*

We stayed two days in Timbuktu. The euphoria of our having arrived there soon faded, for it seemed a disappointingly desolate place. The population of more than 100,000 in the 16th Century, when Timbuktu was a great city, has now shrunk to a few thousand, mainly because the desert has changed the course of the Niger. The mighty river was once the reason for the town's prosperity and growth, where the camel caravans crossing the Sahara reached water at last, but over the centuries the Niger has moved to the south. The distance is increasing year by year, for when we were there in 1958 Kabara, the 'port', was seven miles from Timbuktu while now, apparently, it is more like ten. The loss of the river has left a largely silent, yellow-grey town of dust and sand.

Timbuktu seems to live in and on the past. The human population is small, and camels, brought in by the Tuareg nomads, dominate the place. When we were there, the empty streets were funereal, but no one could fail to admire some of the beautiful centuries-old buildings, in particular the three great mosques. The oldest and most famous of these is the Djinquereber, with its massive mud walls bristling with wooden

Yeji Ferry

Bolgatanga, Northern Territories

Haute Volta, family transport

Ouagadougou

Mopti, our first visit

Goundam, our boat

Goundam

Salifu with guinea-fowl

217

'spines', and the Sidi Yahiya is almost as impressive; but we admired the Sankore most of all. It is built in a similar style, yet, situated as it is on the northern, 'desert' edge of the town, it blends even more perfectly in tone and structure with the encroaching sands. We discovered that the Sankore Mosque was the 'newest' of the three, dating back 'only' to the mid 15th Century! Five hundred years ago it was the site of a huge university, which was then a beacon of Muslim learning. The University is long gone, but traces of its ancient scholarship remain in the large number of Arabic manuscripts that are still present in the town. When we visited Timbuktu there was no central store-place, and we heard that these books were kept in private dwellings. After making careful and tactful requests we were allowed to view and even handle a few of the historic manuscripts, in a pleasant but run-down home in a dark, narrow alleyway. The house was clearly very old, with a beautifully carved and decorated doorway, and the dozen or so books we saw were stacked higgledy-piggledy on a dusty shelf. Most of the volumes were large, with loose pages and cracked, detached leather covers, yet in the dry heat the writing was still clear, and in one of them we examined some beautiful illumination. We felt privileged to see the books, but it seemed incredible that such priceless works should be left almost unprotected. It has been a relief to learn, recently, that not only have many now been removed to safety in Timbuktu's new museum but also that those still kept in private libraries are being copied onto microfilm.

Out of curiosity we searched for the homes of Gordon Laing, Rene Caillié and Heinrich Barth, the 19th Century explorers who helped make Timbuktu known in Europe. We were shown the houses, which are quite close together and all mud-built. They were dilapidated, like much of the town, and uninhabited, and it was disappointing to find that no one seemed very interested in their existence, although in the case of Caillié and Laing commemorative plaques showed us we had found the right buildings. We were not allowed in.

We visited the small post office, where we were permitted to frank our own letters, to ensure that they arrived home with the famous postmark clearly visible. The clerk there said I was the first white man 'not a soldier' he had seen for several months, and he was even more surprised by James, for Africans from the Coast rarely came to Timbuktu. We explained that we were indeed soldiers, but on leave. He said he would

218

put us in touch with some French *soldats*. We thanked him, but were unsure what we were letting ourselves in for.

The first night we stayed at the *Campement*, which I believe has since become a hotel. Its facilities were basic: we slept on a sort of landing, where the heat was exhausting but there were no mosquitoes. We obtained good food cheaply from vendors by the roadside, who were cooking chicken and guinea-fowl in large portable ovens. Next morning the post-office clerk introduced us to the Commandant at the ancient Fort Bonnier, who showed us round the garrison and to our surprise invited us to stay our second night there. We never discovered the status of the 'soldiers' he was commanding. At first we thought they must be a detachment of the Foreign Legion, but then concluded they were an outpost of the French Army, presumably stationed there initially to defend French interests along a vulnerable stretch of the Niger. They were so hospitable, and spent so much time asking us about the military in Accra that it seemed embarrassing to ask them who they were! They certainly lived far more comfortably than most of Timbuktu's inhabitants, and our room at the fort was a revelation, with mosquito-nets over the beds, and a bathroom with running water. We were even presented with a jug of extremely good red wine.

When we told the Commandant our plans for the return trip, he suggested we should go at least some of the way by boat from Kabara, so we enquired in Timbuktu about river-transport, but no one could help us with any sort of timetable. Our post-office friend said that when we reached Kabara we would find out whether there was a boat running – or not! Our first problem, in any case, was how to get to the Niger, and it was discouraging to find that there would be no trucks visiting the port for the next two days. We seriously contemplated travelling there by camel, and even had a short 'test run' through the streets of Timbuktu. Then the Commandant learnt of our predicament and himself laid on a truck for us, with uniformed driver and *tricolor* flying.

It was mid-morning when we reached Kabara which, after Timbuktu, seemed like paradise. The village closely resembled a diminutive Mopti, with its harbour jam-packed with colourful house-boats and *pirogues*, small canoe-like craft made from wooden slats 'sewn' together with reeds. On the bank were piles of huge greyish-white salt-slabs, which had come via Timbuktu from the mines of Taodenni, far out in the Sahara, carried there on camel-back. Farther along, the river-bank was brightened by the usual laundry area, with women singing rhythmically as they sloshed their washing in the shallows, beating it on smooth stones in mid-stream before laying it on great boulders to dry. Other women were weaving baskets from reeds, working speedily and singing all the time, while close by, men were also chanting rhythmically as they hauled in cat-fish from the river, beating them to death on the stones and immediately tossing them into a kind of giant barbecue.

In the sand-dunes around Kabara, several nomad families had made camp. They were living in tiny rounded 'tents', smaller and neater than the ones we had seen earlier at Goundam, some made of canvas and others of woven reeds, none tall enough for an adult to stand upright, although multitudes of small children were running in and out. These extremely poor people were in strong contrast to the groups of Tuareg tribesmen, swaggering in fine robes, who had brought the salt-slabs from the desert, and who always seemed either to be riding on camels or to have just alighted from them. Near the nomad habitations small buff-coloured birds raced to and fro over the sand, seemingly catching flies. A closer look showed them to be Cream-coloured Coursers, and I remember thinking that back in England the sight of just one of these vagrants would have brought every bird-watcher, for miles around, helter-skelter to see it. When I mentioned this to James, his comment, delivered uncannily in the accents of our Goundam host, was "Zese is not good birds. Zey is not for eating."

I had been told that big passenger boats regularly called in at Kabara en route between Gau and Mopti – but now we learnt that this only happened from August to November, when the water was at its highest. James said he didn't think we could afford to wait six months, since we had only a week in which to get back to Accra... Perhaps if we could travel on a smaller boat to somewhere near Goundam... and from there "We fly again!" declared my friend, hopefully.

We asked the owners of several *pinasses* if they could help us reach Goundam. These boats were medium-sized craft, brightly-painted, mostly with proper seats and some sort of roof. The vessels looked quite comfortable, but none could take us. Then a charming family on a houseboat asked if we would like to come with them. They were leaving that afternoon for Mopti, a journey which would take them many days, but perhaps we would like to travel as far as Diré? From there to Goundam was only a little way. "And from there we fly!" said James once again. The only problem, our new friends said, was that they would be taking fifty or more salt-slabs on board, so it would not be comfortable. We accepted with alacrity, nonetheless.

Their houseboat was a long, remarkably graceful vessel, with an arched roof of plaited reeds. The main deck was divided into five sections by solid wooden struts. By the time James and I went on board in mid afternoon, two of these 'compartments', one at each end, had been filled with the salt-slabs, stacked lengthwise like office-files in a drawer. The family of four lived in the three middle sections of this surprisingly sturdy craft, and were obviously prosperous people, for they told us they owned a house in Mopti and another in Gau, bought from the valuable traffic in salt-slabs. The husband and wife were wonderfully hospitable, although we could communicate only slowly, for their French was even worse than mine. James could not follow their tribal language, and made little headway with Fanti or Twi, although they did understand some of his barrack-Hausa. The two delightful children chattered incessantly, seemingly unworried that we understood little of what they were saying. The girl, aged about eight, was serious-minded and determined that we should be well looked-after, which meant that we were always given the first offerings of food and drink. She had an attractive smile and would be beautiful; the boy, rather younger, was mischievous and funny.

The amount of possessions this family managed to stow neatly on board was impressive. The centrepiece of the living-quarters was a large stove, around which were set several benches, together with some piles of bedding. There were also two cupboards, in one of which they kept innumerable calabashes, used for serving food and drink, and an impressive display of bottled beer. The other was a food-store, with dried pulse and rice, yams and other fresh vegetables, spices and a huge calabash bowl of diced goat's meat. In addition there were large boxes with lids, which contained family possessions but also doubled as extra seats. This was clearly a working-vessel, but our conditions on board were far more luxurious than most of the *pinasses* could offer. There

Timbuktu

The Sankore Mosque

Timbuktu, 'Book Street'

Kabara harbour, with salt-slabs

Kabara, nomad homes

Kabara silhouette

Pirogues

James and I at Kabara

was even radio music!

That night James and I slept little, although there was plenty of floor-space. After a wonderful meal of goat-stew, washed down with a Niger-version of palm wine, we sat and watched the river as the boat headed west, the engine purring softly. It was a magical journey. As it grew dark, flights of wildfowl drifted past in skeins and splashed down around us; then the stars came out and shone with a brilliance one sees only in the desert. From some recess on board the family produced a big paraffin-lamp, which they lit and hung in the prow of the boat. There it served to illuminate the area under the canopy but also to attract an array of flies, midges, moths and beetles – and to keep them and the mosquitoes away from the passengers. Many insects from this winged cascade landed on the water nearby, and we could see the ripples and hear the slurping sound as big fish gathered them in. Our new friends did not waste the opportunity: they threw out lines and quickly made several impressive captures – in form and colour like a kind of gigantic roach – which became our breakfast. At one stage there was loud splashing in midstream, and big shapes were visible at a distance, black against the silvery water. Our hosts told us they were hippos, but that they would not harm us. Fortunately I did not then realise just how dangerous those giant animals can be.

James and I must have drifted off to sleep, eventually, because we were woken suddenly about three a.m. by shouts from the river nearby. Apparently another houseboat was shipping water and was in danger of sinking. Our family reacted swiftly, changing course so that we drew alongside, whereupon with ropes made of plaited reeds the two boats were tied securely together. It was not easy to follow what was said, but the gist seemed to be that if we could tow the stricken vessel to the nearest riverside village, they could repair the damage there. By first light we had reached a habitation of half a dozen huts, where what was probably the entire population turned out to help in the rescue. The houseboat was hauled into a small creek, then, to loud goodbyes and thankyous from the bank, we moved out into the river again and continued on our way.

We hugged the north bank, chugging slowly upstream, past massive reed-beds where herons and egrets were fishing, and giant sand-banks on which crocodiles basked. Then we were moving into desert, with

226

sand stretching far into the distance. The Niger here was so wide that the southern bank was only just visible. Towards noon we reached Diré, where there was a small harbour and a landing-stage.

As so often on our journey, our hosts would accept no payment. We could not even thank them properly. The best we could manage was to give them one of our Frontier Force cap-badges and a few palm-tree buttons, which seemed to please all the family. Then they headed off towards Mopti with their salt-slabs and our gratitude, and we made our way into the little town.

❖   ❖   ❖

Travel-guides either seem to ignore Diré utterly or to disparage it, but we found it an attractive place. Although so near to the Niger, it was a real desert town, set in miles of empty sand, but far more lively than Timbuktu. We decided to have some food before inquiring about vehicles leaving for Goundam, and in a chaotic and dirty chop-bar near the market we ate a superb meal, sitting on a rickety bench beside a bar crawling with flies and cockroaches. We were served a delicious curry, washed down with iced lager from a portable kerosene refrigerator. It was a deservedly popular chop-bar, filled with smiling patrons, most of whom took their bowls of food outside and sat cross-legged on the sand to eat it.

"The dirtiest chop-bars really are the best!" said James.

Replete and satisfied we walked round Diré, enjoying the bustling market. It was interesting to see mounds of peppers and even tomatoes and pineapples, as well as the expected yams and cassava, all brought by boat to this desert township. We had just begun to enquire about transport to Goundam when our military connections and the good luck that seemed to follow us everywhere took yet another turn. At the Lorry Station we met a charming, elderly man, who asked in excellent English if we would like to visit the Residence. He proved to be the steward of Diré's Commandant. The invitation was surprising, he knew, but he was looking after this very big house, much of which was empty, and they were always happy to see visitors, particularly those who had come from far. From listening to us he had realised we were from Ghana, and wondered if we would like to stay the night. This seemed too good to be true, but we were worried about the delay in reaching Goundam. He said that was not a problem, either. The Commandant himself was 'on tour' in Gau, but he was due to return by air to Goundam early next morning, and if we wished, we could travel to the town in the microbus that was going to collect him. From there an efficient 'bus service' would take us on to Mopti very swiftly. James was disappointed that we should not be travelling by air again, but cheered up considerably when he learnt that the bus would get us to Mopti long before the next flight, which was not for two days.

The Residence was massive, open and cool, and the steward's hospitality marvellous. We had comfortable beds on a veranda, with a wash-room nearby, and cool drinks were brought to us whenever we wished. The old man and his wife seemed glad of our company. On a lower balcony lived the Commandant's pet cheetah! It reclined on a bed, purring like a cat when the Steward stroked it. At first we thought it was completely free, and were not keen to go close, but the animal was in fact tethered by a rope. Apparently the Commandant had been accustomed to take the cheetah for daily walks in Diré, like a dog on a lead, until it had playfully swiped at an old woman, removing half her arm... Now he was planning to release his pet far in the Sahel, but needed to know for sure that there were other cheetahs in the chosen locality.

It was not his only unusual pet. He also owned a beautiful Crowned Crane, which lived in the courtyard, where it was looked after by a very small boy. The Steward disliked this bird intensely, for it often tried to attack its reflection in his shiny black shoes...

After Diré fatigue set in. We had been treated with astonishing kindness and hospitality throughout our trip, had eaten well and for much of the journey had slept in comfort. Physically we were in good shape, but mentally we were exhausted. We would have liked to stay in the desert towns, unhurried and unworried, but always there was the necessity of reporting back to Accra in a week's time. We found this urgency particularly saddening at Goundam, when we returned to the *campement* at the edge of the marshes, for the caretaker and his wife greeted us like old friends. We stayed in the same room, revisited the same chop-bar, took the boat out on the water again, and later watched

228

the jumping mice in the moonlight. Despite our worries about the return trip, the *campement* was already beginning to feel like home. We would have loved to stay at least another night there and 'recharge batteries' but a *camion* was indeed leaving for Mopti in the morning and we could not afford to waste the opportunity.

We were ready early, with time to wander round Goundam, and decided to take a closer look at the 'Palace', which was such a fine land-mark for the town. We had reached the dazzlingly white walls and were following a path around them to see if there was a way in, when we came across a party of about a dozen Tuareg tribesmen in dashing white robes, like extras from a film of *Beau Geste*. They were lounging in the shade of some trees right by the Palace wall, while an entourage of slaves saw to the watering of their camels at a well twenty yards away. The warriors seemed to be 'comparing swords', discussing the significance of the patterns etched on their dazzling blades. James was keen to examine one of these beautiful weapons, and approached the nearest Tuareg, signalling his request. He made the mistake, however, of touching the elaborately decorated scabbard as he asked.

The effect was frightening. The man stepped back as if stung, hand on hilt and glowering, and I had visions of my friend being beheaded before my eyes. My frantic French made no impression on the angry tribesman, but astonishingly, one of the Tuareg could speak English! "I see American films…" was his surprising explanation.

He explained that it was a mortal crime to touch a blade without fol-lowing the correct etiquette. We apologised so successfully that several of the desert warriors, including the offended party, now became keen to show us their beautifully engraved weapons, and what had begun badly ended with their offering us refreshment of dates and sweet tea. Throughout this whole episode James had kept remarkably calm. He was not even sweating.

"But weren't you scared?" I asked.

"Terrified!"

The *camion* that took us to Mopti was the most comfortable we had travelled in thus far. It carried just seven passengers, when it could have taken forty, and as a result we were able to sit where we wished, so chose seats near an open side of the vehicle. Occasionally we were choked with red dust, but for the most part it was breezy and cool. There was also a huge pile of Fulani camel-hair blankets at the back, for sale in Mopti, and mid-way through our journey James and I settled down on this cosy heap and slept for several hours. Once again it was dark when we reached Mopti, and again we were received at the *campement* as if arriving at such unsocial hours was perfectly normal. Better still, our driver had told us that he would be driving his *camion* to Ouagadugu the following evening, which was a huge boost to our confidence – and would also allow us to explore Mopti thoroughly. Suddenly, we felt far less tired and worried.

❖   ❖   ❖

So, after settling our accommodation with Monsieur Jormel, we went out to see Mopti by night. We had had no time to examine the place properly on our first brief visit, but now we found ourselves in a wonderfully lively and unrestricted town, an exciting link between the desert to the north, and Haute Volta and Ghana to the south. Looking back from today's less trusting society it seems remarkable that James and I could wander quite as we did then, with total acceptance, talking to a multiplicity of races and tribes, and watching a range of free entertainment that included juggling and fire-eating, and sophisticated mime and dumb-show. It was an exhilarating time. We walked for about a mile beside the Bani river, and in that space we counted seven chop-bars, most of them thriving and exuberant, with customers of both sexes ranging in age from white-haired octogenarians to small children of not more than five or six.

At several of these chop-bars we sampled the food. We tried spiced cat-fish, much tastier than the ones we had eaten on our previous visit, delicious guinea-fowl kebabs with peppers and sweet potato, and a sort of warm mousse, pink and delicious, made of a fruit that was new to both of us. Mopti seemed to have a very tolerant attitude to liquor, and with such a cosmopolitan population everything seemed available there beside the river. A group of smartly-dressed Frenchmen, both black and white, were sitting in comfort on the wide veranda of a small but sophisticated wine-bar, and there were several stalls where beer and a form of palm wine were the staple. Especially popular was a ramshackle lean-to where all-male customers in tattered garments were drinking what appeared to be locally-distilled spirits from very small cups, which were being filled from a large petrol drum. Prudence dictated that we avoid the stuff, but curiosity won, and we shared a tiny cup. The liquid was almost tasteless, but with a powerful kick. "French *akpeteshie*," James called it.

There was a peculiar innocence about this waterside society. We saw no boorishness or loud behaviour, and no hint of drunkenness. It was noticeable that although there were innumerable children present, some of them very young, none were in the bars. I wondered about the Muslim population in this riverside promenade, and whether their abstemiousness was put severely to the test. At one chop-bar James and I became (for the umpteenth time) the magnet for would-be English speakers, of whom we asked this very question.

"I am myself Muslim," said one young Arab with a strong American accent. "I do not drink only water! Our faith says we should take no beer or wine, but truly here people are not troubled if sometimes we do."

We encountered *boules* (or *petanque*) for the first time, and were intrigued enough by the spectacle and the simplicity of the rules to try it for ourselves, although only briefly, as we did not wish to ruin the game we had been invited to join. We returned to the *campement* about 2 a.m., exhilarated and considerably refreshed. Sure enough, some of the residents, including M. Jormel, were still up, drinking in the bar.

Next morning we walked beside the same stretch of the Bani, and to our surprise found that many of the stalls we had seen the night before were now completely empty, while others had simply vanished, reduced to neat and remarkably small piles of timber stacked against trees, ready to be resurrected in the evening. The riverside path was thronged with working-people, men and women, striding into town, many carrying gigantic loads on their heads, and the water was crowded with vessels of all shapes and sizes, but very few cars or trucks passed us on the road.

While the old part of Mopti was one of the most lively and colourful places I have seen anywhere in the world, the 'new town' was less attractive, with brick-built houses and shops little different from those in Ouagadougou – or Accra. We visited the post office and again were allowed to stamp our own passports. This was becoming something of an obsession, for there was absolutely no need for the documentation, except to prove to our friends back in Accra that we had been to these places.

We returned to the marshes for an hour or two and again marvelled at the flowers and bird-life. This time, in addition to countless herons and egrets, we saw harriers gliding over the reed-beds, and pelicans in the open water, and besides the big pied kingfishers we had seen before, now there were also several of a smaller species, resembling our European birds, but of an even more dazzling electric blue. I learnt later that these beautiful birds, which were acrobatically catching dragonflies, were Malachite Kingfishers. Wide stretches of this shallow lagoon were covered in water lilies, white, yellow and pale mauve, and we watched the jacanas striding across the big leaves without causing a ripple. Several had small, dark fluffy chicks with them, with enormous feet, totally out of proportion, which enabled them to scamper over the water plants as if on dry land.

We travelled to Ouagadougou overnight. The *camion* carried twelve passengers this time, but still seemed almost empty. The pile of Fulani blankets had been exchanged for an even bigger heap of camel-skins, which James and I and two other passengers commandeered to sleep on and in. We were glad of the warmth, even more than the comfort, for the temperature dropped rapidly and it became very cold.

This part of the journey, which had taken us two full days as we travelled North, we now covered in a single night. No doubt the *camion* stopped several times to collect water, and perhaps to refuel, but we did not wake. Apparently there was also quite a long halt at Ouahigouya, but as we knew that our Education Officer friend was still on tour we had no reason to be woken up for that stop. We emerged from our 'hibernation' at sunrise to find that we were already trundling through the dusty outskirts of Ouagadougou.

We spent a lazy day in the town, and enjoyed a different kind of informality from that of Mopti. 1950s Ouagadougou was a town of bicycles, and the first in West Africa to have special 'cycle-lanes'. The lack of cars was immediately apparent and made for a leisurely way of life, and the bustling market in the centre of town gave a feeling of involvement, for all roads seemed to lead to the *Grand Marché*. We had been intrigued by this market on our first visit, and were pleased to have more time to see it properly. Since 1958, apparently, a new *marché* has been constructed on an even bigger scale: suffice to say that we found the old one a most impressive affair, and spent several hours simply walking from stall to stall, viewing the incredible range of goods for sale. Had we not been committed to several days' more travelling, I am sure we should have purchased many things, for clothes, ornaments, paintings, carvings, pottery and especially wall-masks, all of fine quality, were in profusion – and astonishingly cheap. The food displays were impressive, too, and this time we avoided the main meat-hall. It was a shock therefore, to find, alongside the palm wine section, a counter specialising in monkey flesh, with the severed heads placed in a row at the back to ensure that nobody could fail to recognise what kind of meat was on display. Equally fascinating were stalls which offered goods with magical properties. We had seen many such *juju* shows at village markets in Ghana, but the stalls in Ouagadugu were on an altogether vaster scale, with vials of evil-looking liquid, sacks of powdered bones, skulls, grotesque fetish-dolls, and shrivelled parts of countless animals, birds and reptiles.

We played *boules* twice more in Ouagadougou, once by daylight, and once at night, and found it a satisfying game. Its major advantage for an arid landscape seemed to be the lack of facilities needed, for any patch of dust or sand was suitable. In the lorry-park, where we played, there were three games taking place at the same time. One of the 'stars' was the driver who had brought us from Mopti.

After a night in Ouagadougou we headed south in yet another *camion*. When we stopped at Po, our last halt on the Haute Volta side of the border, we met up with Chris, a friend from the Signals Brigade at Giffard Camp, who had set off three days after us, and was travelling alone. His money was running out, and he was thinking of trying to reach Ouagadougou before heading home.

"You planned better than I did," he said, "but I've got to French Territory, anyway, and maintenant je suis knackered."

We had little time to share experiences before our truck set off for

Navrongo. We did discover, however, that the reason for Chris's money-shortage was that he had spent three nights at an expensive hotel in Kumasi, which he had enjoyed greatly. He had also stayed overnight at Tamale with the First Battalion.

"They are expecting you two," he said. "They know you are heading north. Peter and Tom will be disappointed if you don't call in on your way back, and apparently there are lots of Takoradi people hoping to see James."

After leaving Po, we crossed the border to Paga, where we had so narrowly escaped a long delay on our way north. This time there was no hold-up at all, and we had time to visit the pools of the 'sacred crocodiles'. Back in Accra, our friends from the Northern Territories had told us that this was a spectacle we must not miss, but James and I both felt that the sight of these reptiles being tormented by visitors, before devouring whole live chickens thrown to them, was thoroughly unedifying. We were glad to resume our journey to Navrongo.

We spent a pleasant but uneventful night in the town, staying at a spotlessly clean rest-house that seemed to be some sort of Catholic foundation, before going on to Bolgatanga next morning. There we changed transport, and continued to Tamale by government bus, arriving in mid-afternoon. This time we did stop the night with the First Battalion. It was an enjoyable visit altogether, for both of us. Within moments of our arrival, James was surrounded by old school-friends from Takoradi, who whisked him away, all chattering loudly, to stay with them in the barracks. I was given a spare room at the Junior Officers' Quarters, and Tom and Peter, who had been with me at Eaton Hall, then took me to the Mess, where they managed to book me in for an evening meal. They also lent me some clean clothes! The usual luck cut in, for it transpired that Tom would be going to Kumasi next day, to take some maps to the Infantry Training School there. He offered us a lift.

He drove us to Kumasi in a smart land rover, and James and I suddenly realised that, at last, we could sit back and stop worrying about our next destination. On the way, Tom quizzed us about our trip, and we found ourselves carried away by the excitement of the past fortnight.

"Pete and I have our leave coming up soon," he said, when he could get a word in. "We'd also been thinking seriously about trying to get to Timbuktu, and listening to you two has certainly convinced *me*!"

"We've been incredibly lucky the whole way..." I started to say, but then we both pointed out that it was less due to luck than the fact that we were 'black and white'.

We had to explain this very carefully, and I am not sure that Tom was convinced.

We reached Kumasi by late afternoon, where we said goodbye to our friend and wished him luck with his own journey north. And since we had spent so little on our own round trip, we decided to spend a night in a hotel. The luxury was wasted on us, however. The room was too hot – and the beds too soft! The food looked good but tasted insipid.

The following morning we boarded a government-transport bus to Accra. We slept much of the way. The driver dropped us at the Ambassador Hotel, from where we telephoned the guard room at the barracks. Jeremy was Orderly Officer, and came in the duty land rover to collect us.

He could tell from our grins that we had had a successful trip.

"I presume you got there?" We nodded.

In the log-book Jeremy recorded that the duty truck had made a journey to the Ambassador Hotel 'to rescue explorers returning from Timbuktu...'

Our houseboat

Diré

Diré, the
commandant's crane

... and his cheetah!

Diré, Chop-bar fine pass-all

237

Goundam again, James at the Campement

Mopti, again, beside the River Bani

Mopti, trade and fishing vessels

Mopti, the Great Mosque

Chapter Nine

FAREWELL

The weeks after our Timbuktu trip were very satisfying. James and I felt a real sense of achievement, and I was thrilled to find that the photos I had taken had turned out well, so that people could see where we had been and what we had done. Everyone seemed pleased for us, and in addition to Colonel Harding and Major Ives, several senior officers whom I only knew slightly came up and offered congratulations, while James reckoned that he didn't have to pay for a drink for weeks.

There was a sudden rush of junior officers planning their own expeditions to the Far North... A postcard came from Tom and Pete, who had reached the Niger but had got no further – "You were spot-on about Mopti! It was such a fantastic place that we spent three days there and didn't feel bad about not getting to Timbuktu."

This idyllic time could not last, however, for I soon had to begin the sad count-down to leaving Ghana. Without doubt, if I had not already had my university place settled, and if I could have stayed with the West African Frontier Force, I would have done so, for I felt greatly at home in the Ghanaian army. The country's prospects seemed good, also, with Nkrumah just the charismatic leader the nation needed.

I realise now that I and most of my young English colleagues were naïve in our belief that the new state was perfect. Only Rob, budding politician and historian, kept saying "It's not as lovely in the garden as you think." The African officers were more aware than we were of unrest simmering. Emmanuel had often talked of corruption in government in a way that we made too little effort to understand. Now he had gone to England, on a mortar course, but Albert, who was still with us, several times spoke with a similar voice, arguing that the Nkrumah government "did not seem to understand the military." Some of the European senior officers also read the signs, and Douglas Ives said that, much as he liked the Battalion and his life in Accra, he was actually looking forward to his own departure in six month's time. His political antennae told him the government 'smelt wrong', and he foresaw, correctly, that the steady 'Africanisation' of the military, expected and necessary as it was currently, would soon accelerate out of control.

Perhaps we subalterns should have been more aware in our assessment of Nkrumah. The signs had been clear enough – indeed I remember an occasion much earlier when the Prime Minister had left on a visit to England, and the Police and the Army had been alerted, because an anti-Nkrumah crowd had gathered in Accra and it was deemed necessary to put down any sign of insurrection before it really started. I recall our driving into Accra in a convoy, and the unfurling of banners saying *DISPERSE OR WE FIRE,* much as in our Internal Security practices, and Colonel Harding even issuing live ammunition – but the crowd did disperse very quickly when the banners appeared, and one stone through a truck window was the sum of the damage. The Army was popular: the disquiet was with Government. Hindsight says we should have heeded the warning signs – and in fact this event, with Nkrumah out of the country, was remarkably similar to how he was to be ousted eight years later – but at the time it was 'an incident', frightening for an hour or so, but nothing to worry about, long term.

Most of my close African friends, James, BB, William Stevens and the rest, were not political people, and even the two Josephs, Halm and Mensah, who certainly were, told me later that their own perspective had been too narrow for them to see what was going on.

The time came for me to hand over my dual posts of Assistant Adjutant and Intelligence Officer. I had learnt a great deal while working for Douglas Ives, had been proud of both jobs, and had come to value my position in the Battalion. I was delighted, therefore, that my successor was to be – Albert Ocran! He was an obvious choice, much better qualified than me, in fact, and got on well with both the Adjutant and Colonel Harding.

Without being asked, the Colonel wrote me an over-complimentary testimonial, "to help in your job-hunting back in England, if you do feel you must leave the army and become an academic."

Goodbyes were difficult and sad, as in many cases I thought I should never see most of my African friends again. Joseph Halm and James Ankumah were shortly to visit London, however, on courses at the military School of Music at Kneller Hall, and Albert was also going to England on yet another course, so I had hopes of seeing them again soon. Many of the others gave me photos of their families, which I still treasure, and we all promised to write. My lasting regret is that I was unable to say goodbye to Emmanuel Kotoka, for he was in England already, and returned to Ghana just as I left. I never saw him again.

The dreamtime ended for me in February 1958. Originally I had planned to break my flight home by stopping for a few days at Beirut and then Rome, but I was feeling so depressed at leaving Ghana that I decided to fly straight back to England.

I would then have time to pay a short visit to my home in Devon, before reporting to the Lancashire Fusiliers' Depot in Bury for my last days of commissioned service. While on our Timbuktu trip, I had told James that one of the things I was looking forward to on my return was a visit to Old Trafford to see Manchester United play, especially as some of those I had known from my early days in Lancashire were now in the side. When my 'plane landed at Kano in Northern Nigeria, I had time to purchase a four-days-old English newspaper at the airport before flying on to Tripoli, and there was a column about the team's prospects in the European Cup. When we reached London, however, I learnt the shocking news of the Munich crash, which had destroyed the United team...

Despite that sadness, and what seemed the appalling cold of Lancashire in February, my visit to Bury was enjoyable, and was made especially pleasant by Captain David Lloyd Jones, whom I had last met at Formby during my basic training. He was now stationed at the Lancashire Fusiliers' depot, and went out of his way to be helpful and encouraging – he was keen to hear about Ghana and Independence, and had certainly not forgotten the episode of the Very pistol!

So I ceased to be a soldier, and returned home to Devon.

PART THREE
A LONG POSTSCRIPT

Chapter One

RUMOURS

The story might easily have ended there, but it didn't. During the summer of 1958, before taking up my place at Oxford, I taught for a term in a small school near Tiverton, and in my spare time explored Exmoor and the North Devon coast. In the evenings I talked to a fellow teacher, Gerald Hamilton, who in 1940 had sailed a tiny fishing-boat several times to Dunkirk, and had brought back many soldiers safely. He was reticent about his own exploits, but was keen to hear about my time in West Africa, which helped me to put Ghana into proper perspective.

In the summer holidays, with a group of friends, I camped on Lundy, the lovely island in the Bristol Channel, where we swam and climbed cliffs, watched peregrine falcons and innumerable seabirds, and enjoyed the friendliness of the Marisco Tavern. With fewer than fifty residents, Lundy was wonderfully therapeutic. To my surprise and pleasure, a letter from Joseph Halm reached me on the tiny island, forwarded from my home and brought over to Lundy on a paddle-steamer of day-trippers from Ilfracombe. The letter began *I hope you get this, wherever you are now* … and ended *from J and all the Sunshine People…*

That October, I settled in at Worcester College, Oxford, where my study course was supposed to be in French and German, but having recently spent time learning Twi and Hausa, albeit in a minor way, I wanted a break from languages. At a social gathering before my first term began I met the brilliant young tutor, Christopher Ricks, and decided I would prefer to study English with him, instead. No one seemed to mind my changing subjects at one day's notice! Christopher has since had a distinguished career as Professor of English, at Bristol first, then Cambridge, then as Professor of Humanities at Boston University, and he has recently been Professor of Poetry at Oxford, as well as a doughty champion of Bob Dylan. In 1958, however, he was in only his second year as a tutor at Worcester College. He was easily the most intelligent person I had met (and still is!) and his enthusiasm did much to return me to an academic life. He had also completed two years' national service as an officer in the Green Howards, and the three of us in his tutor group who had been commissioned felt a kinship with him, although he seldom spoke of his time in the army, and we were far too much in awe of him to introduce the subject.

I enjoyed my first year at Oxford in a muted way, for I found some of my colleagues who had not yet done their military service both frivolous and immature. The fault was mine, I now realise, although I know my opinion was shared by many who, like me, had been in the forces. Because of this I did not, at first, make the most of an extremely friendly, sociable college. Thoughts of Ghana and the world I had left behind continually intruded, and indeed, this was when, in the evenings, I started to collect up my ideas on the months I had spent there, using notes made at the time. Joseph Halm in a characteristically forthright letter asked 'Are you still half African?' which shook me, as I realised that indeed in some ways I was, although I remember sending him a postcard of the beautiful college cloisters, on which I had written, defensively 'This is my home now!'

I was extremely lucky to have chosen Worcester College, not only for its friendliness and lack of snobbery, but for its situation. It was near to the centre of Oxford, and to the bus and train stations, yet it was surrounded by the most wonderful gardens, with a picturesque lake, beside which it was possible to relax completely. I also came to love the city itself, with its historic buildings and wonderful amenities, and the beautiful countryside around it, which I explored thoroughly during the summer weekends.

While I was at university, Joseph and James each came to England at different times, to study at Kneller Hall. I was disappointed to miss James's visit, as I was then holidaying in Scotland and he was only in England briefly. With Joseph, however, I visited many parts of London, and I have a photo of my friend, looking apprehensive, posing in front of the gorilla, at the zoo in Regent's Park. I recall his saying, with typical self-mockery, "He is probably very gentle, but I have an inbuilt fear of apes – particularly very large ones!"

Albert Ocran went a stage further for, while on a course in Wiltshire during my Oxford vacation, he came to stay with me and my family in Devon. He charmed everybody, and created excitement and no little admiration in parochial Tavistock, by walking around the grounds of my father's preparatory school wearing a dazzling golden *kente*-cloth – and teaching the children to snare rabbits!

I kept up a written correspondence with several African friends. Their letters grew increasingly despondent, and I learnt from them, long before the press and radio news reported it, of Nkrumah's obsessive dallying with communist states, and how his infatuation with Russian and Chinese regimes was ruining Ghana through the undertaking of impractical projects. He was swiftly turning a prosperous country into one that was struggling financially, if not yet quite broke, and he was doing it not merely by grandiose state projects, but also by squandering vast sums on private buildings and gardens for his own gratification. The army was having a hard time, too, since Nkrumah was pouring money into his own Russian-trained 'praetorian guard' at the expense of the regular battalions. Boadu Bekoe proved a fine correspondent, and kept me up-to-date with what was happening in the Battalion. He had ambitions to become a doctor, and was particularly upset about the poor funding of 37 Military Hospital, to which he had been recently transferred as a trainee-physiotherapist: "Medical supplies are hopeless – in fact there are hardly any!" In a letter that surprised me, the normally placid Joseph Mensah was abusive about the newly-created Young Pioneer Movement – "All it's for is to make Nkrumah look even bigger..." adding, in a postscript, "if you don't get this, it'll be because I've been arrested by Nk's spies... Anyone who disagrees with him is shoved in gaol." Joseph Halm was even more pointed. When we had met in England his views had been comparatively mild, but in letters he wrote of how Nkrumah "spends all his time talking about African

Unity, when actually he's starting these secret camps to train soldiers to sabotage other independent countries. We aren't supposed to know these camps exist – or why! ... He's even closed the borders to the north, east and west. JB says you'd never have got to Timbuktu as things are now!" As almost an afterthought, he had added "We are still the Sunshine People, though, even if the Land isn't very sunny."

In 1961 Nkrumah had sacked all his European army and police officers. This was what Douglas Ives had predicted three years earlier, although the sudden finality of it was a shock. The sacking was apparently hastened by Ghana's sending of a peace-keeping force to the Congo, for Nkrumah had been embarrassed by comments from other black African leaders, that his army was still 'ruled by whites'... What Emmanuel Kotoka had called 'fast blacking' destabilised the armed forces, but it did mean that many of my Ghanaian friends gained rapid promotion, even before the dismissal of the Europeans – in fact some moved up two ranks virtually overnight. By the start of the Congo expedition both Emmanuel and Albert were majors, and by the end, colonels.

After leaving Oxford, I was appointed to a teaching post in Shropshire, which I found challenging and stimulating, and I also joined the Combined Cadet Force, as an officer attached to the King's Shropshire Light Infantry, so retaining my military connections. Meanwhile I continued my Ghana correspondence, albeit not as conscientiously as I would have wished, and wrote the first of numerous articles, mainly for natural history journals in Britain, about the wildlife I had seen in different regions and terrains in West Africa. I wrote little about my attitude to the people, however, and nothing at all about politics, as the information I was receiving, while obviously of public interest, would have caused trouble for my African friends had I chosen to publish it.

I half expected some sort of uprising in Ghana, but was still astonished to learn that on 24th February 1966 there had been a *coup d'etat* by the armed forces, mainly involving people who had been in my own Second Battalion. Prime Minister Kwame Nkrumah had been deposed in his absence, while on a visit to Hanoi. Furthermore, the *coup* had been led by Colonel Emmanuel Kotoka, with Colonel Albert Ocran playing an important role...

In the period following this event, I received few letters from Ghana. The *coup*-leaders were reticent, understandably, and were anyway too busy to reply, so it was left to James, the two Josephs and especially BB, to keep me in the picture. The country now had a military government, with *Generals* Kotoka and Ocran in key roles. I learnt via BB that Peter Kamerling was an *aide* to Brigadier Afrifa, one of the masterminds of the *coup,* and that his friends had not seen him for several weeks...

In the main, although times were hard, the new regime seemed popular. From England, however, it was difficult to judge the reaction of other nations to what had happened. Then there was a brief 'counter-*coup*' in 1967, led by a small number of Nkrumah's more fanatical supporters, which was quickly put down – but resulted in the death of Emmanuel Kotoka... I heard the news via the television, and felt stunned and sick. The blow was made worse by the increased difficulty of communication, and for several months I could not make contact with Ghana at all. Not one of my letters received a reply, and I was glad that full-time teaching helped to take my mind off the situation, although my colleagues told me later that it was obvious that I was very worried.

In 1968 my school generously allowed me a 'sabbatical term' so that I could return to Ghana, to learn first-hand what had been happening. I would be able to leave in August, at the start of the summer holidays – and a sympathetic colleague, Patrick Cormack, would take over my English Department for a term. It was kind of him to undertake the job at such short notice as, at the time, in addition to his teaching duties, he was newly married, and was also canvassing to become a Member of Parliament (but as he is now *Sir* Patrick, long-time Conservative MP for South Staffordshire, it cannot have harmed his chances unduly...)

Chapter Two

ACCRA AGAIN, AUGUST 1968

I decided to go by sea, to 'recharge batteries' after the teaching year and put my thoughts in order during the long journey, so as soon as the summer term had ended I set out from Liverpool on the *SS Apapa*. I had never been on a real sea voyage before, and was determined to enjoy it. During the first few days I had long conversations with Ghanaians returning home, from whom I learnt further details about the *coup*, the new government and the current political situation. I was surprised, however, by how uninterested many of these people seemed to be in what was going on in their own land. Their conversation was full of details about financial possibilities in Accra, and the size of their new cars. Ten years earlier African friends had talked about arrogant 'been-tos', people who had been to England or USA, and had then returned to boast about their travels and often to disparage their own country for its inadequacies. Now I was meeting them, and as the voyage continued, my astonishment grew as I realised that several of these Ghanaians, who had at first insisted on being seen on deck, wearing smart European suits, were increasingly retiring to their cabins and ordering huge amounts of food and drink from Room Service.

In contrast, however, I met a delightful Lebanese family, the Olari-ibigbes. Father was wonderfully articulate and exuberant, and worked at the University of Ghana, at Legon, a place that brought back happy memories; mother was beautiful and effervescent, as was their daughter Valerie; and their teenage son, Malcolm, promised to show me around the university campus.

Among other places, the *Apapa* called in at Bathurst (now Banjul) in the Gambia and Freetown in Sierra Leone, against both of which countries I had played hockey and rugby ten years before, so it was interesting to visit their capitals as a civilian... I found Bathurst a chaotic town, friendly and convivial, but irritating, too, because all visitors were accosted by small children incessantly asking for 'dash'. Freetown, however, was almost 'Ghanaian', like a small version of Accra in colour and liveliness – and I found the inhabitants understood my 'rusty' pidgin-English!

After twelve magical days on board the *Apapa* we reached the new port of Tema. The previous night we had passed along the Ghana coast, and had seen myriads of small fishing-boats to *seaward* of us, their lights like a line of glow-worms. I was up at 4 a.m. with Malcolm and Valerie, ready for our arrival. With the dawn we watched the shoals of flying-fish first, silver-blue and mysterious, then came the fishing-boats (some power-assisted, under the new state scheme) and soon we were passing the long, brilliant 'milky way' of Accra's lights. We arrived eventually at the skyline of Tema, very modern, neon-lit, with its huge cranes along the dock, so different from Freetown's steamy indolence and the friendly shambles of Bathurst.

I had been apprehensive about what I might find in Ghana. My main worry was that I would not possibly be able to recapture the wonderful atmosphere of ten years earlier, and the lack of correspondence in recent months troubled me, especially having had no recent communication with the Josephs, BB or James. I was all too aware that I had not tried hard enough to get in touch with them again, until I had sent some frantic last-minute letters which might or might not have arrived... I had decided to stay at the *Star Hotel,* some way from the barracks, and feel my way gradually, exploring Accra afresh before starting to look for my friends. As I left the boat at Tema, the faces were friendly but strange, and I wondered momentarily if the whole visit was a mistake...

I need not have worried, however, for within minutes of my arrival I was whisked through customs with "Welcome back, sir!" by an ebullient young man named John, whose face was familiar. He proved to have been one of our junior orderly-room clerks at Giffard Camp...

In Accra, as I had expected, much had changed in the ten years. There were, of course, fewer white people in the streets, and the billboard advertisements now featured only smiling black faces, although many of these were clearly not African at all, but had 'darkened' European features with slicked-back straight black hair, something I had been prepared for by the hilarious illustrated menus on board the *Apapa*. Independence Square had now become Black Star Square, and Independence Arch in its whirl of traffic had a number of new monuments nearby, commemorating 24th February and the *coup*. The sea-front was dominated by 'Job 600', last and most futile of Nkrumah's extravagant buildings, a giant conference-hall intended to seat thousands, which would never be used – or even completed. Some of the old landmarks of Accra, which previously I had been able to visit at will, I now found to be out of bounds, although I discovered later that by persistence I could usually gain entry. I discovered, too, that I would now have to pay to swim at Labadi, but as 'our' beach was deserted and forbidding, I chose not to.

The currency had altered: *cedis* had replaced pounds, and everything in the city was extremely expensive.... The colour, noise and laughter were the same, however, and I was pleased and relieved to find the ordinary people in Accra as welcoming and courteous as ever.

My first visit was to Emmanuel Kotoka's grave, in the military cemetery. It was unpretentious, in grey marble, but stood out strongly from the bare white crosses surrounding it, and beautiful Red-for-Morning-Time flowers were growing around and over the tomb. I found myself very moved, and was glad to be on my own, except for an elderly caretaker, with whom I had a long conversation. He had been a great admirer of 'the General', and seemed almost overawed when I said Emmanuel had been a colleague of mine.

After that, I set out to find my friends, and went first to the records office at Burma (formerly Giffard) Camp, where the clerks were extremely helpful, and on the first afternoon worked a full hour over-time to locate names and addresses. One sad thing they told me straight away: Seidu Grumah, who had looked after the Battalion mascot, had died, back in 1964. He had cared devotedly for Charles the Ram, given to the Second Battalion at Independence by the departing Governor, and within a few days of his master's death, the ram had also passed away…

Albert Ocran did know I was coming. He was now GOC, commanding the whole army, living in what had been General Paley's house. At his gate I was greeted by a sentry with fixed bayonet, and in support there was a full guard in ceremonial dress. Albert was bearded and looked very distinguished, although much older than his 38 years. His wife, Agnes, told me that he was perpetually tired, and that his work necessitated his rising every morning at 4.30 a.m. The guard at the gate was a direct result of the 1967 counter-*coup*, and Albert found the excessive security wearing. In person he had changed little, however, with the same sense of humour and the same astonishing recall of small details about people and events. He said that as soon as the military regime 'had things in order' well enough to hand over to a civilian government, he would retire from the army, and go to Oxford to study law – a promise he was to keep… Characteristically, Albert told me very little about the *coup*, and nothing at all about his own part in it.

Lunch with the Ocrans consisted of my favourite groundnut stew – something I had failed to find in England in the past ten years… I took photos of the whole family, Albert in General's uniform, with Agnes and the six children, on the balcony of their enormous house. The last time I had used a camera there had been when I had sneaked photos of my fellow officers at a drinks party given by General Paley, to show friends that we had been socializing with the Top Brass!

Malcolm Olaribigbe did indeed show me around the University, in company with his great friend George Harlley, who proved to be the son of the Chief of Police, whom I had known slightly, and who had worked closely with Albert and Emmanuel at the time of the *coup*. Small world, again… We went all over the campus. I had forgotten how attractive the place was, and my visit brought back vivid memories of the map-reading exercise there in 1957. In particular the many ponds, with goldfish and blue water-lilies, and the ornamental flower-beds and intricate walk-ways seemed miraculously beautiful. In the big library I was pleased to find the complete works of Christopher Ricks... Malcolm told me how the students, in dire financial circumstances, had been tearing key pages from relevant volumes of all subjects and smuggling them out under their shirts, which was sad to hear about such an idyllic place.

I went to watch Malcolm and George play football for Achimota School (theirs) v the Academicals (largely a European team) but the rain tipped down, the stadium flooded, and the game was abandoned, so George and I went home with the Olaribigbes, for a pleasant evening, during which I learnt a lot more about Ghana politics from the parents, and even more about Achimota International School from George and Malcolm. The previous day I had been impressed by a Ghana TV programme, *Kaleidoscope*, anchored by Cromwell Quist, who seemed a brilliant man, so I was intrigued to learn that his wife had been teaching *Romeo and Juliet* and *The Warden* to Malcolm and George, and that they apparently behaved very badly in her classes... A few days later, at the Star Hotel, I actually met the Quists, who proved to be a charming, friendly couple. They told me that Malcolm and George were in fact delightful youngsters, and not at all badly behaved!

I had informed James and Boadu by letter that I was coming, but had no idea whether they had received the information. At the Military Hospital, BB greeted me exuberantly. He said he and James had both written several times in the past few months, and were worried because they hadn't heard from me! With great pride he guided me around his workplace in the hospital, greeting patients with a friendliness and rapport that showed how happy he was in his job. Then he took me in his new electric-blue Morris to Burma Camp, where I was welcomed by Binchiti Lobi (now Regimental Sergeant-Major) and had far too many beers in the Sergeants' Mess. I was greeted by many old friends, who told me that I was the first European to enter the Barracks since 1961... and the first *ever* to visit their new Mess. I was particularly pleased to meet Eben Tawiah again. In 1957-8 he had been a private soldier, working in Military Transport, and one of my best boxers – now he was a Staff-Sergeant Parachutist, smart, extremely fit and very happy. He was soon to be commissioned. I had no idea that there was now a parachute detachment in the Ghana Army, but from his effervescent account it was clearly thriving.

Then we went to Buttler Lines, which proved to be the same Junior Officers' Quarters in which I had so much enjoyed living, ten years before. The whole place was now more luxurious, with smart white walls and balconies, and a fine array of climbing plants around the doorways. To my astonishment (and his glee,) James and his family were now housed in what had been my rooms and Jeremy's, while William Stevens and his large family lived next door! This was a pleasant surprise, and it was quite an achievement for BB to have kept the secret, even for a few hours...

Then we went to BB's own house in Accra, where his wife Beatrice plied us with enough food and drink for a week, and I met their delightful children (Beatrice Two and Bright Boadu Two, so the alliteration would continue in the family!)

With the BBs I explored some of my old Accra haunts, and particularly enjoyed revisiting parts of James Town and the fishing port, where nets and buoys were hung everywhere, and catches varying between huge hammer-head sharks and tiny, transparent shrimps were spread out on the sand. I was keen to see Christiansborg Castle again, but BB declared "No one is allowed there nowadays, and anyway it's called Osu Castle!" – the place had apparently been closed to 'outsiders' for several years. We went, all the same, and I had a minor triumph, after chatting to a pleasant sentry at the gate. I said I had been used to inspecting the guard at the Castle ten years before, and explained the procedure – and he nervously allowed me to enter the courtyard, although I could go no further.

A few days later James, BB and Peter Kamerling took me on a marvellous three-day trip to Akosombo, where we saw the new Volta dam and the vast plant that was providing electricity for much of Ghana ("one of Nkrumah's really worthwhile projects, I have to admit," Peter said), and the village that had sprung up to house the workmen. I felt that progress had come at a cost, however, for ten years before, that area had been virgin forest... We also saw how the gigantic new Lake Volta, above the dam, was spreading. It had already caused the town of Kete Krachi to be re-built further north (twice!) to avoid being inundated. The rising waters were drowning miles of forest-land, and skeletal trees were still visible above the surface, but it was obviously going to become a scenic wonder and a huge tourist attraction, especially when the hippos and crocodiles had moved in... James said: "Next time you come, we'll take a boat trip hundreds of miles up Lake Volta," and the idea seemed delightful, although improbable.

On the way to Akosombo we had followed the Tema 'motorway' (a smooth dual-carriageway) and called in at the recently established 4th Battalion, which had the most modern barracks in the Ghana Army, with lovely *en-suite* accommodation, lots of green grass between the neat sloping homes, and pawpaw trees as hedges. The only setback was that the Battalion was rather a long way from Tema and Accra, but state transport apparently took care of that. We searched for Godson Fiawatsror, who had been posted there, but he was on leave. We did see Michael Williams Adjei, however, who greeted me with his familiar huge grin, and was now a rather plump but very happy Staff-Sergeant.

James, BB and Peter told me much about their own service in the Congo and some more details about the *coup*. From them I learnt more than I could expect to gather from Albert, and Peter, naturally, had a very personal view. "You'll have to wait for the book about it, though!" he said, and in fact in an Accra bookshop we found two rather good A4-sized booklets, both of which I purchased. *Price of Freedom* was a cheap but lively cartoon 'life' of Emmanuel Kotoka, by Yaw Boakye Ghanatta, which gave a vivid account of Emma's early days, much of which I knew already, but also an over-simplified but clear picture of the events of 24th February 1966. Even better (and not much more expensive) was *Kotoka and Ghana* by Robert Carlton Ashun, which had just been published and, mainly through photographs and reports of speeches and tributes, told the story of the period between the *coup* and the death of Emmanuel. The photos were fascinating, as my friends could identify almost all the soldiers in most of the shots.

James and BB seemed happy in their careers, and were prospering, although they were not optimistic about the country's future, if and when a civilian government took over again. Peter had indeed been an *aide* to Brigadier Afrifa, one of the organisers of the *coup*, but he had quarrelled with his master and had left his service. He was still a very confident person, however, and felt sure that he would be successful in whatever job he undertook. To my surprise, he told me he had become a Muslim. "I used to drink too much," he said. "Now I don't drink at all!" James and BB confirmed this. Before I returned to England Peter gave me a relic from the ousting of Nkrumah, an eighteen-inch-high statue of a chief's 'linguist', beautifully carved out of ebony, which has stood in a prominent place wherever I have lived in the nearly 40 years since. As his friends pointed out, the face of the carving does look remarkably like Peter Kamerling's!

Albert's driver took me to see Peduasi Lodge, one of Nkrumah's private 'rest homes', high on a hilltop near Aburi. Apparently most Army personnel had refused to enter the place more than once, being frightened by the senseless opulence. Indeed, some felt that a *juju* spirit haunted it. The day I visited the Lodge, Albert had agreed to play golf with the Attorney General, although I think this was in part an excuse not to go inside Peduasi again. My other friends said they had seen it once but would not come with me – although they were adamant that I ought to visit the place, if only to banish any doubts that the *coup* was justified.

As I was starting to write this account of Peduasi, I found myself wondering whether perhaps my reactions at the time had been governed by hysteria and even a wish to find it a megalomaniac nightmare. Maybe it was not as extravagant a place as I had then felt it to be? But re-reading my notebook from 2nd September 1968 put me straight. I had written: *The word 'Lodge' is an obscene misnomer, since it is really a castle. You enter through sliding gates. Normally, a sentry stops you – but if like me you are in a General's car, he salutes instead! You follow a winding drive through hibiscus groves, and halt in a huge porch. Ahead of you there is glass and marble, marble and glass, which seem to go on for miles... You wander along a colossal veranda to a door which leads into just one of the buildings surrounding a courtyard. There seem to be dozens of swimming pools, around which are growing (indoors!) full-sized trees...*

There is a hall of mirrors and, everywhere, red carpets. There are soaring windows with fantastic curtains... You travel between the floors by lifts, and on one occasion the driver and I got lost, and actually found ourselves on the wrong floor... On every level there are spectacular balconies with enormous plush sofas... All this for one man's self-aggrandisement – and apparently Peduasi isn't unique, for Nkrumah seemingly built himself several other 'rest homes' like this...!

I went round the vast edifice with the driver, and found the extravagance truly astonishing, in particular a series of what appeared to be 'orgy rooms' – in one of which even the walls were decorated in red velvet – each suite complete with giant beds, monster TVs and 'fridges, and private swimming pools, where Nkrumah and his cronies could dally with their mistresses while the country sank into poverty. Aptly, while we were at Peduasi a massive thunderstorm broke on the Aburi Escarpment, and the rain came down in hissing torrents... I could see that the driver was awestruck and actually scared, so as soon as we had found our bearings we beat a hasty retreat.

I accompanied BB to the hospital in Mampong, where his father was gravely ill. The doctors had just removed several enormous tapeworms from the old man, who was in his mid-70s, a big age for Ghanaians then. He was cheerful, and touchingly grateful for our visit, but as we were coming away BB said "I think he will die in less than a week..." He was correct... A few evenings later, I went with Joseph Mensah to a concert at the Star Hotel, where five bands were playing, including the Armed Forces outfit, which included James, William Stevens and others, and was conducted by Budu Larbi, now a captain and a superb showman. I had expected BB to come with me and Joseph, but he arrived late, said quietly "My father has died," then explained to us that the old man had been glad to go, and was now happy again and that therefore he himself refused to be miserable...

The concert was billed as a 'Rollicking Melodrama of Music', entitled *Yesterday, Today and Tomorrow,* and the bands were all of a very high standard. Pat Koto, the soloist for the Armed Forces, had a wonderful tenor voice. I didn't know him well, but James and William brought him over to our table at the first interval. He was a tiny, birdlike man, but with an enormous personality, and I could see how much the success (and massive record-sales!) of the Armed Forces Band owed to him. The Heart Beats ensemble I had experienced already, as they had been entertaining us on board the *Apapa*, smooth and sophisticated, while the Rolling Beats were fascinating, doing 'moonwalking' long before Michael Jackson apparently 'invented' it.

I have several vivid memories of that concert, in addition to the different bands: firstly, I had forgotten how enjoyable it was to 'dance' to *Highlife* music, although my brief efforts were put in the shade by my African friends. Also, during one interval the MC announced 'Riddles!' and declared that small prizes would be awarded for correct answers. The puzzles were not very subtle: for example 'Someone was 16 but had had only four birthdays. How could that be?' and our table kept answering very quickly, but not bothering to go up to the MC – so our neighbours began to 'borrow' our answers and collected two prizes! At the end of the concert, the staff at the Star told us with glee that overnight a burglar had been doing the rounds of the hotel, but had made the mistake of breaking into the suite where the boxing champion Johnny Cooke was staying... My own room would have been next but one!

BB and I went to see General Ankrah, the Head of State, leaving to tour the Ivory Coast. Albert wasn't with him, as he had another important visit lined up in the North. There was a big turnout, and I noted at the time that the General's Ghana Airways state aircraft looked like a yellow-and-black flying lizard. As BB and I walked across the runway to gatecrash the VIP party, a security man wanted to know what we were doing (and I certainly did feel out of place in my red shirt, blue shorts and flipflops, amid the starched formality of the officials.) Then Ankrah's car and motorcade came swooping by, and as luck would have it the General was looking out my side and waved and grinned with obvious recognition (which I thought was impressive, since I'd not seen him for ten years, had not known him well – and he'd no idea I was in the country...) The security official was not in the least embarrassed. He smiled and said "I tink General be your friend." The Commander of the guard seeing Ankrah off proved to be my old driver, Amadu Fulani, so again I couldn't help feeling the world was getting smaller and smaller.

A day or so later BB told me he planned to take his family and me to the *Ga Homowo* harvest festival at Labadi.

"I'm not from Accra, so I don't understand it any more than you will!" he said. "It's exciting, though!"

It was an event I had been disappointed to have missed during my army days. I had heard much about the *Homowo* and had been keen to see it, so now was my chance. James was busy with rehearsals for another concert, so couldn't join us. Nor could Joseph Mensah. "I went to it once, long ago, and was very confused," he said, "so I shall look forward to hearing what an Englishman thinks of it!"

In truth I was mightily impressed.

I saw not a single other white person during the day, in a crowd of many thousands... It was a privilege to be there, and I found it fascinating, but without the Bekoe family I would have got lost in the melee more than once. What happens at the *Homowo* is indeed hard to describe in European terms, and I have since (several times!) read explanations of its symbolism in a little explanatory booklet by Charles Ammah, without being much the wiser... Apparently, different versions of the *Homowo* ceremony take place at the various main centres of the Ga people around Accra, of which the Labadi *La Kpaa* is said to be the most spectacular. For those Africans who say that the description that follows is incoherent, and no English viewer can possibly do justice to the *Homowo,* I would agree wholeheartedly! – but it was a memorable occasion for me, so I offer the best I can, from a distance of forty years...

It seemed to have little to do with harvest. My main impression was of a kaleidoscope of people, many in white robes, others in dazzling clothes, dancing in huge groups very slowly along the roadway. Some of these groups were headed by banners; others by village elders carrying painted branches resembling horns; others by women fabulously attired in gold *kente*, their faces daubed with red ochre. Much of the pageantry was beautiful, while a performance of 'ghost dancers', their faces smeared with white clay, was sinister. The people in the vast crowd passed in and out, in and out between the dancers. We were swept along in a tidal wave that reminded me of the Notting Hill Carnival. At one surreal point we were confronted by a fetish shrine in the middle of the roadway, with daubed white walls, conical reed thatch and scrubbed stones in front of the entrance curtains. Before this shrine an old, old woman danced, progressing nowhere, eyes glazed, face ashen, bare breasts flapping, the only thing about her which was feminine. She was in a profound trance, and near her, several children jogged up and down blankly, also trance-bound and ashen, heads lolling, utterly unaware of where – or who – they were, but keeping the rhythm of the Homowo drums. We were in Labadi for more than three hours, and I believe these drums never once ceased.

It is a tradition that at one stage in the *La Kpaa,* the entire crowd becomes involved in an extraordinary dance. In theory every adult or teenage male is allowed (encouraged!) to 'embrace, fondle or caress' any and every woman or teenage girl who is dancing... This *La Kpaa Ekpee Yo ('Labadi's god has married')* is supposed to signify that 'the god of Labadi has fallen in love with every woman who comes to the spot where the dance is being held.' In reality what happens is that everyone, regardless of sex, embraces everyone else, while maintaining the dance. BB said "It is proof of being happy." My British reserve at first forbade such intimacy with total strangers, and I was worried that in the intervening ten years I might have lost my ability to participate. I felt I needed a drink, and grabbed a coconut shell of palm wine from a stall. The effect was almost instantaneous! The involvement of the huge crowd, and the realisation that colour and creed mattered nothing at all in this context, were infectious, and I found myself joining in, with increasing abandon. I then discovered that I was enjoying the experience.

What I found surprising about this powerful ceremony was that there was nothing at all lewd about it. With every excuse for licentious behaviour, there seemed to be none at all. As everyone swayed in a sort of gigantic conga along the road and around the fetish shrine, I was reminded less of Notting Hill Carnival, and more of the Helston 'Furry Dance'.

We had travelled to Labadi in BB's car. I could not remember even vaguely where he had parked it, and had visions of walking several miles back to his home, or the Star – supposing I could find either! – in much the same way that I had returned on foot after listening to Nkrumah on Independence Night. I no longer cared how lost I was. The Bekoe

Family had kept close, however, and we bundled into their Morris in a sense of total exhilaration.

"Quite, totally mad!" BB said. "But a good day!"

❖   ❖   ❖

This was the time of the 'd'Oliviera Affair' and many of my African friends were concerned about whether Basil d'O had been omitted from the English cricket touring party to South Africa purely on racist grounds. Albert said that he had noticed more racism on his last trip to England (to have a medical check) – and wanted to know whether I had felt the same in reverse about Ghana. I was able to say quite genuinely "Not at all," from my personal experience, and especially in the light of the *Ga Homowa*...

The question of race relations arose again, indirectly, when I was invited to a 'light supper' by a white Canadian couple, cousins of a Devonshire friend of mine, who were teaching at Accra Polytechnic. The meal proved to be a far more elaborate affair than I had expected, and there were two other guests, also Canadian. Chris and Colette had just been to Timbuktu – five days by boat from Mopti, but in 'state rooms' in a big passenger ship, not our houseboat! The other couple had motor-cycled around a large part of Nigeria, which they had found 'gruesome'... There was much to hear about and compare. To my surprise, all four agreed that they did not really enjoy Accra, although a car and higher pay would make a big difference! It was a pleasant evening, but I was saddened that, despite their impressive travels, they seemed inhibited about mixing with Africans. Their attitude was in no way racist. They all declared that they would like to be more sociable, especially in Accra, but they felt it 'wasn't safe'. I imagined this to be a kick-back from Nkrumah's anti-white policy, so did not ask them to elaborate, and to avoid embarrassment I tried to tone down my own enthusiasm for Ghana and Ghanaians. At one stage, however, Colette said "My uncle tells me you have lots of African friends. He met one of them, called Albert, a few years ago and liked him very much. I wish Chris and I could socialise more." I felt it strange that they should feel this inhibition in a teaching-staff that was almost entirely African. I realised too late that I had wasted a great chance to introduce them to some of my particular friends. An evening in the company of James, BB and their families would have removed a lot of hang-ups – and perhaps Colette could have met Albert himself...

The time went by all too quickly, and I still had not seen Joseph Halm.

For my return journey I was to catch the *SS Aureol* from Takoradi, so travelled by government bus to the town almost a week before departure, since Joseph had recently left the army and was now a senior fire officer at the port. It was wonderful to see him again, but he looked ill, and was unhappy, for he was finding the work too boring for someone of his intellect, and I think he greatly regretted being so far from his military friends. Joseph's decision to leave the army was a tragedy, James and BB had told me, as he had looked set to become the next Director of the Regimental Band... They had been surprised and shocked by his decision. I tried to talk to Joseph about it, without much success. "My friends are my friends still," was all he would say.

With Joseph I explored Takoradi, a place I had seen little of in 1956-8. The town reminded me of Dublin in its juxtaposition of sacred and profane. Two almost-identical buildings side by side emphasised this: one was *The Holy Church of Spiritual Movement* and the other *The Highway Akpeteshie Bar*, both well patronised, with plenty of people going straight from one to the other and vice-versa. With Joseph's help I added a 'Takoradi section' to my catalogue of *tro-tro* slogans, and listed nearly a hundred new ones. We felt that pride of place should go to a smart red, gold and green truck on which was blazoned the one word *WHY?*

We explored the surrounding coast, and found some wonderful wildlife, including an incredible lizard or skink that seemed straight out of Gerald Durrell. It was big, more than a foot long, and stretched motionless on a fallen palm trunk, brilliant scarlet with black markings. We were able to get quite close. The creature was so bizarre that I thought it must be a plastic model, until it skittered along the trunk and disappeared into some bushes. We asked a group of children playing nearby if they had seen this extraordinary reptile. They looked at us wide-eyed, then concluded we were making it up, and burst out laughing.

Along the beach many people were surfing, a few on proper boards, but the majority on planks from packing-cases, and having a wonderful time. When I had been in Ghana before, the Europeans had spent countless hours surfing at Labadi, but this was the first time I had seen Africans doing it. Joseph explained that a recent TV programme had encouraged the craze! He said that he was determined to try it for himself.

We were both fascinated by the innovative ways quite small children were fishing in the streams that ran down to the shore. Several very young boys were making small tributaries, into which they chased the little fish, and were then using further channels to drain the water and leave their catch stranded. Another group were using 'nets' of brushwood very successfully. The children were also playing a remarkable 'otter-sliding' game, just like Tarka on snow, but in their case down the sandy cliffs, ending at the tide's edge in a higgledy-piggledy laughing mass...

One morning we met the First Battalion boxing team working-out on Takoradi beach, and Amani Baz, their trainer, asked if I would help them. I am sure he was being 'tongue-in-cheek', but it was a nice moment. In 1957 the same Amani had lost a close fight with Sam Osei from our Second Battalion team, before Sam went on to box in the Commonwealth Games – and later, the Olympics.

Joseph came to look round the *Aureol* before we sailed, and it was no surprise that he knew several of the crew. "I think I'll stow-away!" he said. Sadly, it was the last time I was to see him, for he died less than a year later. Quite what caused his death I never discovered, and even BB, with his medical training, could not tell me – illnesses in West Africa could then strike very suddenly, and there was seldom a *post-mortem* – but I cannot help feeling that part of the cause, in Joseph's case, was loneliness: what could almost be called a broken heart. He was a gentle, unassuming, yet extremely amusing person, whose wit was never offensive. His friends revered him. It was perhaps fitting that when I saw Joseph for the last time, in Takoradi, he should have been reading Milton's *Paradise Lost*...

❖ ❖ ❖

While on board the *Aureol* I put down my thoughts on 'second time round'. Ghana was still the Sunshine Land, but the confidence of the country had taken a knock. Nkrumah's violent anti-white rule had given place to a regime that now seemed to wish for more white help and 'stiffening', but was perhaps not morally secure enough to risk asking for it. RSM Binchity had said he thought the new young African officers were 'too soft'… Albert hinted the same. He wondered if they were trying too hard not to be unpopular…

On the plus side, since the *coup,* pay for the Army and Police had risen greatly, and was at last adequate. Although we did not know it at the time, in 1956-8 we, the young European amateurs, had been earning more than African career officers like Emmanuel Kotoka, which was preposterous, and it was good to know that now my army friends felt their services were being better rewarded. But the Army ruled the country, and outside the forces there seemed still to be a lot of grossly unjust poverty, with many labouring jobs appearing to hold no prospects at all of improved circumstances. Joseph had suggested that a military government was poorly qualified to cope with this side of things. "Now I'm not a soldier I can say this!" he observed. But he admitted that under the military regime things were much better than under Nkrumah.

Certainly, in 1968 there was more 'foreigner-consciousness' in the country, although when I was with African friends I still felt totally at ease, and when by myself I was never worried or inhibited.

In one respect the ending of the 'Nkrumah years' seemed to have stimulated the nation's creativity. The bookshops in Accra were full of home-grown novels, some mere potboilers but others, like Cameron Duodu's *The Gab Boys*, brilliantly inventive and funny. Many writers seemed to be using their work to rid themselves of long-pent-up frustrations…

The future of Ghana's aspiring authors also seemed assured. Before I left him at Takoradi, Joseph had given me a small magazine called *The New Generation*, which I read on my journey home. It was an anthology of prose and verse from the secondary schools and training colleges of Ghana, the results of a literary competition. "I think you will find it good," Joseph had said. I found it excellent – and this year, almost four decades later, I have re-read it with undimmed enthusiasm. The stories, short plays and poems were beautifully written, in vivid, powerful

English, which did not surprise me. What I found amazing, however, was the variety of styles and subject matter, and the way these young students had used their own experiences to create memorable pictures that reflected their country. The seventeen works were equally spread between boys and girls. In *A Tiger who was Fooled Twice,* a very young pupil had ingeniously adapted the Brer Rabbit legend to involve a tiger throwing a hare into the long grass... A fine poem, *Was it a Dream?* told poignantly of a couple's much-longed-for child who lived less than a year – an experience all too common in West Africa. There were several brilliantly-observed 'been-to' stories which, after my outward journey in the *Apapa,* I was well able to appreciate. The tale which I found most startling in its maturity, however, was called *The Incest.* It told of a Gold Coast soldier on the Burma Campaign who fell in love with a white American, leaving her pregnant when he returned home at the end of the war. The daughter, of whom he knew nothing, came to Africa and unwittingly fell in love with the soldier's son... What could easily have turned into a mere string of coincidences was so carefully plotted, and convincingly told, that the incest of the story became true tragedy.

Typically, Albert had not let on that he too had been writing, and had recently put the finishing touches to *A Myth is Broken,* his clear and concise analysis of the 1966 *coup.* It received brilliant reviews, and was described as a 'definitive account'. My father, who had liked Albert very much when he had visited us in Devon, read the book with great interest some months later, and said wryly: "Your friend does have a bit of an advantage, doesn't he, writing about a *coup* that he actually helped organise!" (Albert's second volume, with its evocative title *The Politics of the Sword,* is a shrewd assessment of West African military governments – again an insider's view.)

The return trip passed with less excitement and interest than the outward journey. One difference was that this time, in addition to stopping at Freetown and Bathurst, we called in at Monrovia, the Liberian capital, which hardly seemed a West African town at all. It had none of the colour and brightness of the ex-British capitals, and the monochrome streets were full of black American cars. I enjoyed my visit, however, for I was shown around the town by a beautiful girl called

Venus Harper, who had lived there until moving to Accra to work, and was now travelling to England on the *Aureol*, before going on to New York. She already had a strong American accent – but said that this was hardly surprising. "We Liberians are all descended from American slaves!" she declared.

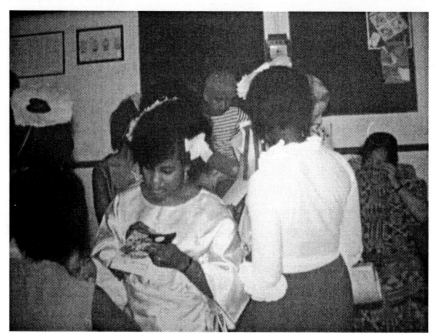

1968, on board the Apapa

'Carnival Night'!

Armed Forces Band

The Ga Homowo

Peter, James and BB at Akosombo

The New Ghana, the Dam at Akasombo by day

...and by night

Farewell, Emmanuel Kotoka

Chapter Three

THE LAST TIME

In 1969 the Army handed over, as planned, and after a democratic election Kofi Busia took charge of a new civilian government. In August 1971, again during the summer holidays, I returned to Accra once more, for a final, much shorter, visit. This time I went by air, and Boadu Bekoe and Peter Kamerling met me at the airport with their usual exuberance.

I stayed in BB's smart green and red house in the city, and found it delightful, my time there enhanced by some marvellous choral singing from the neighbours in the evening, which went on until late at night. I thought there might be surprised faces the first morning, when a European emerged from BB's front door, but was greeted by "Did you sleep well?" from a girl sweeping the next courtyard – so in that sense things hadn't changed… I was impressed by my friend's status as a physiotherapist-cum-doctor. All day, when he was at home, people from the neighbourhood called for treatment and medical advice, which BB gave willingly and with confidence. "I am glad to be a doctor, as well as a soldier," he said.

It struck me early on that there was a strange atmosphere in Accra, and even more so at Burma Camp.

"When we were just the army, everybody liked us," Joseph Mensah said. "Then we became the government, as well, and soon they wanted to be rid of us and we wanted to go. Now they seem to want us back again…"

Peter Kamerling was not happy, but in his case the malaise came from inaction. When he had been ADC to Brigadier Afrifa he had visited London (twice) and New York for conferences, and had been much in the limelight. He still missed the excitement.

Albert was in England already, planning what he had long intended, to take a law degree...

BB came with me to Akasombo again, hoping this time to do the Lake Volta trip. We stayed overnight at the new Volta Hotel, and our room had a balcony with fantastic views over the dam and the lake.

But there was no passenger ship to Kete Krachi for almost a week!

We hired a small boat which took us around the Akasombo area and gave a flavour of 'lake atmosphere', but it wasn't the same. Then we had a contest to find (and climb) the tallest termite hill, but after an hour or so, this palled too. So we decided to head for Kumasi – and what had started as a disappointing trip became a marvellous one...

Next morning we left Akasombo at 7.30 a.m., and a young American staying at the hotel gave us a lift to the village – where we boarded a *tro-tro* for Somanya and from there went on to Koforidua. The truck had a passenger limit of twenty-one, and we had more than thirty on board! After a brief stop in Koforidua, which brought back many memories, especially of my visits to the Government Agent George Levack, we went on to Kumasi, this time in a less-crowded *tro-tro*. There, we decided to 'do it in style' so stayed at the City Hotel, an impressive place, and remarkably cheap.

We called on Maurice Essien and Godson Fiawatsror at the Band Lines – two good friends I had missed in 1968 – and had a joyous couple of days, with far too much food and drink, and hours and hours of talk. Maurice and Godson had done well for themselves. In addition to their music (which included making a lot of rather good *Highlife* records, copies of which they gave me), they had gone into property. Maurice now owned three attractive houses in Kumasi, and Godson two. Wherever we needed to go in the area, Maurice laid on a truck for us... As Godson said, "Essien is now the money-man!" While we were with them, many of the old Corps of Drums people turned up – it was exhausting – but exhilarating.

Back in Accra I talked further about the *coup* with James and Peter, and also William Stevens, whose clearly-expressed erudition reminded me greatly of Joseph Halm. I learnt that none of them had had any idea that the *coup* was taking place until it had happened, not even Peter, who had been part of it! The discovery of Nkrumah's gold bars made a good story – and explained why many of the Second Battalion seemed so prosperous… "Afrifa has most of all," Peter said, without rancour.

James, BB, William and Peter came to see me off at the airport, and although we tried hard to be cheerful, it was difficult to dispel the gloomy feeling that we would not see each other again. "Perhaps when I am a Big Man, in charge of the hospital," BB said, "I will come to England."

"And perhaps when Ghana is fifty years old, you will come back and we will all meet together again, here in Accra," added William.

He spoke jokingly, but I remembered his words when I started to put together these memories. I have not been back, but who knows – 2007?

Which is where the story ought to end – but there is one final detail to record. In 1972, I married Rosalind, and we moved to Marlow, in Buckinghamshire, where we took charge of a school boarding-house at the edge of the beautiful Chilterns and quite near to Oxford. Meanwhile, General Albert Ocran was now retired from the army and, as he had promised, had come to the University to study law…

So we took the boarding children over to see him…

Albert was living in a big house at the back of the Oxfam building in Banbury Road. He was on his own, although his family would join him later – and already he looked younger, and less ill, with the cares of high office steadily slipping away. He was greatly enjoying his legal studies, with many plans for what needed doing in that field in Ghana.

As always, his rapport with youngsters was brilliant.

That evening I overheard an eleven-year-old ringing his parents on our house 'phone:

"We had a fantastic day in Oxford. I'm a Chief now! We met an African General – yes, a real one – and he gave me a chief's fly-whisk…"

The End

Printed in the United Kingdom
by Lightning Source UK Ltd.
118641UK00001B/175-195

9 781425 980306